Stuttering: The Search for a Cause and Cure

OLIVER BLOODSTEIN
Brooklyn College of the City University of New York

ALLYN AND BACON
Boston London Toronto Sydney Tokyo Singapore

Series Editor: Ray Short
Production Administrator: Marjorie Payne
Editorial-Production Service: Chestnut Hill Enterprises, Inc.
Cover Administrator: Linda Dickinson
Composition Buyer: Linda Cox
Manufacturing Buyer: Megan Cochran

Library of Congress Catologing-in-Publication Data

Bloodstein, Oliver.
    Stuttering : the search for a cause and cure / Oliver Bloodstein.
      p. cm.
    Includes bibliographical references and index.
    ISBN 0–205–13845–4
    [DNLM: 1. Stuttering—etiology. 2. Stuttering—therapy. WM 475
B655sa]
    RC424.B56 1993
    616.85'54—dc20
    DNLM/DLC
    for Library of Congress   92–1153
                                         CIP

Printed in the United States of America

10 9 8 7 6 5 4 3 2   98 97 96 95 94 93

Contents

Preface

In the brief autobiography that he wrote as a young man, Wendell Johnson, the distinguished speech pathologist who was my teacher, wrote, "I am a stutterer. I am not like other people. I must think differently, act differently, live differently—because I stutter."

Johnson was giving words to an age-old human anguish. One of the most handicapping of disabilities, stuttering, or stammering as it is sometimes called, has been with us at all times and in all places. The Bible knows of it, and references to it have been read in cuneiform tablets and Egyptian papyri. But, it is only in very recent times that some light has been shed on it through scientific investigations. This book is the story of modern efforts, including a few of my own as a speech clinician and researcher, to understand stuttering and to find better ways of alleviating it.

The science of speech and its aberrations crosses many disciplines, and research on stuttering has been carried on by speech pathologists, psychologists, linguists, neurologists, geneticists, psychiatrists, sociologists, anthropologists, and even electronic engineers. As a result, the literature on the subject abounds in conflicting theories. Medicine, psychoanalysis, and the psychology of learning have provided whole domains for the study of stuttering with such unique research methodologies, theories, treatments, terminologies, and basic assumptions about the nature of maladaptive behavior that almost no communication has taken place between these domains. Crossing from one to the other, it is sometimes hard to believe that they have been concerned with the same speech disorder. Yet, despite the disagreement and confusion, and although much remains to be learned about stuttering, a great deal is known. In recent years, most researchers have come to the conclusion that stuttering probably comes about through an interaction of hereditary and environmental factors. We also have some clues as to what some of these factors might be, and we can offer some informed speculations about what stutterers are doing when they block and what children are doing when they are first observed to stutter. Finally, we can dispel some prevalent notions about the disorder that are harmful and untrue.

With respect to treatment, too, there are hopeful signs of progress to report. It is true that deep divisions of philosophy exist, chiefly between speech clinicians who teach stutterers to speak differently and those who teach them to stutter differently. And the extravagant claims for supposedly new cures that are a popular subject for TV segments are not to be taken seriously. Nevertheless, we are at present capable of helping a large proportion of stutterers to overcome the problem in childhood and to alleviate it very considerably in adolescence and adulthood.

Stuttering: The Search for a Cause and Cure is for all those who have reason to be interested in the subject of stuttering. It is also intended for everyone who is drawn to intellectual adventure and fascinated by scientific puzzles.

O. B.

CHAPTER ONE

The Problem

Dictionaries generally define stuttering as involuntary hesitations, repetitions, and prolongations of sounds. One of the shortcomings of such a definition is that it fails to differentiate stuttering, as the term is used in speech pathology, from other kinds of interruptions in speech. A common example of such other kinds of interruptions is normal disfluency. Careful observation shows that almost all of us have hesitations, repetitions, and prolongations in our normal conversational speech from time to time. These disfluencies generally go unnoticed by the speaker and the listener. We become aware of them only when we are so tense, embarrassed, guilty, or confused that the disfluency becomes extreme. But this is not what speech pathologists call stuttering. What is the difference? To begin with, people who stutter know precisely what word they wish to say. For the moment they are simply unable to say it. They can say some other word, or the same word at some other time, but not that word at that moment. Also, stutterers usually anticipate their moments of stuttering, or blocks. As they approach the stuttered word, they are likely to have a sense of impending difficulty that we call *expectancy* or *anticipation*.

Stuttering also differs from *cluttering*, a jerky, indistinct pattern in which speech erupts in rapid bursts full of hesitations and repetitions and the speaker seems to be trying to say one word before finishing the last. We don't know exactly what causes cluttering, but unlike stuttering, it is a diffuse disfluency that is hard to localize to specific words. And unlike most stutterers, clutterers tend to be unperturbed by their speech difficulty, when they are aware of it at all.

Finally there is so-called neurogenic stuttering, which may appear suddenly in adulthood after a brain injury. How far it differs from the usual variety of stuttering is something about which we are still uncertain, but at least one major distinction is that ordinary stuttering virtually always develops in childhood.

The subject of this book, then, is a specific disorder of speech fluency with distinctive characteristics. It usually begins between the ages of 2 and 5 years, and rarely starts after the onset of adolescence. As age increases, the risk that a child will begin to stutter diminishes. Parents generally describe the onset of stuttering as gradual. Only in rare cases does stuttering seem to develop with dramatic suddenness following some traumatic event.

A surprising fact is that the majority of stuttering children recover spontaneously. According to some research, as many as 80 percent of those who ever stutter have stopped by the time they reach adulthood. The cases that persist into later life are numerous enough, constituting nearly one percent of the population, but they are a minority. We wish we knew why some children gradually "grow out of" episodes of months or years of stuttering and why some do not. Questioning the parents of children who recover has not given us much enlightenment. Many have no explanation. Others have told of the child's being treated for tongue-tie, cured of intestinal worms, operated on for enlarged tonsils, taken to a chiropractor, or the like. Powerful suggestion may have been at work in such cases, or perhaps they are examples of mere coincidence. What we do know is that the younger the child, the greater the chances of spontaneous recovery. Quite a few preschool children stutter for no more than a few weeks or months. In one study of nearly one thousand children entering the first grade, over eight percent were said to have already recovered from stuttering.

The problem often tends to run in families. Many more stutterers than nonstutterers know of stuttering relatives or ancestors. It is not uncommon to encounter a family that has produced stutterers for several generations. A question that was debated for many years is whether the inheritance of stuttering is primarily biological or mainly due to the transmission of certain family environments. At the present time most workers believe that genes play a major part, in some unknown way.

Boys who stutter outnumber girls by about three to one. The reason is not known. Boys and girls differ in physiology, social and physical development, and the parental attitudes to which they are exposed, so almost any theory of stuttering can be reconciled with the sex ratio. Among the explanations that have been proposed for the sex ratio are genetic inheritance, higher parental expectations for boys, higher levels of testosterone in the male fetus, the difference in the rate of speech and language development in the sexes, and contrasting unconscious psychodynamics. It has not escaped notice that boys exceed girls in an impressive number of things that are bad.

Stuttering is an intermittent disorder that comes and goes in response to the subtlest situational factors. Most stutterers are usually fluent when they are alone, when they speak to an infant or an animal, when they sing, whisper, or imitate a foreign accent or the speech of another person, or when they adopt any unaccustomed manner of speaking. They generally speak normally when repeating a word on which they have just stuttered, when reading in unison with another person, when carried away by enthusiasm or overcome by fear, in loud noise, and under many other conditions.

So far as controlled scientific investigation has disclosed, there are few if any differences between stutterers and normal speakers in physical constitution, birth and developmental history, intelligence, and personality. By and large, stutterers tend to be very ordinary individuals. There may be some exceptions to this, notably in certain subtle factors of brain organization, as we will see in later chapters. There is one difference that we are sure of. Although the majority of stutterers acquire speech normally, an unexpectedly large minority are slow in beginning to speak or persist rather late in infantile errors in their articulation of speech sounds.

Symptomatology

When stuttering has assumed its fully developed form, the interruptions, or blocks, consist chiefly of repetitions or prolongations of sounds or syllables, explosive initiations of syllables, and pauses during which the stutterer is helpless to utter a sound. The block usually occurs on the first syllable of the word. Ordinary stuttering is never heard on the last sound of a word. So the difficulty apparently has something to do with the initiation of words in most cases, and of syllables within words occasionally.

Many stutterers engage in various kinds of associated movements when they block. They may jerk their heads, shut their eyes, stick out their tongues, clench their fists, gasp, or empty their lungs with sudden expiratory thrusts of air. These represent efforts to get started on words or to terminate blocks. Stutterers may also interject extraneous sounds or words such as "er," "well," or "you know" for similar reasons or in order to postpone the attempt on a word until they feel able to say it. Many devices for starting words seem to owe what effectiveness they have to their potential for distracting the stutterer's attention, because they seem to wear out when they become fully automatic and lose their novelty. For this reason, some stutterers acquire whole accretions of interjections or associated movements which have become so habitual that the stutterer is not aware of them. In some cases, such secondary symptoms, as they are called, constitute most of the abnormality of the stutterer's speech.

The problem varies greatly in severity. Some stutterers are literally helpless to utter a word in some situations and have to resort to writing notes in order to communicate. A few engage in struggle behavior that might be mistaken for a mild convulsive seizure. At the other extreme, stuttering may be so mild that it is little more than an occasional nuisance to the speaker. But the mere fact that the difficulty seems mild to the observer is no guarantee that the stutterer perceives it that way. In fact, some of the most severe problems are presented by people who seem to talk with perfectly normal fluency. These individuals are haunted by continual fearful anticipations of stuttering as they speak. And interruptions so slight that they pass unnoticed by others seem to them to be shameful failures. These so-called interiorized stutterers are generally adults who stuttered overtly as children. In time they suppressed their outward symptoms, but not the inner experience of stuttering.

It is the subjective experience of stuttering that is by far the most disagreeable aspect of the disorder. If we ask stutterers what it feels like to have a block, they will generally tell us first and foremost that they experience a feeling of loss of control over their speech organs. It is as if their tongue, lips, and jaw are momentarily paralyzed or acting of their own accord. This is evidently far from an actual paralysis or involuntary spasm of some sort, because the stutterer can stop the block to say some other word fluently. But the loss of control is quite real, and is as baffling and demoralizing to the stutterer as it would be to anyone who repeatedly experienced a sudden paralysis of part of their body. Another prominent feature is muscular tension, which stutterers universally report, usually in their speech organs, often in the chest or the pit of the stomach, and occasionally in their limbs. "It's like a rock inside," one stutterer said. Stutterers also describe strong emotional reactions. Before the block there is that feeling of fearful anticipation which can mount to panic, and afterward there is humiliation and frustration. During a severe block, stutterers sometimes say that they feel cut off from their surroundings, and experiments have shown that, during prolonged blocking, manual activity involuntarily stops and subjects may fail to perceive visual and auditory stimuli. One young man commented that having a block was like taking a plunge in the dark. The impression we get of a stutterer during a severe block is one of rigid immobility and deep absorption.

Attitudes and Adaptations

To be a stutterer is more than to be merely a person with a certain way of talking. Few normal speakers have any inkling of how lives can be affected by the need to improvise ways of coping with stuttering and by the attitudes and assumptions that people are apt to acquire because they stutter.

The process begins early. By age seven, many children articulate the assumption that they are an unusual kind of person by saying "I don't talk good." One child I examined had urged his mother to take him to a doctor. Throughout life, for as long as individuals continue to stutter, that self-concept as a defective speaker will be a dominating factor. They will stutter more when made self-conscious about their speech and they will talk with normal fluency on occasions when they forget that they are stutterers.

A person with a self-concept as a stutterer expects to stutter. Quite soon, this anticipation becomes attached to certain specific words as a result of memorable experiences of failure in trying to say them. Once a stutterer anticipates trouble on a word, the anticipation alone is often enough to evoke stuttering. Almost every stutterer has his or her own private list of difficult words. As times goes on, this may amount to a substantial part of the person's vocabulary. One reason for this is the normal process of generalization. A stutterer who incurs a stinging social penalty because of failure to say "Poughkeepsie" may conclude that words beginning with "p" are hard to say, with the result that they may become so. A revealing aspect of this effect is that "pneumonia" may become difficult, even though there is no p-sound in it. And a stutterer who has trouble with "f" words may say "photo" fluently even though the word begins with an f-sound. These are striking examples of the role that perceptions and expectations play in stuttering.

The hardest word that most stutterers ever have to say is their name. The familiar proposal, "Let's all introduce ourselves," is likely to strike cold fear to a stutterer's heart. Scarcely less difficult are their age, address, and telephone number. The reason for this is twofold. These are words stutterers have often had to use in circumstances in which failure to say them has been acutely embarrassing. And there is no other way to say them.

If a stutterer expects to block on "tonight," the substitution of "this evening" offers an unobtrusive way out. Since language abounds in synonyms, word substitution is one of the most common ways that stutterers have of coping with their disability. Some stutterers think they have developed peerless vocabularies in the effort to avoid difficult words. Unfortunately, this device often becomes part of the stutterer's problem. Beginning as an occasional expedient that a child may use when already blocking on a word, word substitution soon comes to be employed in response to the anticipation of stuttering. In the end, stutterers may continually look ahead as they speak, scanning intended utterances for dangerous words and searching for synonyms. If no synonyms are available, they may revise the whole sentence so that a difficult word at the beginning occurs less conspicuously at the end. Or the stutterer may resort to circumlocutions. One young man who had difficulty with "cousin" said he was going to spend the weekend with his mother's sister's son. Failing to find apt synonyms or circumlocutions, some stutterers settle for only approximately what they intended to say. The most memorable example in my experience was an adult who spoke perfectly fluently, but made so little sense that I wondered if he was mentally ill before it became clear that he was avoiding stuttering by doggedly substituting words, whether they were appropriate or not. Another extreme example of word substitution was a college student who attended all the dances and social events that stutterers normally avoid because they know they will frequently have to introduce themselves in such situations. When asked how he managed it, he said it was no problem—he simply gave any name he thought of that he could say. Although these are unusual cases, it is not uncommon for stutterers to pass themselves off successfully as normal speakers with many of their acquaintances by using word substitutions and circumlocutions. As a result, they are compelled to cope from day to day and moment to moment with the constant threat of exposure.

Most stutterers learn early that there are social penalties for the way they speak. Other children imitate them, strangers wring their hands in sympathy, busy storekeepers hurry them, teachers avoid calling on them, and the entertainment media sometimes capitalize on their frustration in order to make people laugh. As adults, they are often faced with listeners who look away from them when they stutter, compress their lips in an effort to keep from smiling, or try to help them by interjecting words or confidently advising them to "take it easy." Many stutterers become so sensitized by such behavior that they imagine that all listeners react unfavorably to their speech. They may see amusement, embarrassment, annoyance, impatience, or pity in almost every face.

To avoid social penalties, almost all stutterers resort to the avoidance of speaking situations at times. For some, avoidance has already become habituated by late pre-adolescence. They may balk at being sent on errands requiring speech. They will send a younger brother or sister to buy a comic book for them. In the classroom they may avoid reciting by pretending that they don't know the answer or didn't do the homework, and they may even play truant from school on a day when an oral report is due. Adult stutterers often avoid dating, using the telephone, and asking strangers for directions. When stutterers can't manage to avoid dining in a restaurant, they may order from the menu whatever they can say. A stutterer's choice of a vocation is often influenced, in large part, by the amount of speaking it will entail.

Many years ago, when fewer people attended college than do today, stutterers frequently avoided any higher education because of their problems in oral recitation. This showed up in a remarkable way. Studies done at various universities in the 1930s indicated that students who stuttered had considerably higher average scores on tests of intelligence than their normal speaking classmates. Yet, at the grade-school level, stutterers and nonstutterers tested alike. This was puzzling until it was realized that a selective factor was at work: many stutterers did not attend college unless they had superior intelligence to compensate for their defective speech. It is doubtful whether this difference in I.Q. still exists today in view of the pressures on young people to get a college education.

A good deal of the problem of coping with stuttering was summed up by Stephen, a college freshman, in a story he told about his last term in high school. That term he had an English teacher who put a great deal of emphasis on oral English. On the first day of class she announced that there were to be four oral book reports during the course of the term. From that moment, Stephen began to worry. As the time for the first book report began to approach, he found himself worrying while he was having breakfast, when he was on his way to school, during his classes, and while he was doing his homework in the evening. Finally, the first thought he had when he awoke in the morning and the last thought he had before falling asleep at night was about the book report. Stephen's worries were typical. What words was he going to have to say? Could he say them? If not, what words could he use in their place? By careful planning he managed to prepare a report that he thought he could give without much stuttering and was a good piece of work as well. But there was still some time left, so he began to worry about the words he had chosen to avoid stuttering. And then he began to feel that he would stutter on more and more of them, and to search for still other words to use instead. Finally the day came for the book report. Unfortunately, it was a large class and the teacher did not call on Stephen that day. Again the following day he sat waiting and wondering if he would be the next to recite. He could have volunteered to recite and gotten it over with, but he never managed to raise his hand. So it was not until the third day that the teacher called on him. He dragged himself to the front of the room, began to speak, and was overcome by panic. Words of one syllable were relatively easy for him to say, so he began to look for monosyllabic synonyms of many of his words. As a result, he said, what came out was such nonsense that when he had finished he went to his seat in abject shame. Stephen's performance seemed to him so disgraceful that he immediately began to brood about it. He brooded about it almost continually, every day, at home, at school, at all hours of the day. For a time, the first thought he had when awakening and the last thought he had before falling asleep was about the awful humiliation he had suffered in his English class. But after a while, he said, he stopped brooding. It was time to begin worrying about the next book report.

Theories of Stuttering

What exactly are stutterers doing, or what is happening to them, when they block? And how does the disorder get its start in the first place? One would think that behavior as unusual as stuttering would have a highly visible cause. Yet the cause, or causes, are subtle enough to be still, to a considerable extent, in the realm of theory despite almost a century of research and the exercise of a vast amount of imaginative thought by scientists and scholars. We can, however, narrow down the possibilities. To start with, all of the folk theories are probably wrong. Few if any children stutter because they think faster than they can talk, talk faster than they can think, have been tickled too much, have imitated another child who stutters, are tongue-tied, are "nervous," lack confidence, or are trying to get attention. The causes that have been suggested by serious students of the problem in this century cover a wide range of factors including an enlarged thymus gland, faulty visual imagery, conflicts over oral-erotic gratification, enforced right-handedness, labeling a child a stutterer, various forms of conditioning, brain abnormality, parental overprotection, communicative pressures, and high fetal levels of the male hormone testosterone. This is merely a sample. So many different theories can hardly all be right, even if stuttering has multiple causes as some have suggested. Clearly, much of the speculation on the subject that has appeared in scientific journals has consisted merely of ideas that occurred to someone while shaving. But a few common threads run through all of this speculation. Virtually all theories of stuttering can be reduced to three basic ideas about the nature of the stuttering block. In the order in which they appeared historically, these are the concepts that stuttering is:

1. A breakdown of coordination of speech muscles
2. A reaction of struggle or avoidance performed in the anticipation of imagined speech difficulty
3. An attempt to satisfy an unconscious neurotic need

The breakdown hypothesis rests on the fact that normal speech demands an exquisitely timed integration of a multitude of muscles of the oral structures, larynx, and respiratory system. It is easy to imagine that, under momentary stress, the coordination of all these muscles might fail. But why does it do so in some individuals and not others? The answer given is that some individuals possess a neuromuscular speech apparatus that is particularly prone to break down. So this concept of the stuttering block is generally found together with the assumption that stutterers have a defect of some kind in their physical constitution. But how can stuttering be an organic disorder when stutterers speak fluently so much of the time? The explanation is that the stutterer's vulnerable speech system performs normally as long as stress is absent. Stress means any emotional arousal, whether from psychological elements in an interpersonal relationship, fear of stuttering, or anything else. The breakdown hypothesis accords well with the stutterer's feeling of loss of control over his speech organs and with evidence that heredity plays a part in stuttering.

The anticipatory struggle hypothesis rests on the premise that human behavior can stray in maladaptive ways because of the things we know that aren't so. In the stutterer's case, it is the private superstition that speech is difficult that is alleged to be at the heart of the problem. If the word "Mississippi" is judged sufficiently hard to say, there may seem to be no other way to say it than with effort and caution. As a result, the word is bound to be produced in a labored and hesitant way, according to the theory. From this point of view, stuttering is considered to be similar to the failures by which certain accomplished musicians are afflicted when they perform in front of an audience, or the typing errors that most of us make when we are made self-conscious about the way we are typing. Almost anyone would be able to walk the length of a wooden plank without stepping off if the plank was on the ground. But put the plank fifty feet in the air, and it becomes an entirely different matter. Our gait would probably become so awkward that we would be in danger of falling off. Yet if someone were to inquire of us why we weren't walking normally, we would have to say it was because we were trying to keep from falling off. It is much the same paradox that stuttering presents, according to the anticipatory struggle hypothesis. The concept accords well with the observation that stutterers have little difficulty with their speech when they forget that they are stutterers, and with the belief of many stutterers that their speech is generally at its worst when it is most important to speak well. It is also consistent with clinical case reports suggesting that children often begin to stutter after adults have attempted to correct their articulation of speech sounds or tried to hasten their language development.

The unconscious need hypothesis assumes that the stuttering block is a purposeful, goal-directed act that performs a function in the psychic economy of a conflicted, neurotic individual. Theories based on this concept have been elaborated almost entirely within the framework of classical psychoanalysis, and so the needs that stuttering has been said to fulfill revolve chiefly around the Freudian themes of sex and aggression. The notion that stuttering is a symptom of neurosis is not as popular as it was in an era when the social environment was assigned a greater burden of responsibility for human ills than it bears today, but it is still current, particularly among psychotherapists, psychiatrists, and the educated public. On the surface at least, the hypothesis derives some plausibility from the observation that stutterers often appear anxious and the fact that they are apt to stutter more when they are socially ill at ease, feel inferior, or anticipate rejection, but its main support is to be found in psychoanalysts' assertions about the stutterer's neurotic conflicts as these are revealed to them through the psychoanalytic process.

The breakdown, anticipatory struggle, and neurotic need hypotheses have formed the basis of a vast amount of theory and research on stuttering for nearly a century. Speculations about stuttering have taken a myriad of forms, but most of them come down to the question of which of these three conceptions of the stuttering block is valid.

CHAPTER TWO

From Aristotle
to Freud

Early Theories

It was the Greeks, as usual, who made the first observations on stuttering that were remotely scientific. Hippocrates (c. 460–377 B.C.), traditionally regarded as the father of medicine, referred briefly in his works to *trauloi*, by which he apparently meant stuttering or several speech difficulties that included stuttering. Somewhat later Aristotle, who wrote about practically everything, discussed stuttering unambiguously. He offered the suggestion that stuttering is due to a weak tongue that acts too sluggishly to keep up with the conceptions of the mind. Not to discredit Aristotle, this sounds a bit like what Athenian mothers were undoubtedly saying about their stuttering children. The notion that in stuttering thinking outruns speech recurred repeatedly in learned speculations well into the nineteenth century, when we find Andrew Combe, an Englishman, stating that stuttering results from "the ineffectual struggle of a small organ of language to keep pace with the workings of larger organs of intellect." The tongue continued to be viewed as the major source of the trouble from the time of Aristotle onward. In the second century A.D., Galen, the renowned Greek physician of Pergamum, thought that stutterers' tongues were either too short or too thick and swollen. Although Galen is thought to have founded the modern science of experimental physiology, he evidently neglected to measure stutterers' tongues in any number.

Galen's observations were couched in the terms of the ancient humoral system of medicine according to which the four significant properties of the body were moisture, dryness, heat, and cold. This system continued to be the basis of scholarly views about stuttering throughout the Middle Ages and Renaissance. In Venice, in 1583, Mercurialis published a volume on the diseases of children in which he recommended applying either moisture or warming and drying substances to the tongue, depending on circumstances. He believed that stuttering might be caused by excessive moisture or dryness of the tongue, brain, or muscles, or by a missing tooth, and advocated a variety of therapeutic measures including diet and vocal exercises. In 1627, Sir Francis Bacon attributed stuttering simply to coldness or dryness of the tongue and prescribed wine in moderation "because it heateth."

With the coming of the scientific revolution in the seventeenth century, more was learned about the physiology of speech production, and the tongue was gradually joined by the larynx, the breathing mechanism, the nerves, and eventually the brain as suspects in the causation of stuttering. It is evident that from Aristotle to the nineteenth century, almost all workers who addressed themselves to the problem considered it to be an organic disorder consisting of the recurrent breakdown of a weak, vulnerable speech apparatus. At the beginning of the nineteenth century, there was a rapid development of the modern science of neurophysiology. As a result, the brain largely supplanted the peripheral speech organs in theories of stuttering, and the breakdown hypothesis assumed more or less its present form. In nineteenth-century France, Britain, and Germany, physiologists and physicians offered theories in which a defect of one or another part of the brain was said to cause stuttering through its effect on breathing, the functioning of the tongue, or the action of the larynx.

A New Approach to the Problem

In the meantime, a wholly new outlook on stuttering had slowly been in the making. In the eighteenth century, some early forerunners of the psychologists of today came to be known as "associationists" because they were influenced by the belief of the philosopher John Locke that our knowledge and personality result from a process of association of ideas. Chief among the associationists were the physician and philosopher David Hartley, the physician Erasmus Darwin (grandfather of Charles), and the German-Jewish philosopher Moses Mendelssohn. All three of these thinkers were interested in speech and language, both normal and abnormal, and all of them wrote about stuttering as a disorder in which learning, emotions, and mental processes played the principal part. Here, in embryo, was a conception of stuttering that was ultimately to lead to both the anticipatory struggle and the unconscious need hypotheses.

It was in the nineteenth century that the anticipatory struggle hypothesis first appeared in any clear, explicit form. Probably it was no accident that the individuals who broached it were so often stutterers themselves. No one understands as well as the stutterer the irony of stuttering that is captured in that hypothesis, the irony that a Frenchman once expressed when he said that he had one faculty that he could make use of only when he didn't need it, and that was speech. In 1830, Schulthess, a Swiss physician and physiologist, and a stutterer, called stuttering a "lalophobia," a phobia regarding articulation of speech sounds. In 1842, Merkel, a professor of medicine at Leipzig University, and a stutterer, wrote that stuttering blocks were caused by a failure of confidence in the ability to communicate. He surmised that the disorder originated in early traumatic experiences during speaking. Beesel, a Prussian teacher, suggested in 1845 that the stutterer's struggles in the anticipation and the act of stuttering represent an effort to overcome a real or imagined difficulty. In 1869, Wyneken, a German physician who stuttered, called the stutterer a *Sprachzweifler* or speech doubter. He said the stutterer is like a person who, at the moment that he decides to leap over a chasm, is tormented by doubts that he will make it. In 1890, Denhardt, director of a German institute for stutterers, blamed the problem on the stutterer's fixed belief in the difficulty of speech. He noted that words and situations associated with stuttering in the past may acquire the power to evoke stuttering on later occasions, an entirely up-to-date observation.

As the nineteenth century drew to a close, psychoanalysis appeared on the scene and the way was prepared for a third hypothesis about the nature of the stuttering block. Freud himself wrote very little about stuttering and we have only fragmentary reports on his views about it. We know that in 1888 and 1890 he treated a 40-year-old widow, Frau Emmy von N., who had a stutter, among other problems. It appears from his account of the case that the stutter decreased after a traumatic event associated with its onset was brought to consciousness. The stuttering was not eradicated, however, and we are told that Freud believed psychoanalysis had not found an explanation for stuttering or been effective in treating it. In a personal letter to his close associate Ferenczi in 1915, he theorized that stuttering is due to conflicts over excremental functions. At any rate, in the early years of the twentieth century, some of Freud's students wrote extensively about stuttering as a symptom of emotional conflicts and gave a rich elaboration to the concept that the stutterer blocks in order to satisfy deep and complex psychic needs. The story of that development belongs to another chapter.

Treatment in the Nineteenth Century

The nineteenth century was notable for a greatly increased effort to treat stutterers. The new emphasis on mind and emotion in stuttering almost certainly had something to do with this. Also, there was that optimistic intellectual climate of the time, with its faith in progress and the attitude that science and education together could overcome most of the ills of humankind. Stuttering suddenly seemed curable, and many old and new methods were tried. Some of these were touted by commercial institutions for treating the disorder. Others were employed by physicians, particularly in Germany, where speech pathology flourished as a province of medicine. Although the techniques used were varied and numerous, they were all examples of three general approaches: suggestion, relaxation, and distraction.

Suggestion

Many of the most common practices, such as speech drills, almost certainly owed whatever effectiveness they had to the stutterer's belief that they would help. A striking characteristic of stuttering is its readiness to respond to suggestion. The most blatant examples involve hypnosis. Experience in the nineteenth century showed that if stutterers are hypnotized and told that they will be fluent when they awake, they will usually speak without stuttering following the hypnotic session, though for all too short a time. But post-hypnotic suggestions are only an extreme example of an influence that others exert over us continually in greater or lesser degree in our daily lives. In the case of stuttering, the most powerful suggestions emanate from therapies in which the stutterer has strong faith or from therapists who advocate them. We can set it down as an axiom that anything the stutterer firmly believes will help is very likely to do so—temporarily in most cases. There is hardly any other way to explain the repeated use of some of the remedies that were employed in the 1800s. Vocal exercises, breathing exercises, and articulatory drills were used regularly. These must, at times, have resulted in some apparent benefit. Yet we know that as a rule there is nothing wrong with the stutterer's voice, breathing, or articulation of speech sounds, except when stuttering or its anticipation interferes with them. Some physicians prescribed diets. In many cases, stutterers were prohibited from speaking for periods of weeks. Various other forms of hocus-pocus were invented and some still make their appearance from time to time.

The most bizarre therapy in which suggestion played a part was tongue surgery. In one remarkable year, 1841, well over 200 stutterers had their tongues operated on. The principal figure in this episode was a famous Prussian surgeon, Johannes Dieffenbach. He believed that removing a portion of the base of the tongue would interrupt nerve impulses causing what he perceived to be spasms of the tongue or vocal cords. For a short time the operation was hailed as a brilliant success. When they had recovered from the operation, the patients spoke without stuttering. A number of other surgeons began operating on stutterers' tongues in France, Britain, and the United States, and one or two claimed priority as originators of the procedure. But by the time the year was up, this enthusiastic activity had all but ceased. The patients, it seems, were stuttering again. What had caused their short-lived fluency? Perhaps the distraction of post-operative pain and swelling had some effect, but it is more than likely that the stutterer's belief in the operation played a major part. In 1841, anesthetic techniques were still in their infancy. And surgery was far more dangerous than it is today; several stutterers died of hemorrhage on the operating table. We can be sure that any person who submitted to this treatment believed in its effectiveness.

Today, suggestion as a treatment for stuttering has largely been abandoned as without value in the long run. We still hear of hypnosis being advocated for stuttering from time to time, but rarely by professional speech pathologists. Most of us not only reject the use of suggestion in any form, but are at pains to avoid using it unwittingly. It is all too easy to employ suggestion inadvertently. Anyone with the title of doctor may impart it to a susceptible subject. It can stem from the fervor of a speech clinician possessed of a new method. Often, its source is the personality of a clinician who happens to be naturally endowed with a quality that inspires faith. As a speech pathologist I am not excessively burdened by that problem, and yet, I remember a young student who came to me after our very first session and announced that I had cured him. I prepared him gently for relapse.

Since this is the last time suggestion will be mentioned at any length in this book, let us give it its due. Clinical experience indicates that children may derive more lasting benefit from it than adults. We occasionally encounter incidents like the one reported in an old book by Heltman in which a little girl stopped stuttering when she was advised by a friend's father to tie a string around her finger. In essence, suggestion involves the uncritical acceptance of what another person tells us, and this is what children habitually do. Perhaps this helps to explain why children so much more often than adults overcome stuttering completely through therapy, regardless of the method.

Relaxation

General bodily relaxation is another treatment that the nineteenth century knew about. Stuttering is a struggle reaction. There is a basic appropriateness about relaxation as a remedy for it. Without muscular tension, it is impossible to stutter. Relaxation can be taught. Some stutterers learn the knack so well that they can turn it on when they need it. As a practical matter, however, simple training in relaxation has not proved very effective for most stutterers. The reason is that tension and anxiety go hand in hand. Most stutterers can speak fluently while lying relaxed on a cot in the speech clinic, but when a bustling waitress with her pencil poised demands their order, their ability to relax tends to desert them. Despite this drawback, attempts have been made for many years to incorporate relaxation into treatment programs. In two recent efforts, stutterers have been conditioned to react to feared situations by relaxing, or have been taught to relax speech muscles by biofeedback. We will describe these methods briefly later.

Distraction

Stuttering absorbs attention; other activity stops during a block. Stuttering therefore ceases if the speaker's attention is focused with enough concentration elsewhere. Stutterers know this. They invent ways of distracting themselves from anticipated stutterings. An object clutched in the pocket at critical moments may serve. One stutterer I knew mentally hummed themes from symphonies. Some assume an artificial manner. Others habitually speak with a pipe or cigarette in the mouth. One stutterer spoke fluently for a time by adopting a Texas drawl. Another, who was from Texas, managed fairly well whenever she abandoned her hometown speech.

Of all distractors, few work as quickly and conveniently as novel speech patterns. For this reason, it has always been tempting to try to help stutterers by teaching them to talk differently. During the nineteenth century this method was adopted very widely. Stutterers were instructed to: intone their utterances slowly by prolonging every syllable; time each syllable to a rhythmic movement of a finger; use a monotone or a sing-song inflection; slur the consonants and prolong the vowels; shorten the vowels and stress the consonants; modify their breathing for speech; and so forth. To be sure, a few of these patterns may owe their effectiveness to more than distraction alone. For example, slow or rhythmic speech may work partly because stutterers generally have less difficulty with utterances that require simple motor planning. But essentially any change that can be imagined in the stutterer's articulation, voice, or breathing, whether easy or difficult, will produce immediate fluency, and very few of them offer anything more than novelty. It may seem odd that something as simple as talking on a higher or lower pitch can serve to distract a person from stuttering. In all probability, it is not so much the effort involved that does it, but the perception of oneself in a strange role. It is akin to the freedom from inhibitions that travelers sometimes feel when they speak a foreign language. The author John Updike, writing about his own stuttering, put it well: "Any mechanism which displaces your customary voice—singing, having a sore throat, affecting a funny accent—eliminates the stoppage; the captive tongue is released into *Maskenfreiheit*, the freedom conferred by masks."

This masquerade effect is illustrated exceptionally well by an incident recorded in an early work on speech disorders by Scripture. He was visited by a stutterer who was humiliated by his inability to give dictation to his secretary. Discovering that this individual had utterly no singing voice, Scripture taught him to sing whatever he wished to say. The man did this with complete freedom from stuttering as long as he thought he was singing, although his voice was indistinguishable from an ordinary speaking voice. The treatment was a failure, because he refused to make a fool of himself by singing to his secretary.

The idea of designing appliances to be worn in the mouth is also very old. The U.S. Patent Office alone lists over fifty such devices for the cure of stuttering resembling surreal corkscrews, dental appliances, or animal traps. Most of them date from the early 1900s, but a century earlier the famous French physician Jean-Marc-Gaspard Itard, among others, was placing ivory forks under stutterers' tongues. The rationale for these various contraptions was that they supported the tongue, exercised the speech organs, or helped to control them; but if they were of any help it was because stutterers were distracted by the objects in their mouths and the distorted speech that resulted. No doubt, an element of suggestion also contributed.

The one great advantage of distraction as a basis for therapy is that it produces immediate and total fluency. This is especially true of novel speech patterns such as syllable prolongation, rhythmic speech, and the like, and of all the old methods these have been the most enduring. But they also have disadvantages. In the majority of cases, there is some degree of relapse after a number of months. They tend to interfere with the spontaneity of speech by requiring stutterers to give a great deal of attention to how they are speaking. And they generally impart an unnatural quality to speech.

By the beginning of the twentieth century, it was possible to look back on many years of experience with the methods of suggestion, relaxation, and distraction. Some stutterers had apparently been helped, but it was clear that the methods had limitations and drawbacks, despite the extravagant claims that had often been made for them. In the early decades of the twentieth century, two separate waves of reaction developed against them. One had its source in the new psychoanalytic perception of stuttering. Psychoanalysts asserted that the old techniques not only failed to bring lasting benefit, but could actually be harmful. They argued that since stuttering was a neurotic symptom, as they believed, it served as a defense against impulses from the unconscious that threatened the individual's psychic equilibrium, and that removing the symptom by methods other than psychoanalysis might therefore precipitate a more serious emotional disorder. The second reaction against the old methods came later, with the advent of speech pathology as a scientific and academic discipline in the United States and the rise of the Iowa school of stuttering therapy.

CHAPTER THREE

The Search for Psychodynamics

Psychoanalytic Theories

Despite the doubts Freud may have had about stuttering, several of his followers in the early decades of the twentieth century confidently advanced theories about its underlying dynamics. Prominent among these theorists were Isador H. Coriat and Otto Fenichel.

Coriat and Fenichel based their interpretations of stuttering on Freud's theory of neurosis as psychosexual fixation. Freud attached deep psychological importance to the sexual needs of human beings and believed that such needs are present in early infancy in the form of a desire for oral gratification. In the earliest of Freud's well known stages of psychosexual development, the oral-dependent phase, an infant's oral-erotic desires are freely indulged in the act of sucking, and complete dependence on the mother is taken for granted. But soon weaning takes place, and the necessity arises for some separation from the mother. The child ordinarily resolves the conflicts that result from these deprivations. But, on occasion, the deprivations are unduly harsh or early, symptomatic of a disturbed relationship with a neurotic mother. In these cases, according to classical Freudian theory, the oral-dependent needs may be repressed rather than resolved and may manifest themselves in adulthood as neurotic overeating, excessive talking or smoking, emotional dependency, and the like.

Normally the child makes its peace with oral-dependent deprivation and progresses to the anal-sadistic stage. Now the emotional crises arise from parental meddling with anal-erotic gratification in the form of toilet training. Also, at this time, the child learns that the expression of anger and hostility must be limited to socially acceptable forms. According to the theory, psychosexual fixation at this stage leads in adulthood to the so-called anal character traits of excessive orderliness, cleanliness, and punctiliousness and in extreme cases to obsessive-compulsive neuroses like hand-washing compulsions. On the "sadistic" side, neurotic conflicts over expressions of anger at this stage may lead in adulthood to latent hostility and covert aggression beneath a veneer of exaggerated sweetness and amiability. Under normal conditions, children resolve these conflicts too. After a period in which sexuality lies dormant, they are said to enter the Oedipal or Elektra stage marked by sexual attraction to the parent of the opposite sex. Following this, they emerge into adult genital sexuality.

Coriat, writing between 1915 and 1930, was apparently the first to expand fully on stuttering within this classic Freudian scheme. He advanced the theory that stuttering is an attempt to satisfy unresolved oral-erotic needs. Stuttering, he said, is oral activity and hence may be perceived unconsciously as pleasurable. In stuttering, a person may gain partial satisfaction for oral cravings without admitting their forbidden nature. He depicted the stuttering block as a symbolic sucking activity or molding as of a bolus of food.

In 1945, Fenichel, one of several major figures in psychoanalysis who were repatriated to the United States from Germany in the 1930s, devoted a chapter to stuttering in his famous work, *The Psychoanalytic Theory of Neurosis*. In contrast to Coriat, Fenichel attributed stuttering mainly to fixation on the anal-sadistic level. This conformed to Freud's speculation that the disorder represented a "displacement upward" of conflicts surrounding the anal sphincter, the implication being that in withholding or forcefully expelling words, the stutterer engages in a kind of symbolic constipation or diarrhea. But Fenichel's view of stuttering placed greater emphasis on conflicts over hostility and aggression. He asserted that we all unconsciously regard speech as a hostile act, since virtually all of the outlets we are normally permitted for aggression are verbal—quarreling, insulting, slandering, and so on. Moreover, to be aggressive is to be outspoken. Stutterers, he said, differ from others in harboring an unusual amount of latent hostility and abnormal guilt and anxiety about revealing it. As a result, stutterers are caught between two opposing urges. Consciously, they wish to speak, but unconsciously, they fear that by speaking they will inflict injury on the listener. From this conflict, blocked, hesitant speech emerges. Fenichel expressed the concept succinctly by saying that words are weapons and the stutterer unconsciously feels that such powerful weapons must be handled with care.

Conflict regarding the expression of hostility proved to be the most frequent theme in further psychoanalytic writings about stuttering. A common observation in psychoanalytic therapy with stutterers was that they suddenly spoke fluently when they became angry. This was taken to indicate that the symptom disappeared when they overcame their inhibitions about being openly hostile.

This by no means exhausts the subject of psychoanalytic ideas about stuttering. For example, the disorder was viewed as a defense against the impulse to utter sexual, oral, or anal words. Stutterers were also said to be symbolically chewing up their parents as they chewed up their words. Conflicts on the Oedipal level were invoked. The boy might unconsciously wish to suppress speech; to speak is to be potent, and the boy might fear to provoke the wrath of the father with whom he was in sexual rivalry. To speak is to be aggressive and male, so the girl at this stage might stutter out of fear of punishment for attempting to adopt the role of a sexually potent male.

It must be said that many psychoanalysts have discarded much of Freud's theory of psychosexual development and would reject many of these notions about stuttering. We can be sure that when psychoanalysts try to help stutterers, they often proceed on assumptions about the problem that are in keeping with Neo-Freudian theories of neurosis. But no new psychoanalytic theories of stuttering have been advanced.

Research on the Stutterer's Personality

The growth of psychoanalysis from a small, embattled movement to a discipline of great prestige in the first half of the twentieth century was an event of incalculable moment for stutterers and their parents. It meant that a generation or two of stutterers would live their lives thinking of themselves as "nervous" or neurotic and that untold numbers of stutterers' parents would wonder what they had done wrong. The word that stuttering is an emotional disorder was carried to the public by way of medicine, social work, psychotherapy, and other helping professions. During World War II, stutterers were rejected from the armed services because it was assumed that they were apt to break down under stress. Even speech pathologists, who knew better than most that there were conflicting theories about stuttering, were influenced. In the 1930s and 1940s, many speech pathologists disclaimed any qualifications for treating stutterers and vowed that any stutterer who came to them for help would be referred to a psychotherapist without delay. Eventually the climate of opinion in the field of speech pathology changed, but that was not until a vast amount of labor had been expended on the scientific investigation of the stutterer's personality.

The bulk of this research was done in the three decades between 1930 and 1960. During this period almost every test of personality known to clinical psychology was administered to groups of stutterers and control groups of nonstutterers. The researchers were for the most part clinical psychologists and speech pathologists. Many seemed eager to demonstrate the neurotic nature of stuttering. Some were skeptics. Some were certainly motivated by the purest scientific objectivity. Any number simply wanted to get their doctoral dissertations done. No doubt, this disparity accounts for much of the conflicting nature of the conclusions to which they came. Here and there investigators seemed to find evidence of distinct emotional ill health among stutterers. For example, one researcher found stutterers to be more neurotic, more introverted, less dominant, less self-confident, and less sociable than nonstutterers. Another inferred that they were seriously disturbed, emotionally immature, and repressed, and that they showed many signs of neurotic involvement. Yet in many more cases investigators found no differences between stutterers and control subjects. Still others pointed to deviations in some isolated aspects of stutterers' test performances, but there was little uniformity about such findings. We can now look back on this research from enough distance to see it as a whole, and despite all the disagreement, certain broad conclusions stand out clearly. They are best discussed in relation to the two kinds of personality tests that psychologists have devised: personality inventories and projective tests.

Personality Inventories

The structured tests, or personality inventories as they are called, consist of a series of questions such as "Does it make you uneasy to cross a bridge over water?" or a series of statements to be marked true or false, for example "I have difficulty in starting to do things." These pencil-and-paper tests deal chiefly with what is generally referred to as adjustment, although they are usually subdivided into categories such as morale, family relations, and social adjustment, or into scales that measure depression, hypochondriasis, social introversion, and the like. On the large number of occasions on which such tests were given to stutterers in research investigations, the great majority of individuals scored well within the normal range of adjustment. In many of these studies, the stutterers as a group achieved an average score equal to that of their normal speaking control groups. In certain other studies their mean score was somewhat lower. Even in those cases, the stutterers and controls markedly overlapped: Many stutterers were in better emotional health than many of the nonstutterers. To the extent that their test performance sometimes suggested mild degrees of maladjustment, it is arguable that this was not the cause but the result of stuttering. One fact about the research findings tends to support this inference: When stutterers seemed less well adjusted than nonstutterers, this was usually in the area of social adjustment and social skills. Some tests in effect penalized stutterers for stuttering. One inventory on which stutterers achieved relatively low scores in several studies contained items such as "Do you find it difficult to speak in public?" "If you are dining out, do you prefer someone else to order dinner for you?" "Are you often in a state of excitement?" and "Can you usually express yourself better in speech than in writing?" Another test assessed the subject's freedom from "nervous symptoms" and counted stuttering as one.

The results of one study summed up particularly well what we have learned about stutterers from these structured personality tests. In 1952, Dahlstrom and Craven administered the *Minnesota Multiphasic Personality Inventory* to 100 stutterers enrolled in the University of Iowa Speech Clinic and compared their test performance with that of 100 university freshmen, a group of psychiatric patients, and a sample of college students who had applied for counseling because of personal problems. The stutterers did not differ significantly from the freshmen; they were in distinctly better emotional health than the psychiatric patients; and they performed most similarly to the students with personal problems.

Projective Techniques

From the first, pencil-and-paper tests have been criticized on the grounds that they fail to probe beneath relatively superficial aspects of personality and that subjects can too easily fake responses that are socially acceptable. At an early date, psychologists tried to find a remedy for these defects in so-called projective tests. The principle underlying such tests is quite plausible. Under ordinary conditions, our behavior is largely determined by social learning and convention. Most of our behavior therefore reveals little of importance about us as individuals. But put us in a situation in which society gives us no clue to how to react, and what we do is apt to reveal unique aspects of our personality, possibly significant ones. This, for example, is the basis of the famous Rorschach Test, in which the subject is shown an inkblot and asked, "What might this be?" From such aspects of the subject's responses as the perception of movement, the use of color, the use of the whole blot or of details, and many others, the psychologist who interprets the test draws inferences about a variety of character traits. The result is a richer insight into a subject's personality than is obtained through a structured test. For this, a price must be paid. On the whole, projective tests are not as reliable as personality inventories. Psychologists may disagree about the meaning of the results. The validity of interpretations are often open to question. For these reasons, psychologists generally consider such tests best used as part of a total diagnostic examination in which the results can be verified by other tests, interviews, and clinical observation.

It is little wonder, then, that the results of the Rorschach investigations of stutterers proved to be so conflicting. In a series of such studies one researcher found poor control of intellectual functioning of an emotional origin. One found a failure to recognize inner promptings and respond impulsively to the environment. One emphasized stutterers' obsessive-compulsive make-up. Another found lower self-awareness and empathic ability. And various others found little or nothing to distinguish stutterers from normal speakers. Writers who later reviewed the Rorschach findings and tried to make sense of them have generally been baffled. One complained that workers sometimes drew the same inferences from diametrically opposed findings. Another concluded that the Rorschach Test seems to offer "an amorphous flux from which any desired interpretation could be pulled."

The *TAT*, or *Thematic Apperception Test*, is another well known projective technique. Here the subject is asked to make up a story about each of a series of pictures which contain human figures of ambiguous age and sex. The stories lend themselves to inferences about the subject's psychological needs, attitudes, and strivings. A comprehensive TAT study by Richardson in 1944 found no differences between stutterers and normal speakers in needs, reactions to frustration, attitudes toward the environment, adequacy of the central character, and unsatisfactory endings. In further studies the TAT and various other projective techniques were used principally in attempts to verify specific psychoanalytic assertions about stutterers. Researchers found no differences between stutterers and nonstutterers in passive-dependency or anal character traits. With regard to oral and anal eroticism and latent hostility, the results were equivocal or sharply conflicting.

Conclusion

After the 1950s, few personality studies of stutterers were done. A tacit understanding had developed that it would be futile to do any more. And to anyone who drew back from the confusion of conflicting and ambiguous findings to view them as a whole, several facts seemed to be conclusively established. First, stutterers are not typically malad-justed, except to the extent that their speech difficulty makes them so. Second, stutterers rarely present the picture of any of the known psy-choneuroses (anxiety, depression, hysteria, obsessive-compulsivity, and so on) that is so clearly evident on many personality tests. Third, stutter-ers do not share any specific character structure or set of personality traits; they are as different from each other as any group of individuals are likely to be.

The Effectiveness of Psychotherapy

By the 1960s, few speech pathologists thought of stuttering as a neurotic disorder, but the message of the personality research was much slower to reach other helping professions and the educated public. When psycho-analysts did take notice of the research, it was usually to argue that no personality tests could probe the underlying psychodynamics of stutter-ing as well as the psychoanalytic process itself. And so psychoanalysis and other forms of psychotherapy continued to be used to treat some stutterers.

How effective has psychotherapy been? Factual information on this question is scarce. In 1923, A. A. Brill, who helped to introduce Freud's work to the United States, reported on his treatment of 69 adult stutterers by psychoanalysis. The majority gained normal speech during therapy, but after a period of eleven years only five were "really well." Most of the others, he wrote, "seem to be satisfied that they have been improved, although they have their ups and downs." There seem to have been no further follow-up reports comparable to Brill's. From time to time ac-counts of successful psychotherapy with single cases have appeared. Claims of success in individual cases have also been published for many other kinds of therapy for stuttering. In the field of psychotherapy stut-tering seems to have acquired a reputation for being difficult to treat. This is sometimes imputed to the stutterer's unconscious resistance to re-covery.

CHAPTER FOUR

The Orton-Travis Theory of Cerebral Dominance

In the 1920s, great changes in ideas about the nature of certain human illnesses were in store. The Freudian outlook had not yet reached that pinnacle of influence that caused a variety of physical aberrations from allergy to autism to be regarded for such a long time as emotional in origin, but it was about to. The medical outlook of the nineteenth century which viewed emotional or behavioral disturbances as "nervous" disorders in the literal sense was soon to go into decline. But it still prevailed. In the last years of this decade there emerged a neurological theory of stuttering that enjoyed very wide acceptance for a brief period. Some medical texts still cite it as a current theory. We still sometimes hear it stated as fact that changing children's handedness may cause them to stutter. And certain features of the theory are reflected in some of the most current hypotheses about the disorder.

Lee Edward Travis

Although the broad outlines of the theory were suggested by Samuel T. Orton, it was the research and teaching of Lee Edward Travis that were mainly responsible for the theory's influence. The story of Lee Travis is bound up with that of another figure, Carl Emil Seashore, who played an important role in the origin of speech pathology as a non-medical discipline in the United States. Seashore was a psychologist who had

Lee Edward Travis

done distinguished work on voice, hearing, and the testing of musical ability around the turn of the century. In the 1920s, he was the Dean of the Graduate College at the State University of Iowa. In the course of his career the subject of speech disorders had impressed itself upon him and he saw that there was inadequate knowledge about their cause and treatment. Seashore possessed the imagination to think forth a whole new profession and field of research.[1] Aware that no existing academic department of the university could teach all that could then be learned about speech and its disorders, he proceeded to break down interdepartmental barriers to establish a new academic discipline. Selecting a promising young graduate student in psychology, he had him take courses in the department of speech, the department of psychology, and various departments of the university medical school. In 1924 the student became the first person ever to be awarded the Ph.D. as a specialist in the scientific study and clinical treatment of speech disorders. That student was Lee Edward Travis.

In 1925, at Seashore's invitation, a small group of scholars with an interest in speech disorders met in Travis's living room to discuss the founding of a scientific academy for the study of speech disorders. They came from various institutions and from fields as disparate as psychiatry, voice science, and the teaching of language to the deaf. Among the guests was Robert West of the University of Wisconsin. In a few years, the academy grew into a small association that held periodic conventions and published a journal devoted to research on stuttering and other speech disorders. Eventually this became the American Speech-Language-Hearing Association, which today numbers over 60,000 members. Travis and West founded the profession of speech pathology and audiology in the United States. West was the association's first president and kept it going when conventions were sometimes attended by as few as six people. Travis was the preeminent teacher and researcher in the growing field and did more than any other single person to establish it as a research-oriented discipline. He was a tall, handsome, compelling man whose students sat at his feet. Years later one of them wrote that he taught them to question accepted beliefs and made them feel like comrades in the search for truth. Until the rapid growth of the profession after World War II, the University of Iowa was one of the few institutions in the country at which one could study speech pathology. As a result, probably the majority of young people studying the subject in the United States today are students of students of students of Lee Travis.

In 1927 one of the first university speech clinics in the country was established at the University of Iowa and Travis was named its director. True to Seashore's original purpose, one of its foremost missions was research, and Travis, aided by his devoted students, set about doing it with energy and zeal. His main interest was in stuttering, and he brought

1. Seashore lived to see his vision become a reality. Many years later, as one of a small group of students and teachers who were huddled around a radio in the University of Iowa's East Hall listening to the news of Pearl Harbor, I saw a distinguished-looking elderly man who was pointed out to me as Dean Emeritus Seashore.

stutterers into the laboratory for neurophysiological study with the most advanced instrumentation of the day. His subjects were for the most part university students, among whom many severe stutterers were to be found. A number of the stutterers who attended the University of Iowa speech clinic in those days and served as subjects in Travis's studies stayed on to earn doctorates in speech pathology and eventually became noted authorities on their speech difficulty.

An Ingenious Theory About Doubtful Facts

Travis was eager to test a speculation that had been advanced by Samuel Orton, the head of the University Department of Psychiatry. Orton's theory provided an explanation for the alleged fact that stutterers were apt to be left-handed or ambidextrous and that many of them had had their handedness changed from left to right in childhood. The prevailing opinion today is that there is little basis for these assumptions, but they were accepted by many at the time. A survey of schoolchildren in London in 1912 and another in St. Louis in 1916 seemed to show that an unusual number of stutterers had been forced to write with the right hand. And there was much anecdotal evidence. A boy was supposed to have begun to stutter while training himself in left-handed skills in his determination to become a "southpaw" pitcher. Several institutionalized mentally retarded children were reported to have begun to stutter when some months of left-handed training was given to them on the theory that this would open up additional centers in the brain. There was even a story about a 58-year-old right-handed man who stuttered after his right arm was amputated.

The explanation, as elaborated by Travis in 1931 in his book, *Speech Pathology*, was that stuttering is caused by a lack of sufficient dominance of one half of the brain over the other. Travis pointed out that the human body is symmetrical, the structures and muscles on one side generally duplicating those on the other. This symmetry extends to midline structures like the tongue, lips, jaw, and palate, in which muscle fibers on the left side of the organ mirror those on the right. The nerve impulses that activate the body's voluntary muscles come from the two halves of the cerebrum, the left cerebral hemisphere controlling the muscles on the right half of the body and the right hemisphere controlling those on the left. This much is fact. The rest was theory. Orton and Travis reasoned that a mechanism had to exist for synchronizing the nerve impulses from the two halves of the brain. Otherwise, they thought, nerve impulses would arrive at the two halves of the speech organs at different times, interfering with their smooth functioning. No difficulty would be apparent in gross movements of these structures, as in eating, but the rapid, precise coordinations of speech would tend to break down.

Orton and Travis hypothesized that the synchronization came about because one half of the brain was normally dominant over the other. Cerebral dominance was already a familiar concept in two other connections. It was well known that in most individuals one hemisphere, usually the left, is dominant for language functions. Autopsies on patients with aphasia who had lost some of these functions because of brain damage had proved that. Cerebral dominance also had something to do with handedness. Although there was some doubt about the ultimate cause of hand preference, it was obvious that if the right hand was preferred for most activities, this signified the dominance of the left hemisphere for handedness. Orton and Travis suggested that the same hemisphere that was dominant for language and handedness was also dominant for timing the nerve impulses to the paired musculatures. In other words, the dominant hemisphere determined the precise moment when both hemispheres would fire their impulses to the right and left sides of the speech mechanism.

The Orton-Travis theory asserted that stutterers differed from normal speakers in the lack of a safe margin of dominance of one hemisphere over the other. This resulted in conflict between the hemispheres, inadequate synchronization of the nerve impulses to the paired speech muscles, and a predisposition to stuttering. Such a theory implied a number of things about stutterers' handedness. First, a person with deficient cerebral dominance would be likely to be a relatively ambidextrous person. Orton and Travis theorized that many stutterers had inborn ambidextrous tendencies. Second, forcing children to write with the nonpreferred hand risked causing them to stutter. Such training, they thought, exercised the nondominant hemisphere at the expense of the dominant one, and thus reduced the margin of hemispheric dominance. Finally, the theory accounted for the alleged prevalence of left-handedness among stutterers. It might seem that a left-handed person with a dominant right hemisphere ought to have as safe a margin of cerebral dominance as a right-handed individual. Orton and Travis argued that the left-handed person often does not, simply because of the pressures in a right-handed society to use the right hand. In fact, it is quite true that left-handed individuals as a group tend to be more ambidextrous than right-handed people. Many who call themselves left-handed use the right hand for a considerable number of activities. Some use the left hand only for writing.

So the theory achieved a resounding success in accounting for what were then believed to be significant facts about stuttering. This marked the beginning of an episode of over a decade in which the attention of both researchers and clinicians was focused on stutterers' handedness. By the time it was over, there was serious doubt about the facts, and the theory had lost favor. But this was not before the concept of insufficient cerebral dominance had scored a further triumph. In 1934, Travis announced that he had obtained laboratory verification of the theory by means of a new device called an electromyograph. The electromyograph detects the electrical potentials that are present in a muscle when the arrival of nerve impulses causes the muscle to contract. Its invention gave Travis the opportunity to make a direct test of the assumption that the nerve impulses reaching the two halves of the paired speech muscles were not synchronized during stuttering. Attaching electrical contacts to subjects' right and left masseter muscles (muscles that elevate the jaw), he recorded the precise instants that the muscles began to contract. He found that during the normal speech of both stutterers and nonstutterers, there was precise synchronization of the nerve impulses. But during stuttering, just as he had predicted, the impulses reached the left and right masseter muscles at different times. To Travis and his students, the evidence that inadequate cerebral dominance caused stuttering seemed incontrovertible. It was not until twenty years later that the fallacy was exposed. In his enthusiasm, Travis had ignored a truism that was to dog researchers on stuttering repeatedly: abnormalities observed during the act of speech may be a cause, a result, or a feature of stuttering.

Research on Stutterers' Laterality

It was to Travis's credit that, having adopted a theory to explain certain facts, he did not take the facts for granted. He and his students immediately set to work studying stutterers' handedness. Similar studies were done at a few other institutions as interest in the cerebral dominance theory grew. The problem undoubtedly seemed straightforward enough at first: It was merely necessary to determine what percentage of stutterers and nonstutterers were left-handed, were ambidextrous, and had had their handedness changed from left to right in childhood. But researchers soon found that this approach was hopelessly naive. It produced results so diverse that reports of left-handedness among stutterers ranged from 2 percent of subjects to 21 percent; of ambidexterity from 0 percent to 61 percent; and of changed handedness from 5 percent to 73 percent. Obviously, there were various meanings to these terms, and different methods of determining handedness. Subjects were not either left-handed or not; they possessed degrees of left-handedness or right-handedness, degrees of ambidexterity. So the need arose for a standardized, quantitative measure of handedness. The task of devising such a measure fell to Travis's young student, Wendell Johnson. Johnson produced a questionnaire composed of such items as "Which hand do you use to throw a ball?" "Which hand do you use to brush your teeth?" "When you sweep the floor, which hand propels the broom?" The answers yielded a dextrality quotient, or D.Q., which was simply the proportion of right-handed to total responses. If all the items were answered in a right-handed way, the D.Q. was 1; perfect left-handedness was 0; and ambidexterity was in the neighborhood of .5. Johnson's hand-usage questionnaire left little room for ambiguity about what was being measured, and it took only a short time to show that the findings it produced conflicted sharply with the prevailing notions of the time. In a typical study, stutterers achieved a mean D.Q. of .88 as compared with .87 for nonstutterers; both scores pointed unremarkably to relative right-handedness.

If there was nothing unusual about stutterers' handedness, the Orton-Travis theory was left without a reason for its existence. But such an attractive theory was not to be abandoned because of an inconvenient fact. Adherents of the theory pointed out that a hand-usage questionnaire was concerned with activities that are subject to training by a right-handed society. To discover a subject's inborn sidedness, they argued, one had to study activities that are insulated from environmental influences. One example is eyedness. Stretch out your arm and, with both eyes open, line up the end of a finger with a more distant object like a spot on the wall. Then, find out which eye did the sighting by closing each eye alternately. Most people habitually sight with the same eye. Sure enough, many stutterers who were right-handed did prove to be left-eyed on this test. Foot preference is another example. So is thumbedness as revealed by the hand clasp test. It was Wendell Johnson who pointed out that when we clasp our hands it is almost always the same thumb that comes out on top. Again, many stutterers seemed to have left-sided or ambiguous lateral tendencies on these tests.

The test that seemed for a brief time to settle the issue in favor of the Orton-Travis theory involved simultaneous bimanual writing. When we write or draw rapidly with both hands at once, there is a natural tendency to produce a mirror image with the non-preferred hand, unless we are ambidextrous. We can be trained to prefer either hand for writing, but no one teaches us whether or not to mirror with the other. So we can reason that a failure to mirror may reflect an innate ambidexterity. The only trouble with such a test is that almost all of us can write or draw with both hands without mirroring if we do it very slowly and carefully. It was another young student of Travis, Charles Van Riper, who found a way around this difficulty. He first suggested that the subject write on both sides of a vertical board. In that situation it is extremely difficult to write without mirroring, even with considerable care. In fact that was a problem. Now almost everyone mirrored, except those with the most extreme ambidexterity. Van Riper found an ingenious solution. He hinged two boards together so that they could be opened or closed at various angles like the covers of a book. With the board fully open the subject copied a figure simultaneously on each half. The task was then repeated with the halves set at increasing angles from the original plane, so that the subject was drawing as though on the back of a progressively closing book. When the book was fully closed, the subject was drawing the figure on both sides of a vertical board. Van Riper surmised that every person had a critical angle somewhere between the fully open position (0 degrees) and the fully closed position (90 degrees) at which he or she would begin to mirror. The more ambidextrous the subjects, the better able they would be to draw without mirroring as the task approached the vertical board condition, and so the larger their critical angle would be.

The next step was to determine if the critical angle board test was valid. Van Riper did what seemed to be the obvious thing to do. He gave the test to three groups of college students, carefully selected on the basis of the hand-usage questionnaire to represent highly right-handed, highly left-handed, and highly ambidextrous individuals. The results lived up to expectations in the most satisfactory way. The highly right-handed group had an average critical angle of 27 degrees. The average critical angle of the left-handed students was also 27 degrees; they differed only in mirroring with the right hand. The ambidextrous group, however, had an average critical angle of 69 degrees.

The question now was, How would stutterers perform? Van Riper gave the critical angle board test to a group of students who were attending the speech clinic for help for their stuttering. Their average critical angle proved to be 67 degrees. The implications seemed clear: On a hand-usage questionnaire most stutterers may seem right-handed, but give them a test of native laterality and their innate ambidexterity stands out.

For the moment, then, the Orton-Travis theory stood its ground. But the triumph was to last for only a short time. The procedure that Van Riper had followed in conducting his study assumed that people tend to fall into three relatively distinct categories of handedness. In 1940, Elizabeth M. Daniels reported a study of stutterers' and nonstutterers' handedness at Syracuse University. One of her conclusions was distinctly at variance with accepted notions. She wrote, "...the popular concept of kinds of handedness (right, left, and ambidextrous) is inaccurate to a degree of becoming almost meaningless. It was shown that three distinct types of handedness groups do not exist; a concept of widely varying degrees of ambidexterity among all individuals more nearly approaches the actual situation. . . ." If Daniels' interpretation of her findings was correct, it implied that Van Riper's normal speaking subjects, chosen from among several hundred students to represent the most perfect right- or left-handedness and ambidexterity, were far from representative of the population at large. To correct this was simple. One had only to compare stutterers with control subjects who had not been selected to represent particular types of handedness. In 1942, Wendell Johnson made such a comparison with the assistance of his student, Arthur King. They had available the scores of 98 stutterers who had been given the critical angle board test at the University of Iowa speech clinic. The scores were in the form of dextrality quotients, this being an alternative way of scoring the test.[2] The stutterers' average D.Q. was .54. This plainly indicated ambidexterity and was in complete accord with Van Riper's finding of an average critical angle of 67 degrees for a group of stutterers. Johnson and King now gave the test to 71 normal-speaking college students who had not been selected for handedness in any way. Their average D.Q. was .52. On a hand-usage questionnaire both groups were relatively right-handed. The inference was plain for anyone to see. On a test of supposed inborn handedness stutterers turn out to be innately ambidextrous, but that is apparently because almost everybody is.

Handedness Therapy

Very little research was done on stutterers' handedness after 1942 and the enthusiasm that had been stirred up by the cerebral dominance theory gradually died away. It was not the Johnson and King study alone that was responsible for this. Probably an equally important reason was disappointment over the results of the treatment that was based on the theory. It was common practice during the 1930s to train stutterers to be left-handed. Typically, stutterers presented themselves at the speech clinic as right-handed persons, but a test such as the critical angle board test would generally show to the clinician's satisfaction that the individual had innate ambidextrous or left-handed proclivities. Or a left-eyed preference on a test of eyedness would suggest that the stutterer had "confused" or "mixed" laterality. By virtue of one test or another, few stutterers escaped the judgment that they needed to be changed back to

----

2. The dextrality quotient in this case was the proportion of right-handed responses on successive trials as the angle was varied between 0 and 90 degrees.

the left-handed individuals that nature intended them to be, and many of them worked long and hard to acquire left-handed skills. To ensure success, many stutterers had their right hands placed in plaster casts or tied up in leather restraints. Johnson and Van Riper, who were stutterers themselves, were among those whose right hands were tied up. In those early days they were roommates for a time. Years later Wendell Johnson told of how he awoke one morning to face yet another day of left-handed frustration. Saying to Van Riper, "I've got to have more reasons," he removed the restraints and never wore them again. This act of rebellion foreshadowed the independent leap that Johnson himself was soon to take into the realm of theory, though it is unlikely that he knew it at the time.

At the time, the Orton-Travis theory was enjoying the most favorable reception that had ever been accorded to a theory of stuttering and every sign pointed to the effectiveness of handedness change as a method of therapy. Reports of success were not merely anecdotal; they took the form of systematic case studies of groups of stutterers that were published in scholarly journals. Why then, hardly a decade later, were so few speech clinicians attempting to shift stutterers' handedness? Not a single study discrediting the therapy or reporting unfavorable results was ever published. Yet the therapy was quietly discarded as it came to be common knowledge that in the long run it was worthless. The initial successes were evidently just one more example of the power of belief in a method to produce short-lived freedom from stuttering. Due to this power, almost any new and revolutionary movement in stuttering therapy is likely to seem for a time to be the long-sought deliverance from the disorder as the hope and conviction of therapists communicates itself to the people they are treating. We were to witness this phenomenon again in the 1960s.

In 1938, Travis left Iowa for the University of Southern California and in 1940, he startled many of his colleagues by publishing an article entitled "The Need for Stuttering," which was a straightforward espousal of the psychoanalytic point of view. By the mid-1940s, the cerebral dominance theory had few adherents. Yet one last pillar of support for the theory remained standing. No one had disputed the electromyographic evidence that Travis had gathered to show that during stuttering the nerve impulses arrived at different times to the left and right masseter muscles of the jaw. It was not until 1955 that a student of Johnson's, Dean E. Williams, repeated the study with a few additional procedures. During stuttering he observed the same abnormalities that Travis had reported. But he also observed them when normal speakers imitated stuttering and when subjects were merely instructed to perform abnormal movements of the jaw. By that time the Orton-Travis had long since passed into history and another twenty years were to elapse before cerebral dominance would again claim the attention of researchers on stuttering.

CHAPTER FIVE

A Medical Model for Stuttering

Cerebral dominance was by no means the only aspect of the stutterer's physical constitution that came under scrutiny in the 1930s. In that era, the view that stuttering is the symptom of an underlying bodily abnormality was still firmly planted in the minds of most researchers and studies were done on the respiration, heart rate, blood pressure, brain waves, reflexes, basal metabolic rate, motor capacities, and the chemical composition of the blood and saliva of stutterers. These investigations often caused flurries of excitement as one or another physiological measure seemed to differentiate stutterers from control subjects, but always additional findings proved in the end to be conflicting and inconclusive.

Some of this work was carried out at the University of Wisconsin, where Robert West was the director of a speech clinic that had existed for quite some time. West had originally intended to become a physician, but had been prevented from obtaining a medical degree by unfavorable economic circumstances. He had extensive medical knowledge in spite of that, and he lent his resonant voice with evident relish to words such as lalopathology (defective speech), sigmatism (lisping), and anacusis (deafness). West was certain that there was something basically organic about stuttering. In the 1930s, he theorized that stutterers suffered from a biochemical imbalance of some sort, and studies of the chemical constituents of stutterers' blood done under his direction at first suggested that this was so. When this hypothesis failed to be verified by further research, he speculated that stutterings were minuscule convulsive seizures and related the problem to an obscure neurologic disorder known as pyknolepsy.

Robert West

It was West, more than anyone else, who brought logic to the concept of stuttering as an organic disorder. His intellectual rigor could not brook the loose statement that stuttering was inherited, or merely caused by a physical abnormality, when thoughtful consideration dictates that only a structure can be inherited, and that the simple notion of a physical cause fails to account for the extreme intermittency of the disorder. West formulated a general model for organic theories of stuttering that has never been improved upon. He based it on the medical concept that diseases may have both predisposing and precipitating causes. For example, the precipitating cause of an infectious disease is a microorganism, but individuals may differ in their inherited susceptibility to certain diseases. West stated that some children are born with an inherited predisposition to stutter. This predisposition, he said, takes the form of an organic deficit whose exact nature has not yet been discovered. To this deficit he gave the name dysphemia, borrowing a term that has sometimes been used in medical literature for stuttering. Dysphemia, to West, was an inner condition of the body; stuttering was its outward symptom. The amount of dysphemia that individuals possessed was roughly measurable in terms of the number of stuttering relatives they had. Stuttering was actually precipitated, he thought, by environmental factors such as diseases, injuries, or emotional stresses. A person lightly predisposed to stutter by heredity might stutter because of the strong pressure of environmental circumstances in early childhood. A heavily predisposed individual might evade the disorder as a result of favorable circumstances.

West and his students did some of the earliest research on the heredity of stuttering. In 1939, West, Nelson, and Berry found that 51 percent of a large group of stutterers reported stuttering relatives, while among nonstutterers the proportion was only 18 percent. This confirmed earlier observations of a strong familial incidence in stuttering. But a crucial question remained to be answered. Was the transmission of stuttering due to genes or was stuttering inherited like one's religion, as Wendell Johnson was soon to insist? If the inheritance was biological, it seemed reasonable to assume that it would follow certain familiar rules that are learned by high-school boys and girls in their study of genetics. That was the trouble. Stuttering did not seem to follow the rules. If a trait is recessive, most people who have it are the offspring of parents neither of whom outwardly exhibit it, simply because individuals who carry the trait on only one gene are far more common than those who carry it on both. But stutterers very frequently have parents who stutter or have a past history of stuttering. If a trait is a sex-linked recessive, affected males rarely have affected children, since the transmission of such traits is through the mother. Again, it is not at all rare for stutterers to have fathers with a history of stuttering. Facts such as these made it difficult for West to offer convincing evidence for his views. In his day it was not yet well-known that many human traits that recur in successive generations of the same family do not exhibit the classical Mendelian rules because they are caused jointly by heredity and environment.

West did establish that the familial incidence of stuttering could not be accounted for as a result of imitation of older relatives. His student, Severina Nelson, showed conclusively in 1939 that any number of stutterers had had no personal contact with family members who stuttered.

A typical case was that of a father who had stopped stuttering before the subject was born.

In an effort to demonstrate the effect of heredity, West's students did the first study of stuttering in twins. It is well-known that identical twins, resulting from the cleavage of a single fertilized ovum, have identical genes, while fraternal twins, because they are the product of two fertilized ova, are no more alike genetically than ordinary siblings. If both members of a twin pair exhibit a given trait, they are said to be concordant for the trait. When identical twins are consistently concordant for a trait, say brown eyes, while fraternal twins are not concordant for it any more often than ordinary siblings, it is a plausible guess that the trait is hereditary. In 1945, Nelson, Hunter, and Walter found among a large number of twins 40 pairs in which stuttering was present. Among the 10 pairs that were identical, both members stuttered, except in one case. Among the 30 fraternal pairs only one member stuttered, except in two cases. Later other studies confirmed the high concordance of identical twins for stuttering. Always, exceptions were found. The exceptions did not invalidate a genetic hypothesis, because it was not stuttering, but only a predisposition to stuttering that could be presumed to be inherited. But from the very beginning some workers rejected the notion that the high concordance in identical twins reflected any biological influence at all. They argued with some reason that because identical twins look so much alike, people tend to react to them alike, so that not only their genetic makeup, but also their early environmental influences tend to be identical. The way to get around this problem, of course, is to study the occurrence of stuttering in identical twins who have been separated at birth and reared apart. It was not until many years later that a small amount of data on this question came to light (see Chapter 14).

West's thoughts on the heredity of stuttering were influenced by a number of other observations. His student, Mildred Berry, was the first to present evidence that an unexpectedly large number of stuttering children are delayed in beginning to talk. Later research verified the fact that many stutterers lag behind other children in language development and persist longer in infantile articulation of speech sounds. Berry also thought her studies of stutterers' histories showed that they more often had respiratory diseases and more often came from twinning families. On the basis of these and other reports, West speculated that stuttering was part of a hereditary *diathesis,* a medical term meaning a joint congenital predisposition to a set of diseases. This diathesis included left-handedness, twinning, late development of speech, allergies, and respiratory disease, all of which he believed to be interrelated.

West never proved that stuttering was due in part to an inherited dysphemia. The intellectual climate of the times was soon to favor a view of stuttering in which environment played the only essential role, and he did not live to see the revival of a belief in genes as an important factor in the development of stuttering. In 1950, after many years at the University of Wisconsin, he accepted a position at Brooklyn College, where the last years of his career were the first ones of mine. West never stopped ruminating on the enigma of stuttering. One day, reflecting on the vast literature that had accumulated on the subject, he was bemused by the thought that when we know the cause of stuttering, we will be able to state it in a single sentence.

CHAPTER SIX

Iowa Therapy

For stutterers, the most far-reaching event of the 1930s was neither the research of Travis nor the insightful theorizing of West. It was a totally new departure in the treatment of stuttering that was destined to become the standard practice in the United States for the next 30 years and is still the preferred approach for many clinicians. Remarkably, this treatment emerged at the University of Iowa at the height of the fervor over handedness training and had probably been going on for a while before anyone realized that it was a therapy in its own right at all. The new approach aimed at two goals: reducing feelings of shame and anxiety and teaching stutterers to modify the way they stuttered. Nowadays, it is often referred to as Van Riper therapy in recognition of the man who developed it in the form in which it is most often used. I will call it Iowa therapy in deference to others who made major contributions to it. It was the work of three young colleagues of Travis who had been his students: Bryng Bryngelson, Charles Van Riper, and Wendell Johnson.

To understand how this program emerged in the shadow of the cerebral dominance theory, it is necessary to remember the many-faceted course of doctoral studies that Seashore had fashioned for Travis. It had imbued the young scholar with a variety of interests, among which were psychoanalysis and emotional adjustment. Travis was deeply absorbed in the mental hygiene movement that had originated early in the century and had co-authored a book on mental hygiene. There is no doubt that this influenced his clinical assistant Bryng Bryngelson, a former preacher and speech teacher, who was the oldest of the three originators of the new treatment and the first on the scene. Bryngelson laid great stress on helping stutterers to acquire an objective attitude toward stuttering all the while that he trained them in left-handed skills. To Bryngelson, an objective attitude meant above all the ability to discuss one's stuttering openly and frankly with others—to advertise it, as he put it. The door-to-door peddler who dubbed himself Stuttering Sam the Salesman was an example he often cited. He was also the first to advocate voluntary stuttering. The idea came to him from a book by Knight Dunlap called *Habits—Their Making and Unmaking*. Dunlap's thesis was that, because habits are unconscious and automatic, the way to break a bad habit was to practice it deliberately. He called this negative practice. Bryngelson applied the technique in his therapy with the rationale that by stuttering on purpose, stutterers could gain conscious control of their involuntary blocks. Later, voluntary stuttering came to be used both as a method for modifying stuttering and as a means of improving speech attitudes.

Bryngelson soon left to take a position at the University of Minnesota, where he continued to reverse stutterers' handedness for many years, but his program for changing stutterers' attitudes and modifying the way they stuttered caught fire in Johnson and Van Riper. To understand the devotion of these two young men to this wholly new approach to therapy, we need to keep in mind that both of them were severe stutterers, and both had personally experienced the worst drawbacks of the older methods. The therapies of the nineteenth century were still the ones most widely available to the general public. These therapies were to a large extent in the hands of commercial practitioners who extorted large sums of money from stutterers by promising a cure. When stutterers arrived at these so-called stammering schools, they found themselves in an atmosphere that was charged with suggestion. The director often was, or claimed to be, a cured stutterer and evinced not the slightest doubt that the new arrival would be relieved of stuttering in short order. Generally, the stutterer was given a novel speech pattern to practice. Often this was rhythmic speech, produced by timing each syllable to the swing of an arm. The result was immediate fluency. The stutterer next learned to time syllables to the swing of a hand from the wrist, and then of a finger from the hand. Finally, the finger was placed in the pocket and the stutterer was ready to leave for home. Some immediately reverted to stuttering, because outside of the safe refuge of the stammering school stuttering was preferable to talking in rhythmic syllables with a finger in the pocket. Others continued to speak fluently for a time. Some were so imbued with the belief that they could now talk normally, that they did not even need to rely on the technique they had been taught at the stammering school. But all too often, in a matter of weeks or months the stutterer relapsed. Far from the stammering school, with the image of its optimistic director fading from memory, surrounded by the old people and places with their associations with failure, the stutterer's conviction that he could speak fluently usually broke down. He would awake one morning convinced that he could no longer speak without stuttering, and the conviction had its inevitable consequence. The blow was hard. He had thought that the monkey was off his back. A new life had begun. With the crushing disappointment, the stuttering often became more severe than ever. Cases of suicide are known to have followed such a course of treatment.

Van Riper and Johnson had both been victims of stammering schools. Van Riper, growing up in a small town in Michigan, had wanted

Charles Van Riper

Wendell Johnson

to become a school teacher, but his severe stuttering posed an insur-mountable obstacle.[1] His father, a country physician, sent him to a well

1. In the fifth edition of Van Riper's textbook, *Speech Correction; Principles and Methods*, there is a photograph of an elderly man, his eyes shut and his mouth twisted in a severe stuttering block. The caption reads, "An Old Stutterer." Those who know him recognize this as a photograph of Van Riper imitating the way he stuttered as a young man.

advertised stammering school in Indianapolis run by Benjamin Bogue. Van Riper left Bogue's institute speaking well enough to secure a grade school teaching position, but in a short time he relapsed so severely that he was able to finish the term only by writing on the blackboard. He resigned his position and thought seriously of building a cabin on some wooded property of his father's and becoming a recluse. But, in the summer of 1929, seeking help at the University of Minnesota, he met Bryngelson and as a result soon afterward enrolled in the speech clinic at the University of Iowa. Inspired by hearing Travis lecture on his theory and research, Van Riper resolved that if he could learn to control his stuttering, he would enter the new profession of speech pathology and devote himself to finding better ways to treat the disorder.

Wendell Johnson had also attended Bogue's institute, as a teenager with a problem so severe that he was often almost speechless. To illustrate the far-reaching effect of the "cure," hope, and relapse that he experienced, he often told the story of how he was invited many years afterward to give a lecture in Indianapolis. By then he was a well known figure in his field and had long been accustomed to speaking publicly without fear and relatively little stuttering, but as his train approached the scene of his early encounter with Bogue's therapy, he was gripped by acute anxiety. After stopping at a bar for a hasty drink, he got through his lecture, but with more speech difficulty than he had experienced in years.

It is not difficult to understand why both Johnson and Van Riper to the end of their careers spoke with the utmost bitterness about stammering schools and the techniques for inducing fluency that they used. Van Riper warned that any quick cure of stuttering augured quick relapse. He asserted that lasting reduction of stuttering necessitated a reduction of the stutterer's fears. He argued that the old methods tended to increase fear. Those methods all said to the stutterer, "Don't stutter. Talk in any bizarre way at all, as long as you don't stutter." The clear implication was that no way of speaking is more to be feared and avoided than stuttering.

The new way that took form at the University of Iowa was to tell the stutterer to go ahead and stutter, but to do so without fear and without the effort, tension, and the devices for avoiding stuttering that complicated the difficulty and made it more abnormal. Reduction of fear was a dominant concern. It was accomplished mainly by teaching stutterers to bring the problem into the open, to admit to others that they stuttered, to use their feared words and enter their feared situations in order to learn that they were not so fearful, and to stutter on purpose—a practice which was called faking. Stutterers entered stores, made telephone calls, struck up conversations with strangers, asked passersby for directions, and contrived many other speech situations.[2] The stutterer's courage was bolstered for this situational work by frequent group meetings with other stutterers that generated a high level of group morale.

When stutterers succeeded at mastering their fear, they talked more, engaged to a greater extent in constructive relationships with others, and became far less handicapped by their speech difficulty. The severity of their stuttering was often lessened as well in some measure, but it was apparent that if stuttering was to be substantially reduced, something more than anxiety reduction was needed. From the very beginning, an equally important goal was modification of stuttering. The approach to this goal was based on analysis of the stuttering behavior. Although stutterers are acutely conscious of being blocked in their attempts to speak, they tend to be only vaguely aware of precisely what they are doing that prevents them from going ahead—for example, that they are pressing their lips together, jamming the tongue against the roof of the mouth, or tightly compressing their vocal cords. This is not so surprising, since few of us are aware of what we are doing with our speech organs when we speak normally, unless we have studied speech physiology. But stutterers are defeated by their ignorance. It is difficult to change our behavior unless we know clearly what it is we are to change. Johnson and Van Riper believed that as stutterers developed this awareness, they could learn to perform their stutterings more slowly, gently, and simply, and so greatly reduce the severity of their speech difficulty.

Ultimately, they thought, stuttering might continue to be modified in this way until it approximated normal disfluency. But fluency was not the immediate goal. It was a basic principle that immediate fluency was not to be trusted. If improvement was to last, it had to come about gradually. Stutterers had to accept themselves fully as stutterers before they could accept the responsibility, as Van Riper put it, of being normal speakers. There is no mystery about this. The observation that stutterers almost always seem on the verge of being able to talk normally has an unfortunate corollary: when stutterers do suddenly become perfectly fluent, they often report that they feel as if they are walking at the edge of a cliff with danger present at every step. If a person whom everyone present knows to be a stutterer has blocked several times in the course of a conversation, another block may be embarrassing. But if the person sup-

---

2. Stutterers were soon engaging in so many speech situations in the stores of Iowa City, that the chamber of commerce lodged a complaint with the university authorities.

posedly no longer stutters, a block is a disaster. Under such conditions the speaker becomes vulnerable to fear, anticipation, and a recurrence of stuttering.

The immediate goal, then, was not to speak without stuttering, but to stutter differently. In this way, there came into existence the basic conflict between two opposing schools of thought that characterizes stuttering therapy today. One philosophy says change the way you talk. It secures immediate fluency at the expense of some strangeness and loss of spontaneity. The other, developed at the University of Iowa, says change the way you stutter. It sacrifices some fluency for spontaneity and naturalness. Originated in its basic outlines by Bryngelson, it was elaborated in distinctive ways by Van Riper and Johnson.

Van Riper: Cancellations, Pull-outs, and Preparatory Sets

Johnson once remarked to his students that he thought Van Riper was probably the best speech clinician in the country. Without any question, in a profession that abounds in dedicated individuals, it would be hard to find anyone with quite the concern and compassion with which he treated the "poor devils," as he called them, who came to him for help. Equally remarkable was the resourcefulness of the methods and techniques for which he became renowned in his field. They were the product of an inventive mind in the service of a passion for finding an effective therapy for stuttering.

Although Van Riper stuttered somewhat to the end of his career, by about 1932 the severity of his stuttering had lessened sufficiently for him to pursue graduate work in psychology and speech pathology. In 1936, after earning his doctorate and spending two years as a postdoctoral fellow at the University of Iowa, he left the university for a small college in Kalamazoo, now Western Michigan University, where he spent his career in the search to which he had dedicated himself. Each year, with the aid of student clinicians, he administered treatment to a different group of severe stutterers, systematically altering some aspect of his program annually and assessing the results by following up his cases for five years. From the account of this experimentation that he wrote after an interval of twenty years, it is apparent that he devoted himself tirelessly to what he called laboring in the vineyard of therapy. He sat with his stutterers, worked with them, stuttered with them in speech situations, encouraged them, commiserated with them, and when he thought they needed it, inflicted penalties on them.

True to the Iowa concept, Van Riper placed great emphasis on fear reduction through nonavoidance. He sent stutterers into difficult situations on pain of dismissal from the clinic if they failed to carry out their assignments. A favorite device was a stuttering "bath" in which stutterers were required to collect a large number of instances of stuttering, real or faked, within a specified interval of time. When meeting a person for the first time, stutterers were given the choice of either immediately admitting that they stuttered or faking a block. Van Riper believed that stutterers needed to build up psychological barriers against pressures that caused them to stutter. As an example of one of his early assignments, he instructed a stutterer to go to the ticket window at the railroad station moments before a train was due, and with a line of impatient people behind him, to calmly fake long stuttering blocks. In his early years he managed his charges, in his own words, like a Prussian drill sergeant. Later, he softened as, along with others in the speech and hearing profession, he learned from psychotherapists the value of a more permissive clinical relationship.

In his search for ways to combat the effects of fear, he taught stutterers to desensitize themselves to their blocks. In place of panic, they learned to deliberately calm themselves during the moment of stuttering. A videotape that he made shortly before he retired to demonstrate his methods shows Van Riper twiddling his thumbs while faking a severe block.

It was in the modification of stuttering that Van Riper made the highly original contributions for which he is best known. The essence of his approach had its roots in Bryngelson's voluntary stuttering. Van Riper trained stutterers to substitute deliberate prolongations of sound for their old stutterings. The prolongations were simple, effortless, and devoid of any secondary features or signs of hurry or anxiety. Van Riper called this "fluent stuttering." When it was performed successfully, it resulted in a very mild pattern of speech interruptions, and the better it was done, the milder it became.

Many stutterers found it difficult to convert their stutterings to easy prolongations. It is a common observation that even when stutterers try to fake stuttering on words on which they have little tendency to stutter, the simulation sometimes turns into a real block. To make it easier for stutterers to modify their blocks, Van Riper tried to help them to change their preparatory sets. He reasoned that during that critical moment of anticipation of stuttering when a block becomes inevitable, stutterers are like runners on their mark, so poised to perform a set of abnormal behaviors that by the time they begin to articulate the word, it is impossible for them to make any change. It followed that the change had to begin before the attempt on the word.

Drawing, no doubt, on his introspections as a stutterer, Van Riper identified three abnormal aspects of behavior that stutterers engage in while preparing to say a difficult word. First, they tense their speech muscles. Second, in fear that they will be unable to initiate the word, they prepare to say the first sound with a fixed posture of the tongue, lips, and jaw; in normal speech, the articulators are in constant motion as the speaker begins to utter the next sound before quite finishing the first. And third, they silently place their articulators in position for the first sound before attempting to make it audible with voice or breath.

It is easy to see that with preparations like these a stutterer has little chance of saying the word normally. Van Riper proceeded to teach stutterers to adopt more normal preparatory sets when anticipating a block. Before attempting the word, they were to make sure their articulators were at rest. They were to get set to say the first sound as a movement leading into the rest of the word. And they were to initiate voice or breath simultaneously with movement of the articulators. This is clearly a prescription for saying the word normally, but that was not its purpose. It was designed to aid stutterers in substituting "fluent stuttering" for their blocks. If the word was said fluently, Van Riper's response was apt to be, "No—I can give you a hundred tricks for avoiding stuttering. What I want to see is if you can change the way you stutter."

This procedure was often helpful, but it had a notable drawback. Stutterers had to focus a great deal of attention on the mechanics of speech in order to alter even one of their preparatory sets, let alone all three. Van Riper was compelled to look for an easier way. He next invented a technique that he called pull-out. Stutterers waited until they began to block and then used this as a signal to terminate the block with a smooth prolongation. As this became habitual, stutterers automatically began to pull out of the block earlier and earlier. Eventually the stutterer was apt to anticipate pulling out prior to the attempt on the word, and so the preparatory sets often took care of themselves.

Pull-outs frequently worked very well, but Van Riper was not satisfied. Stutterers in a block were often too distracted to think about pulling out until it was too late. His solution was the well-known expedient called cancellation. Stutterers completed the block in the old way, but then paused, reflected on their abnormal behavior and emotional reactions, composed themselves, and immediately cancelled their failure by voluntarily stuttering on the word again calmly and with a "fluent" prolongation. This, too, tended to extend backward in time to facilitate pull-outs. In the end, Van Riper adopted the practice of teaching cancellations first, then pull-outs, and finally new preparatory sets.

These techniques for modifying stuttering proved to be of great benefit to many of the stutterers who came to him for help in increasing numbers as his reputation grew. His methods were also easily understood and applied by the speech therapists who were now being trained everywhere. Even today, when behavior therapy is the dominant approach, they are still widely used. In time, students came to him from abroad, and the Van Riper method is well known among speech clinicians in many countries outside the United States.

Johnson: Semantic Reorientation

Wendell Johnson came to the University of Iowa in 1926, a Kansas farm boy with a gift for language and ideas and a virtual inability to render them into speech much of the time. He intended to become a journalist, but stayed to obtain a doctorate in psychology and speech pathology in 1931 and to pursue a career as a teacher and researcher. During the course of that career his therapy for stuttering changed several times, but it never departed from the Iowa principles of anxiety reduction and modification of stuttering through analysis of the behavior.

Johnson's treatment of stutterers' fears was essentially the same as Bryngelson's and Van Riper's. He challenged stutterers to stop apologizing for stuttering by their avoidances and to learn to admit freely that they stuttered. He thought they needed to develop a sense of humor about their speech difficulty and he himself was not above beginning a talk before a lay audience by saying, "My name is Wendell J-J-Johnson and I don't stutter—my name has that many syllables."

Like Van Riper, Johnson believed in modifying stuttering by substituting a voluntary pattern of disfluency, but the pattern he chose contrasted sharply with Van Riper's. Instead of a prolongation of sound, it consisted of a simple, slow, effortless repetition of the first sound or syllable of a word that came to be known as the bounce. This preference had much to do with some unusual notions that had begun to occupy his mind in the mid-1930s as he pondered his own stuttering with all of the sensations, as he later said, of a cat in a puzzle box. He was struck by the fact that all he observed when he studied his behavior was that he was doing something that prevented him from saying the word, whether it was holding his breath, compressing his lips, or repeating or prolonging a sound. So far from having any "inability" to speak, he was at that very moment able to produce other words that were objectively just as difficult. It all seemed to Johnson to add up to the startling inference that his stuttering was what he did in the effort to avoid stuttering. If that was the case, stutterers had to stop trying to avoid stuttering. And the way to do that was to be disfluent on purpose. A frank repetition of sounds and syllables seemed to Johnson the most effective way to develop a tolerance for stuttering and weaken the tendency to avoid it. He disagreed with Van Riper that stutterers needed to "control" their stuttering. He had come to believe that what stutterers suffered from was too much rather than too little control. The bounce was an exercise in throwing caution to the winds.

This, then, was Johnson's program of therapy until one summer in the late 1930s when he fell ill with pneumonia. While convalescing, he read a ponderous 700-page book that was a turning point in his life and profoundly influenced his approach to treatment. Alfred Korzybski was a brilliant Polish count, mathematician, and philosopher. In his book *Science and Sanity,* he offered a discipline called "general semantics," optimistically designed to mitigate disagreements, wars, maladjustment, personal and institutionalized delusions, and absence of sanity in general. One of the major theses of the book is that ordinary language embodies primitive, false-to-fact assumptions about reality in its very structure, and distorts our perceptions and evaluations. By contrast, the language of science, specifically mathematics, provides a far more valid map of the world around us. In the face of the difficulty of reforming the structure of natural languages, Korzybski's antidote was careful training to counteract our readiness to identify words with things.

In general semantics, Johnson found precisely the conceptual scheme he needed to round out his thinking about stuttering. It was the stutterers' evaluations of words as "difficult" and their conviction that they were basically unable to speak in any other way that was at fault, he believed. And the responsibility for these evaluations lay in large part with the language that stutterers habitually used. They tended to talk about "their stuttering," as though it was something they possessed, or that they were possessed by. They said, "My tongue sticks to the roof of my mouth," "My throat closes," or "The word won't come out." They spoke, in short, as though it was not they themselves who were doing these things, but a demon inside them. They could hardly have used a more animistic manner of expressing themselves, or one better calculated to confirm them in their feeling of helplessness to speak without stuttering or to make any change in the way they stuttered.

From then on, what Johnson called "perceptual and evaluative reorientation" became an integral part of his therapy. He taught stutterers to talk about stuttering as something they did rather than something they had or something that happened to them. They learned to say, not "I had a bad block," but "I stopped myself from saying 'Mississippi' by pressing my lips together tightly." Johnson attended Korzybski's summer institute and became part of a small group of general semanticists. He taught a popular course on the subject and in 1946 wrote *People in Quandaries: the Semantics of Personal Adjustment.* His book was one of several, including his friend S. I. Hayakawa's *Language in Action*, that conveyed Korzybski's thinking to the general public.

Johnson's applications of general semantics to the treatment of stuttering were not limited to the analysis of the symptoms. Korzybski had called attention to the peculiar two-valued, either-or structure of language. Few of us are either beautiful or ugly, popular or unpopular, smart or stupid, and so forth, in any extreme sense. We belong somewhere on a dimension, or continuum, of pulchritude, popularity, intelligence, and fluency. Yet our language makes little allowance for this. As a result, Johnson pointed out, stutterers tend to speak and think as though one is either a stutterer or a perfectly fluent speaker. Because they want so badly not to stutter, they place a very high premium on perfect fluency. They become perfectionists about fluency, and this tends to make them all the more tense and fearful about stuttering. They appear to define normal speech, Johnson said, in a way that makes it almost impossible for them to acquire it. The remedy was a straightforward application of the scientific method. Stutterers were instructed to pretend that some of their professors were stutterers and to record every instance of stuttering during a few minutes of the lecture by means of a tally mark. They generally came back to the speech clinic with a sheet of paper filled with tallies.

Johnson also made use of general semantics in teaching stutterers to be more objective about the way listeners reacted to their speech. Stutterers usually labor under an exaggerated perception that their listeners are "annoyed," "amused," "embarrassed," "impatient," or the like. Johnson saw that their problem was compounded by the subject-predicate structure of language which compels us to utter statements like "the grass is green." Everyone with a minimum of education in basic science knows that the greenness is not in the grass at all, but in us. Where grass is concerned, the deception that language foists on us may be of little practical consequence. But what of a statement like "Martha is annoyed by my stuttering"? If we are aware that such a statement is in part about our own perceptions, it may occur to us to say instead, "Martha seems to me to be annoyed by my stuttering." If we put it that way, it might further occur to us that what we really mean is that Martha is frowning. Once we say that, it is only a short step to the realization that there are any number of reasons why Martha might be frowning. The trouble is that stutterers are apt to regard "Martha is annoyed" naively as a statement entirely about Martha. So Johnson taught stutterers to use the words "to me" more frequently, to be aware that assertions that people were impatient or amused, or the like, are inferences, and to make more use of descriptive statements such as "he tried to help me with words" or "she smiled" or "some people look away when I stutter." Such statements can be verified, and Johnson saw to it that stutterers made a good many scientific observations of listeners' reactions. It was common for a stutterer who thought people were amused to find that only one out of ten listeners smiled. One stutterer who observed that a certain store clerk always smiled when she stuttered persisted in her observations long enough to discover that the clerk smiled in the same way to other customers.

In the early 1950s, Johnson's treatment program underwent another change when he abandoned the bounce and any other form of voluntary stuttering. This development came about because of one of his students. Dean E. Williams came to the University of Iowa as a student on the G.I. Bill of Rights shortly after World War II and enrolled in the speech clinic because he stuttered. Like the other stutterers, he soon began to adopt the bounce pattern of voluntary disfluency in place of his old blocks. But there was an almost unprecedented zeal about the way Williams practiced the bounce. He did it virtually by the hour. Delivering groceries after school, he struck up conversations with housewives in order to use the bounce. Later, he bounced continually to his passengers as he drove a cab. After a while, he had grown so accustomed to using the bounce that he said he could hardly tell when he was stuttering and when he was faking. No doubt, this was a portent of something unusual that happened a few months after he had entered the clinic. One day, to the astonishment of his friends, his clinician, and his wife, he stopped stuttering. It seems that while speaking to his speech clinician during one of their sessions, he found himself repeating the first syllable of the word "clinician." In his usual bouncing way, he was saying "cli cli cli cli..." All at once the thought occurred to him, "I've just said 'cli' perfectly, four or five times. If I can say it perfectly four or five times, why can't I say it once?" He decided to try it, and said "clinician"—fluently. Then he tried it on the next word, and he said that just as fluently, and the next as well. In fact he spoke without stuttering all hour, all day, and the following days, week after week. The only exception occurred one evening while he was talking to his wife as they were leaving a movie theater still deeply involved in the movie. She said to him, "Dean—you know, you're stuttering again." He turned to her in surprise and said, "That's right, I was," and reverted to fluent speech.

The reactions of the other stutterers in the speech clinic are not difficult to imagine. Above all, they wanted to know what Dean Williams was doing so that they could do it too. When he reflected on what it was that he was doing, it turned out to be something exceedingly simple. He was merely doing what all normal speakers do—that is, "going ahead into speech without holding back," as he put it. Strange as it may seem, on this small bit of advice several other stutterers began to speak fluently. Even Johnson tried it and spoke fluently for a time. But they were not able to keep it up for long. Perhaps the speech attitudes that serve to perpetuate stuttering were weaker in Williams' case because of the way he had worked on them. Even his own remarkable fluency ended about a year later, and he stuttered mildly at times from then on. But Johnson was strongly impressed by Williams' demonstration that all a stutterer had to do to speak normally was more of the things that normal speakers do, and it left a lasting mark on his therapy. He discarded voluntary stuttering and devoted himself entirely to the practice of semantic reorientation. Stutterers were rigorously trained to avoid talking about "their stuttering" and to talk descriptively instead about the things they did that prevented them from going ahead into speech. Dean Williams went on to earn a doctorate in speech pathology and eventually joined Johnson on the faculty of the University of Iowa.

The years from the mid-1930s to the mid-1960s were a formative period in the field of speech and language pathology in the United States as workers in large numbers filled a vacuum that existed in schools, hospitals, and rehabilitation centers. The University of Iowa occupied a key position in this development because it sent so many of its graduates to establish training programs at other colleges and universities. As a result, and because of the writings of Charles Van Riper and Wendell Johnson, Iowa therapy came to be virtually the only acceptable way of treating stutterers in the United States during that period. An attitude of stern disapproval of the older methods was widely disseminated. Throughout those years it was considered unprofessional to teach stutterers how to achieve immediate fluency by prolonging syllables, speaking rhythmically, or changing their normal manner of speaking in any way. Almost the only reputable workers who did so were a few who had been trained in European institutions. It was not until thirty years had passed that that attitude suddenly changed. We will resume that story in Chapter 12.

CHAPTER SEVEN

The Diagnosogenic Theory

Although Wendell Johnson made a notable contribution to the therapy that evolved at the University of Iowa, it is chiefly for a theory of stuttering that speech pathology will remember him. A colleague of mine once pointed out the interesting fact that in the early 1930s Travis made Van Riper his research assistant and Johnson his clinical assistant. The irony of his choice is that Van Riper, "weary of theory" as he later professed himself, became world famous for his clinical work, while Johnson's research and theorizing strongly influenced the thinking of a generation of speech pathologists about the origin and nature of stuttering.

Johnson was 36 years old when I came to the University of Iowa in the fall of 1941 to begin graduate study in speech pathology. It was an exciting time in his life. He had only recently become convinced of the unusual theory that stuttering is caused by parents' diagnosis of normal childhood speech hesitancy as a speech disorder. His first paper on the onset and development of stuttering was not to be published until the following year. We students were among the first to be fascinated by what he termed the diagnosogenic theory.

Johnson was one of the most beloved teachers in academia. He was outgoing and informal. He took every opportunity to bandy ideas about with his students in impromptu sessions after class in the local coffee shops. He believed in thinking things out with others, though almost all the thinking on such occasions was his. Students felt free to call him Jack, a nickname that he earned in his boyhood when Jack Johnson was a heavyweight boxing champion and Wendell often got into fist fights because of his stuttering. His manner when he lectured was quiet and re-laxed, but he had his audience chuckling appreciatively at every turn. So far from detracting, his stuttering blocks merely held us in suspense as we waited for the next aphorism or delightful irony. The ingenious sim-plicity of his theory captured our imaginations. He won us over as his teaching and writing would shortly win over almost the whole profes-sion.

The Origin of the Theory

As Johnson told it, his theory had its genesis in a study that had been be-gun under Travis's direction by a team of researchers composed of Johnson, Van Riper, and various others. The purpose of the study was to search for a clue to the cause of stuttering by comparing a group of young children who had recently begun to stutter with a comparable group of young nonstutterers. From 1934 to 1939 the investigators gath-ered information about the subjects' birth conditions and medical histo-ries, physical, social, and speech development, "nervous habits," hand-edness, and the family background of handedness and stuttering. When the data were finally tabulated, they yielded little of interest. Except for the anticipated finding that the stutterers had more stuttering relatives than the nonstutterers, there was no evidence of a notable difference be-tween the two groups. For Johnson, however, the study proved to have immense significance.

Johnson's role in the investigation was to examine the speech of the children. As he continued to do so, he was struck by a puzzling observa-tion: it was sometimes difficult to tell the stuttering children apart from the nonstutterers by listening to the way they spoke. Certainly, the stut-tering children blocked, hesitated, and prolonged and repeated syllables and words, but so did many of the nonstuttering children. To be sure, most of the stutterers spoke with such unusual effort and disfluency that they were easily identifiable, but this was not always the case. Following a bold hypothesis, Johnson went back to the mothers of the stutterers and asked them to describe how the children were speaking when it was first thought that they were stuttering. For the most part, the mothers mentioned effortless repetitions of words, sounds, or syllables. It seemed to Johnson that similar descriptions could have been offered of the speech of most ordinary young children. In short, at the moment that these parents had diagnosed their children as stutterers, they seemed to have been speaking like any number of children who had never been re-garded as other than normal speakers. A remarkable inference took

shape in Johnson's mind. Later he would give it form in words that became familiar to every student of speech pathology: "Stuttering begins,
not in the child's mouth, but in the parent's ear."

Like most new theories, Johnson's was not totally unindebted to
older ones. In 1932, a noted authority on stuttering, the psychiatrist
Charles Sidney Bluemel, had published a landmark paper in which he
stated that when children first begin to stutter they simply repeat words,
syllables, and sounds with little effort, associated symptoms, or signs of
awareness of the interruptions in their speech. He called this "primary
stuttering" and theorized that it would ordinarily disappear in time if it
were not for the fact that parents often try to help children overcome
primary stuttering by badgering them to talk slowly, "think" before they
speak, take a deep breath, stop and start over, and the like. Admonitions
such as these, Bluemel thought, served to make children anticipate and
fear their "primary" interruptions and struggle to avoid them, thus setting the stage for the serious, chronic form of the disorder, which he
termed "secondary stuttering." The famous Viennese physician and
speech pathologist Emil Froeschels had said much the same thing before
he emigrated to the United States from Nazi Austria. Froeschels had
used the term "physiological stuttering" for the early symptoms of the
disorder and had asserted that it was frequently noticeable in the speech
of normal children. From this starting point Wendell Johnson made a
further leap: it was not primary or physiological stuttering that parents
first became concerned about, but simply the normal disfluencies that
almost all children exhibit. Stuttering was the child's effort to avoid normal disfluency.

In his formal statement of the theory, Johnson hypothesized that
first, stuttering is usually diagnosed by a layman, generally a parent;
second, what these laymen diagnose as stuttering in the vast majority of
cases is nothing but normal childhood disfluency; and third, stuttering as
a disorder develops, not before the diagnosis, but after the diagnosis. He
said, "A rose by any other name does not smell as sweet"; once parents
decide that a child is a "stutterer," they tend to react to the ominous label
rather than to the realities of the child's speech. A stutterer needs help,
and the help the parents give in the only way they know how was apt to
make the child tense and guilty about normal speech interruptions.[1]

1. The influence of Korzybski is clear. Around 1938, following his immer-
sion in general semantics, Johnson directed several masters theses on the effect of
evaluative labeling on behavior. In one of these studies a student, Mary Tudor,
found an increase in the disfluency of six normal speaking children in an orphanage after warning them that they were showing signs of stuttering. The effect was small and somewhat equivocal, but afterward one of these children was
reported by the orphanage to have begun to stutter and needed help in regaining

What sorts of parents would mistake normal disfluencies for a speech disorder? Johnson believed they fell into two categories. Most, he thought, were generally perfectionistic or overanxious in their child training policies. He believed that they imposed high standards of fluency on children just as they made excessive demands on them with regard to politeness, obedience, orderliness, and so forth, and expected them to behave like little adults, or worried too much about their health and development. Few of these demanding parents seemed to him to exhibit marked deviations in personality or to be suffering from neurotic conflicts. He considered them merely to embody to a somewhat extreme degree the competitive pressures of our society. Another group of parents were or had been stutterers themselves or came from families with stuttering members. They were likely to believe that stuttering was hereditary in their family, to listen to their children's speech too carefully for signs of it, and to react with abnormal concern when their children hesitated or repeated. In that way Johnson explained the high familial incidence of stuttering.[2]

The distinction that Johnson drew between stuttering and normal disfluency was sharp and categorical, as he often emphasized. To hesitate is normal, he said, but to hesitate to hesitate may become a serious disorder. His definition of normal was extremely liberal. He refused to label young children as stutterers unless they struggled and strained in their attempts at speech, regarded themselves as stutterers, and gave evidence of reacting emotionally to their speech interruptions. Much of his work with the parents was aimed at helping them to re-evaluate their children as normal speakers. He recognized that most of the young children brought to him as stutterers were far more disfluent than other children. But why call them stutterers, he said, when they were merely doing what most children do, only more so? This was not a policy that most other clinical workers were able to carry quite so far, even when they adhered to his theory, but the question of precisely how to distinguish early stuttering from normal childhood disfluency continued to perplex researchers and clinicians fifty years after Johnson made it an issue.

The diagnosogenic theory was as far removed from the prevailing neurologic explanations of stuttering as a theory could be. But it was in harmony with the developing spirit of the times. By the 1940s, Freud's

normal fluency. This incident may have played a part in the development of his theory. He recounted it to his students later in support of the theory, but never mentioned it in his many publications.

2. Johnson stated that it was not only parents who were responsible for stuttering in children, but also other relatives or family friends who labeled the child a stutterer. In his own case, he thought it was a first grade teacher.

influence had pervaded the intellectual life of the western world to such an extent that even people to whom Freud was no more than a famous name were convinced that almost all power over children for good or ill lay with the parents. The same Zeitgeist that made neurotic theories of stuttering so plausible to the general public insured a favorable reception for Johnson's theory among speech pathologists. The theory became so widely accepted in the field that even many years later, when most researchers on stuttering were exploring vastly different ideas in a new intellectual climate, many clinicians still believed that stuttering results from parental mislabeling of normal speaking children as stutterers.

Research on the Diagnosogenic Theory

Some theories that turn out to be wrong are nevertheless very fruitful because they stimulate research and lead to new points of view. In that sense, the diagnosogenic theory was an exceptionally productive one. A great deal of what we know about stuttering today was learned as a result of attempts to verify the theory. One reason for the broad scope of this research was that a theory that says that stuttering is caused by its diagnosis is extraordinarily difficult to verify simply and quickly by a direct investigation. The central assumption of this theory is that at the moment a stutterer's parents first decide that he or she is stuttering, the child's speech does not differ from that of any ordinary child who does not come to be regarded as a stutterer. That and only that is what we must prove or disprove. Unfortunately, we are never there in the role of objective, scientific observers at the moment of original diagnosis, and Johnson argued that if we see the child a month, a week, or even a day afterward, the child's speech may already have begun to exhibit the effects of the diagnosis. For this reason, Johnson and others had to set about trying to verify various implications of the theory.

Normal Childhood Disfluency

One obvious implication of the diagnosogenic theory is that young children normally tend to be highly disfluent, and so Johnson and his students embarked on studies of their speech. They found virtually no normal speaking subject whose speech was free from disfluencies. On the average, the children between the ages of 2 and 8 years whom they examined had over 7 disfluencies per 100 words. This meant that the average child was likely to exhibit several disfluencies during each minute of running speech. These disfluencies consisted of repetitions of sounds, syllables, words, and phrases; interjections such as "well," "uh," or "um"; revisions ("Red Riding Hood went—she was going to her grandmother's"); incomplete phrases ("He huffed and he puffed and— See, those are the three piggies in there"); broken words("Joanne is a b— ig girl"); and prolonged sounds.

Listener Identification of Stuttering

Another implication of the theory is that adult listeners may differ considerably in their evaluations of a speaker's disfluencies. In 1940, a student of Johnson's, Curtis Tuthill, took a recording of stuttered speech to a convention of the American Speech Correction Association, as it was then called. There he played the record to eleven experts on stuttering and asked them to mark each stuttered word on a transcript of the stutterer's speech. The number of words identified as stuttered ranged all the way from 34 to 89. The experts agreed no better than groups of untrained listeners. Incredulous researchers repeated the study from time to time in the years that followed. Always the result was the same; listeners did not agree well on the occurrence of stuttering. Even when judgments of the overall frequency of stuttering were fairly close, there was marked disagreement over which words were stuttered. Evidently, the identification of stuttering is to a considerable extent a subjective process in which personal standards of fluency play a part.

Social Environment

The stutterer's social environment had, of course, been of interest to psychoanalysts for some time, but systematic investigations of it were prompted largely by Johnson's view that the diagnosis of stuttering was generally a byproduct of demanding child-training policies. It was Johnson himself who initiated the research along all three avenues of approach to the question: studies of the influence of parental environment, socio-economic level, and culture.

The Parents Studies of stutterers' parents were of two different kinds. Some probed their emotional adjustment by means of standard personality tests. They disclosed little evidence that parents of stutterers differed as a group from ordinary individuals. The others were concerned more specifically with their child-training attitudes and practices. By far the most extensive of these was conducted by Johnson from 1952 to 1957. Under his direction, a team of assistants interviewed both the mothers and fathers of 150 young stuttering and 150 young nonstuttering children using a list of 800 questions of which the majority dealt with the home environment, parental policies, disciplinary practices, and parental adjustments as related to the children. Although the two groups of parents proved to be very similar in most of these respects, more parents of stutterers appeared to be anxious and perfectionistic, to have high expectations of their children, and to be discontented with their spouse, children, and social and economic status.

A few studies done by others offered some confirmation that many parents of stutterers tend to be dominating, critical, or anxious. The research findings made it clear, however, that there are very many individual exceptions. Johnson was satisfied that the research on the whole supported his theory. Some who questioned the theory asked why the same parents whose child stuttered often had other children who did not. Invoking Heraclitus, who said that you can't step in the same river twice, he replied that people reacting to different children at different times were not the same parents.

The Influence of Culture   Human cultures tend to differ in their child-rearing practices. This fact has long been recognized to afford a means of studying the effect of early social environment on personality. For Johnson and others it seemed to offer a welcome opportunity to test the hypothesis that stuttering is related to high parental expectations. Stuttering is well known throughout western society and in India, China, and Japan. The question that arose was whether it was absent in certain tribal societies, and if so, what kind of societies these were.

The earliest foray into the anthropology of stuttering was concerned with a small group of American Indians. One September, a student of Johnson's took a job as a teacher on a reservation in southeastern Idaho where the Bannock and Shoshone tribes had resided for some time with minimal contact with the outside world. Johnson suggested that she might do a study of stuttering in this population. The suggestion initiated one of the most curious episodes in the history of research on speech disorders. The following June, the student returned with the report that after careful inquiry she had not been able to learn of any stutterers on the reservation, nor had anyone been able to tell her of a word for stuttering in the Bannock and Shoshone languages. To any ordinary way of thinking, the lack of a word for stuttering in the absence of the problem might have seemed less than remarkable, but Johnson was intrigued by the apparent fact that a group of people who did not have a label for defective fluency did not have the disorder. In 1937, he persuaded another student, John C. Snidecor, to carry out a systematic investigation. Snidecor's mission was to see if he could find any stutterers among the Bannock and Shoshone. He began by gaining an audience with the tribal council of chiefs. Not knowing any word for stuttering in their language, he was compelled to imitate it. He reported that the chiefs were very much amused by his behavior, but told him that they had never seen anything like it. Judging from what we now know, it is probable that the chiefs were cozening him. At frequent intervals from then on Snidecor devoted himself to his task with an Indian guide to whom he had promised a reward for any information leading to the identification of a stutterer. After two years, during which he estimated that he had interviewed about 800 persons and obtained information about 1,000 more, he announced that he had failed to find "one pure-blooded Indian who stuttered."

In the meantime, the diagnosogenic theory had been taking shape in Johnson's mind and he seized upon Snidecor's observations as one more piece of supporting evidence. The Indians of the American plains were known to be more lax in their child-training practices than most people of European origin, relatively little being demanded of children by way of conformity to adult standards of behavior until adolescence. In addition, Snidecor had observed that the Bannock and Shoshone rarely felt the need to speak under pressure, for example to keep a conversation going. In a tribal council, a member could express an opinion simply by saying yes or no. They seemed to evaluate the acquisition of speech by children as a "normal developmental process not to be quickened by overanxious parents for purposes of display." That these people did not stutter seemed to Johnson to be in accord with his views on the onset of the problem and he made much of it. Stuttering appeared to him to reflect a society that imposed heavy pressures on children for achievement and conformity and, as a by-product, placed a high premium on fluent speech. When he wrote an article on his views about stuttering in 1944, he entitled it "The Indians Have No Word for It." By 1950, the diagnosogenic theory had gained wide acceptance among speech pathologists and so had the assumption that American Indians don't stutter. One November, Johnson was beginning a talk at a convention of the American Speech and Hearing Association. To his immense enjoyment, a prankster leaped onto the stage in the full regalia of a Sioux chief and stuttered into the microphone in a manner that would have stirred profound feelings of commiseration if it had been genuine. The audience roared.

In 1953, it became clear that the generalization that American Indians don't stutter had to be qualified. A social anthropologist, Edwin M. Lemert, wrote an account of several tribes among whom he had found stuttering to be common. These were the Kwakiutl, Nootka, and Salish, who inhabit the northwest coast of Canada and are known to the world for their imaginative carving of totem poles. Among these people, Lemert found stuttering, native words for stuttering and other speech disorders, and rituals for expelling the evil spirit that prompted a person to stutter. So far from conflicting with Johnson's outlook, however, stuttering among the northwest coast Indians was precisely what he might have predicted. Before their assimilation into Canadian society, they were remarkable to anthropologists for an intense competition for status and prestige that existed among their large kinship groups or clans. One of their unique institutions was the potlatch, a feast to which they invited rival clans and confirmed their social status by giving away or destroying bearskins or pieces of copper that symbolized prestige. Not to be outdone, their guests had to give a potlatch of their own at which they destroyed or gave away even more valued ceremonial possessions. Lemert pointed out that the rivalry for status led to exacting educational practices, especially for children of the nobility who were called upon to participate in solemn rituals under the scrutiny of elders from rival clans. Lemert also noted that the Indians of the northwest exhibited attitudes of amusement, pity, and rejection toward people with deviations such as left-handedness, lameness, obesity, smallness, and speech defects. Such individuals tended to remain in the background for fear of casting shame on their clan. Among the Bannock and Shoshone, Lemert said, a person with a cleft palate could attain a position of eminence; this would never have been possible among the Kwakiutl.

The fact that the northwest coastal Indians stuttered while the Bannock and Shoshone supposedly did not was eminently consistent with Johnson's conception of the cause of stuttering, and it led to some detailed research comparing the parental practices of the two groups. It was only after many years that it became widely known that the assumed absence of stuttering among the Idaho Indians had no basis in fact. The astonishing revelation came from two independent sources. In 1968, Arthur Frank, then a speech pathology student, conducted a survey among the Bannock and Shoshone at the Fort Hall, Pocatello, reservation in his native Idaho. The individuals he interviewed at first denied knowing anyone in their tribe who stuttered and called it a "white man's problem." After he had lived on the reservation for over two months, however, and perhaps in part because he himself stuttered, a number of individuals overcame their reluctance to admit that the problem existed and that it was an object of ridicule and a source of embarrassment to the families of those who were handicapped by it. Arthur Frank learned of some twenty persons at least forty years of age who stuttered and he interviewed two stutterers in their 50s and 60s who were living on the reservation at the time of Snidecor's study. Almost identical observations were made by Sven Liljeblad, an anthropologist who worked on a Bannock and Shoshone dictionary between 1940 and 1960. In addition, he found a number of expressions for stuttering based on the stems *pybya* in Bannock and *cannungu* in Shoshone. One of his informants at first denied any knowledge of a term for stuttering, but confessed with embarrassment that he knew such a term when Liljeblad confronted him with one. It was not until 1983 that Frank and Liljeblad made this information public in a jointly written paper.

Native Americans were by no means the only group who figured in the persistent belief that there are tribal societies in which stuttering is unknown. In 1945, Adelaide Bullen informally surveyed a number of anthropologists including Margaret Meade, Clyde Kluckhohn, and Henry Fortune. Most could recall no stutterers among the aboriginal people whom they had studied in the South Pacific, New Guinea, Australia, and the Arctic, although Meade remembered hearing of a stutterer among the Arapesh of New Guinea.

In 1953, a more systematic survey was carried out by John J. Morgenstern, an American working on a doctoral dissertation in psychology at the University of Edinburgh. Morgenstern sent questionnaires to 258 anthropologists, missionaries, and physicians who were at work among tribal peoples in various parts of the world. Respondents were asked to comment on the prevalence of stuttering in these societies and on the presence of cultural attitudes of relevance to the diagnosogenic theory. True to Johnson's hypothesis, Morgenstern found a significant tendency for societies with reported low incidence of stuttering to be judged relatively tolerant of nonconformity and to have relatively permissive child training practices. Among some thirteen tribes who were said to have no stuttering and no word for it were the Wapashianas of British Guiana; the Garia of New Guinea; the Kelabits of West Borneo; the Senoi of Malaya; and the Gatwas of India.

Morgenstern was also informed of two groups of tribal people among whom stuttering was apparently unusually common. An American anthropologist, Robert Armstrong, reported that he had met "many dozens of people who stammer in some degree" among the Ibo and Idoma of Nigeria. Armstrong commented that the ability to speak well in public is greatly admired in West Africa and that children who stutter are often severely ridiculed by their age-mates.[3]

Fragmentary as they are, the research findings on the anthropology of stuttering have made it clear that the problem occurs in a very wide variety of cultural settings. Some workers have expressed doubt that it is absent from any ethnic group at all. Whether or not any society is totally free from stuttering is not a question that lends itself to scientific study. The question of whether the incidence of the disorder varies in magnitude among different cultures is answerable. However, as of now, the data for answering it are meager. Such as they are, the data seem to suggest that certain kinds of environmental pressures may tend to increase the risk of stuttering in children.

Socioeconomic Level In Johnson's day, the U.S. upper middle class was notorious for a fierce determination to move up on the socioeconomic scale and for an alleged tendency to badger its children to achieve. Not surprisingly, Johnson suggested that stutterers were disproportionately represented on that level. The parents who brought their children to him did often seem to be relatively affluent and well-educated, but this may have reflected little more than the enhanced ability of such people to find help for their children. Systematic research lent only equivocal support to Johnson's hypothesis. A study by Bender in the 1930s had found an unexpectedly high prevalence of stuttering in the U.S. college population. But in the 1940s Johnson's student, Mary Schindler, found little difference in the occupational levels of parents of stutterers and nonstutterers in a survey of Iowa schoolchildren.

In 1956, Morgenstern reported some observations that seemed to him to accord well with Johnson's thinking. A survey by the Scottish

3. These observations were corroborated by a colleague and former student of mine, Mary Harden Umolu. During an extended visit to Nigeria, she was struck by the number of Ibo people who stuttered. At a party given in her honor by Ibo friends when she left, each person rose in turn to make what began as a speech of farewell to the departing guest, but generally turned into a commentary on the political situation in Nigeria. Ms. Umolu described the Ibo as one of the most economically competitive ethnic groups in West Africa. She noted that they attach great value to education for their children and that they are heavily represented among young West Africans who study at European and American universities. One Ibo student of her acquaintance spoke to one of my classes about his early experiences as a stutterer. He related that at the age of five he was sent to live with his uncle, his parents being eager for him to develop leadership ability and afraid that he would be coddled too much at home. His uncle, who was by no means a mean man, slapped him whenever he stuttered in a futile effort to cure him of his stuttering.

Council for Research in Education had determined the distribution of a large number of Scottish schoolchildren among nine categories of occupational status of the father, ranging from unskilled farm laborer to professional worker. This gave Morgenstern the opportunity to make a comparison with stutterers in the Scottish schools. By and large, the two distributions turned out to be similar. The one outstanding deviation occurred on the next to the lowest level, that of the semi-skilled manual wage earner, such as the truck driver or machine operator, where there was an unusually large number of stutterers. Morgenstern's explanation was that this was the only socioeconomic level on which there was a chance for upward mobility. Semi-skilled laborers, or at least their children, could aspire to become skilled workers. This, he inferred, meant that parents on that level tended to be unusually concerned that their children acquire the kinds of advantages that are conferred by acceptable speech.

The implication seemed to be that any upwardly mobile segment of society is at increased risk of producing stutterers. Later, however, Andrews and Harris failed to find a difference in social class or evidence of upward mobility in the families of stutterers in Newcastle-Upon-Tyne, England. It would seem that the influence of socioeconomic status on stuttering, if there is any at all, is not a major one.

The Stuttering Simpsons

Johnson's views did not allow for the influence of biological heredity on stuttering even in the smallest degree. Although well aware that stuttering often runs in families, he attributed that fact chiefly to the anxiety about children's disfluencies that he considered parents were apt to feel when they believed that the disorder was a family trait. His evidence for this was a study of a stuttering family whom he called the stuttering Simpsons.

In 1939, his student, Marcella Gray, earned her bachelor's degree and took a position as a school speech therapist in a town in Iowa. When she let it be known that she would hold evening classes for adults in the community, seven people came for help with their speech. Six of the seven were members of the same family and all six stuttered. It developed that stutterers had appeared in each of five generations of this family. What was of particular interest to Johnson when he learned of it was that the family had a branch in Kansas in which there were said to be few if any stutterers. Johnson reasoned that if there were genes for stuttering, it would only be by the rarest chance that they would appear in one branch of a family and not in another. The argument seemed to him so compelling that he suggested to Marcella Gray that she devote her masters thesis to a study of the stuttering Simpsons.

Gray interviewed various members of the Iowa branch of the family and contacted the Kansas branch by mail. The principal result of her study was a family tree. It appeared that in this Iowa town five generations before, a man with normal speech had married a woman who stuttered. They had two daughters. The elder of the two stuttered, but Marcella Gray could obtain little information about her descendants. The younger daughter spoke normally, but married a man who stuttered. Of their four children, three stuttered. The youngest of the three was a girl whom Gray designated IIIA. When the children grew to adulthood, all except IIIA moved to Kansas. Of the 31 descendants of IIIA, eleven were stutterers or had stuttered at one time. Of the seventeen members of the Kansas branch of the family, only one stuttered.

Gray reported that the Iowa members believed that stuttering was hereditary in their family. There appeared to her to be a climate of anxiety about the fluency of their children's initial attempts at speech. She inferred that their attitudes were influenced particularly by IVE, IIIA's fifth child, by virtue of his very severe stuttering and his dominant position in the family. They said they wondered whether their children would stutter like IVE or commented that they couldn't stand it if they stuttered like IVE.

At the time of Marcella Gray's study, a number of the Iowa Simpsons visited the University of Iowa speech clinic and were given information and counseling along diagnosogenic lines. Twenty years later Johnson initiated a further investigation of the family. By this time many of the children in the fifth generation had married and had children of their own. Of 44 children in the sixth generation of Simpsons, not one was regarded as a stutterer. A fifth generation mother explained, "We know now how it started and we aren't saying anything to the younger generation like they told us when we were little."

Parents' Recollections of the Earliest Symptoms

Johnson was so convinced of the correctness of the diagnosogenic theory, that when he was invited to contribute an entry on stuttering to the fourteenth edition of the Encyclopedia Britannica, his article was a straightforward presentation of the theory with almost no hint that it was anything but fact. Yet none of the many investigations that had been prompted by the theory could be regarded as critical tests of its validity. Only by observing how children spoke at the moment that their parents first diagnosed them as stutterers could the theory be proved or disproved. To do that was hopelessly difficult. Yet so crucial was that information that Johnson resolved to obtain it in the only way that seemed possible—by investigating the memories of the parents. He recognized the shortcomings of such a method. The justification he offered was, "If you don't do it in this way, how do you do it?"

In the study that Johnson and his co-workers conducted, a large number of mothers and fathers of young stutterers were asked to describe and imitate their children's earliest stutterings. These descriptions were compared with those of a large number of nonstutterers' parents who were asked to describe and imitate their children's earliest normal disfluencies. The outcome can be summarized in three statements. First, with the exception of "complete blocks," which were mentioned only by three mothers and fathers of stutterers, not a single type of disfluency that was described by one group of parents was absent from the descriptions of the other group. Second, certain kinds of disfluency were mentioned more often by one group than by the other; parents of stutterers more often reported syllable repetitions and sound prolongations, whereas parents of nonstutterers more often referred to pauses, phrase repetitions, and interjections such as "uh." Third, the two sets of descriptions overlapped considerably; every type of disfluency except "complete blocks" was identified by some parents as stuttering and by others as normal disfluency.

Anyone skeptical about Johnson's theory could have found ample justification in the differences between the groups, and some did. But Johnson himself was undaunted. He attached great importance to the overlapping between the two groups. Pointing out that the same disfluencies that had been identified as stutterings by most parents had been identified as normal disfluencies by others, and that the same disfluencies that had been described as normal by most parents had been described as stutterings by some others, he reaffirmed his belief that stuttering was essentially a perceptual and evaluative problem. He did modify his theory somewhat, however. He went as far as to admit that parental evaluation of normal disfluency as stuttering was not the only factor in the onset of the disorder. The child's disfluency played a part too, he said, and so did the child's sensitivity to the parents' evaluations. He called this his interactional hypothesis. Nevertheless, until his death in 1965 at the age of 59, he continued to hold that the origin of stuttering lay largely in the parents' perfectionism or anxiety about the child's fluency. In one of his last aphorisms, he declared that stuttering is not so much a feature of a child's speech as a problem that arises for a listener. Robert West, who had preserved an air of patient reserve with respect to what he regarded as my old teacher's implausible notions, asked me, "Honestly, don't you think Johnson spins his ideas to gossamer thinness?"

Johnson lived to see the diagnosogenic theory accepted very widely. During his lifetime the membership of the American Speech and Hearing Association grew from a mere handful to a body of over 13,000, and many of the teachers of these workers had been Johnson's devoted students. For some thirty years, a great many speech clinicians disseminated as fact the hypothesis that parents cause children to stutter by making them anxious about their normal speech hesitations. The theory was never disproved, but by the 1970s it had declined markedly in popularity among professional workers. Perhaps the major reason for this disaffection was the growing belief that biological heredity does play some part in the disorder after all. If it does, this is evidently a convincing reason to believe that children who become stutterers do speak differently from others at the initial moment of the parents' diagnosis. In the end, the theory proved ill adapted to a new intellectual climate in which parents were less likely to receive the sole blame for their children's problems.

CHAPTER EIGHT

Stuttering as an Anticipatory Avoidance Reaction

If stuttering begins, as Johnson thought, as a child's effort to avoid normal disfluency, what is the nature of stuttering later, in older childhood and adulthood? Johnson asserted that it was nothing more than the speaker's attempt to avoid stuttering. Faced with a "difficult" word, the stutterer made an effort not to stutter on it. But the very effort that he made was the stuttering. And having stuttered, he was confirmed in the belief that the word was difficult and so was all the more likely to try to avoid stuttering on it the next time. It was the anticipatory struggle hypothesis—the familiar idea that the problem results from a belief in the difficulty of speech—cut somewhat to fit the diagnosogenic theory. Johnson called stuttering an anxious, anticipatory avoidance reaction. He said, "The stutterer is not a person who can't talk fluently—he is a person who can't talk nonfluently." Johnson devoted a good part of his efforts as a researcher to laboratory investigations designed to verify this hypothesis. In the course of these investigations he and his students and co-workers discovered so much about the conditions under which stuttering blocks occur that most of what was found later consisted largely of its elaboration.

Stuttering and Anticipation

What makes the anticipatory struggle concept so plausible to many stutterers, and to many speech clinicians who enter as deeply into the stutterer's experience as nonstutterers can, is the conspicuous place that the phenomenon of anticipation occupies in that experience. As stutterers approach feared words, there is hardly anything that seems to make stuttering more certain than their conviction that they will stutter on them. And almost all stutterers are aware that they have often said the same words fluently when not expecting to have any difficulty. It is easy to draw the inference that when stutterers block, it is mainly because they expect to.

Little wonder, then, that when Johnson set out to verify his anticipatory avoidance hypothesis, one of his first aims was to demonstrate the extent of the relationship between anticipation and stuttering. The method he chose was a simple one. As stutterers read aloud, they signaled with a hand before attempting every word on which they expected to stutter. In this way Johnson and his co-workers showed in 1937 that 94 percent of the stutterings of a group of adult subjects had been anticipated. Van Riper obtained similar results in an independent study. Stuttering was evidently highly related to expectancy, but the results raised a question. What about the 6 percent of stutterings that were apparently unexpected? Can stuttering happen without anticipation? Some of those ostensibly unanticipated blocks could be laid to mere error; the subject had forgotten to signal or had been uncertain of stuttering. But Van Riper observed that on some occasions stutterers reacted to unanticipated blocks with surprise. And occasionally stutterers were encountered who could predict the occurrence of very few of their blocks. Johnson's response to this was that anticipation of stuttering could involve a low degree of consciousness. One day while I was his student, some of us were having coffee with him before class in the basement of East Hall. Someone asked him if he was able to anticipate all of his own stuttering blocks. His reply was something like this: "Yes, in the sense that while I'm talking to you I anticipate that in a few minutes I'm going to go up the stairs, walk down the hall, and go into Room 112—in that sense I anticipate all of my blocks."

Many years later, Franklin H. Silverman and Dean E. Williams showed that failure to signal the occurrence of stuttering in advance is quite common in children of school age. Some could predict the occurrence of virtually all of their blocks, while others could predict few or none. At this writing the questions of whether, in what sense, and at what stage anticipation is the cause of the stuttering block are still unresolved.

The Consistency Effect

The anticipatory avoidance hypothesis implied that stuttering is learned behavior. This was a bold concept in 1937, but Johnson and his colleague, John R. Knott, thought they saw a way to demonstrate it. Suppose a stutterer read a passage aloud repeatedly, say ten times in succession. Would the stutterer block on the same words or on different words from reading to reading? To the uninitiated, the answer is not obvious. As stutterers, Johnson and Knott must certainly have known the answer, but they wanted to have it in the form of reportable data. When they did the study, the subjects showed a distinct tendency to be consistent in their stuttered words in successive readings. In the tenth reading 60 percent of their stuttered words had been stuttered in the first reading and 90 percent had been stuttered in one or more prior readings. Johnson pointed to the consistency effect as evidence that stuttering was not a random, haphazard phenomenon, but a definite response to identifiable stimuli. What made the learned nature of the response all the more compelling was that the words on which the subjects stuttered so consistently differed to a marked degree from subject to subject.

The Influence of Cues Associated with Past Stuttering

To say that stuttering is learned leaves a great deal unexplained about the nature of the behavior. In order to demonstrate that stuttering was the effort to avoid stuttering, Johnson had to show that stutterers learned to do it in response to cues which they associated with past experiences of speech difficulty. In an experiment which he performed in collaboration with Robert P. Larson and John Knott, stutterers read a passage with a colored border to a single experimenter and then to an audience of 30 or more people. Following the audience situation in which stuttering had increased markedly, it was found that a passage with the colored border produced an increase in stuttering when read to a single listener. A control passage without a red border did not.

Did this prove Johnson's hypothesis, or did it simply show that stuttering could be conditioned to a neutral stimulus? The answer is debatable, but a second experiment that Johnson did with his student Lucille Millsapps appeared to be less equivocal. I don't know how Johnson thought of looking for the phenomenon that later came to be known as the adjacency effect, but I have a strong hunch that he found it by accident. I imagine Johnson lying in bed one night and thinking about the consistency effect that he and Knott had recently demonstrated.

Stutterers blocked on many of the same words from reading to reading. But the effect was far from perfect; in each reading stuttering also occurred in most cases on words that had not been stuttered before. What would happen if we gave a subject a passage to read a second time with the previously stuttered words blotted out? Some new stutterings would almost certainly occur. But what if we blotted those out, and did that repeatedly as the subject reread the passage? Would stuttering soon totally disappear or would new stutterings keep cropping up to take the place of old ones on words that had been blotted out?

When Johnson and Millsapps did the study, they had subjects read a passage nine times and blotted out all previously stuttered words after the third and sixth readings. By the last three readings some subjects were completely fluent, but in more than half the cases new stutterings kept appearing to the end. When the experimenters examined these stutterings, they discovered a surprising fact. To a significant degree, these persistent stutterings had occurred on words adjacent to those that had been blotted out. It was as if the subjects had reacted to the blots as reminders that they had stuttered before, and that was the way in which Johnson and Millsapps interpreted the finding.

The adjacency experiment went to the heart of the issue that Johnson had raised about the nature of stuttering as a response to cues indicative of past difficulty. Yet for many years, I felt dissatisfied. The meaning that he had attached to the adjacency effect seemed to me to assume too much about what the subjects were thinking as they encountered the blots. And it was possible to imagine that the blots provoked stuttering merely because of the interruptions they created in the reading material. Finally, in 1971, together with my student Brenda Rappaport De Santis, I put Johnson's interpretation to a further test. We repeated the Johnson and Millsapps experiment with the addition of a second condition in which the subjects read a passage in which some of the words were blotted out simply at random. When you do a study that employs more than one experimental condition, you routinely vary the order in which they are presented, to make sure that the order does not affect the results. So we gave half the subjects the random blots condition first and the other half were first tested for the adjacency effect in the ordinary way. We little suspected that we were manipulating a factor that would prove to be critical. When we analyzed the results, we found, like Johnson and Millsapps, that the blotting out of previously stuttered words had created an adjacency effect. The random blots produced a surprise. They had no tendency to precipitate adjacent stutterings in the subjects who had undergone this condition first. But when random blots followed the condition in which blots had obliterated stuttered words, they produced adjacent stutterings in virtually every case. We had demonstrated that cues associated with past stuttering not only created stuttering in the same passage, but did so also in a passage different from the one in which the association had been made. It would have been difficult to imagine a more resounding confirmation of the inference that Johnson and Millsapps had drawn.

A few years later, my student Dinci Avari and I found the adjacency effect in each of 12 stuttering children half of whom could not signal anticipation of any of their blocks. Again, Johnson's insight appears to have been right. Although half the children did not seem to experience anticipation on a highly conscious level, they all responded to cues that represented past stuttering.

What Words Are Stuttered?

The cues that stutterers encounter in their daily lives are not colored borders or words blotted out in reading passages; they are persons, places, situations, and, above all, words. The fact that stutterers differ so much in the words that give them trouble hints strongly at the influence of each stutterer's personal history of failure on these words, and Johnson and Knott had pointed this out as evidence of the "psychological" aspect of stuttering. But there was still the question of whether there are any attributes of words that make some of them more difficult than others for stutterers as a group, and what such attributes could tell us about the nature of stuttering. Research on this question was initiated by Johnson and his student and colleague, Spencer F. Brown, and carried out by Brown in a series of investigations of the stuttering of adult subjects in oral reading. Brown found a tendency for stuttering to occur on long words, words at the beginning of the sentence, words that begin with certain sounds, and so-called content words—nouns, verbs, adjectives, and adverbs—as opposed to pronouns, conjunctions, prepositions, and articles. He interpreted these results to mean that stutterers tend to have difficulty on words that they perceive as prominent or important and on which they are therefore especially concerned about avoiding stuttering.

Brown's finding about words beginning with certain sounds needs some explanation. The initial sound made a difference; most subjects stuttered considerably more on some initial sounds than on others. But this was a highly individual factor; the sounds differed from subject to subject. Neither Brown nor various later researchers were able to show convincingly that one initial consonant is harder than any other for stutterers as a group. Only a tendency to stutter more on initial consonants than vowels is fairly general. When we try to account for this, two differences between consonants and vowels suggest themselves. One is that consonants are more complex than vowels. The other is that communication of meaning depends more heavily on consonants than on vowels. Perception of an oral or written message would be impaired far more by omission of the consonants than by omission of the vowels, a fact that is reflected in certain orthographies (for example, Hebrew, ancient Egyptian) in which few or no vowels are represented. An important point is that there are stutterers who have special difficulty with words beginning with vowels, which seems to mean that the stutterer's evaluations of a particular sound as difficult may override every other factor. The power of evaluations and perceptions in determining which initial sounds will cause trouble is amply illustrated by stutterers who block on "knowledge" because it is a "k" word or on "psychology" because it begins with a "p". A speaker of substandard New Yorkese who once came to me for help with his stuttering frequently blocked on words beginning with "th", which he pronounced "t" and "d" as in "tank you" and "dem dare tings." Yet words spelled with the letters "t" and "d" rarely gave him any trouble. A fourteen-year-old stutterer, when I asked him if there were any sounds that gave him special difficulty, said, "Yes, the d-d-d-double-u sound—see, I had trouble with it just then."

The greater frequency of stuttering on content words than other grammatical parts of speech is interesting too. Presumably, it is due to the greater importance of nouns, verbs, adjectives, and adverbs in conveying the meaning of an utterance, as witnessed by the way we reduce a message to these words when writing telegrams. The effect of meaningful content of words was demonstrated elegantly in later research on the relation between stuttering and "information load." If the words of a passage are exposed to a reader consecutively word by word and the reader is asked each time to guess what the next word might be, it is evident that some words will be harder to guess at than others. In a significant sense, words that are hard to guess carry more information than words that are easily predictable; the predictable ones don't tell us more than we already know. By using the guesses of a large number of subjects, we can assign a reliable measure of information load to each word of a passage. Beginning in the 1960s, a series of investigations by independent researchers showed that the greater the information load of words, the more likely stutterers were to block on them in oral reading.

Under What Conditions Are Stutterers Fluent?

As Johnson pursued his anticipatory avoidance hypothesis, he recognized that a scientific understanding of a phenomenon consists essentially of knowledge of the conditions under which it varies. The variability of stuttering is reflected very prominently in the many conditions under which stutterers speak fluently, and so he felt the need for a broad study of these conditions. The task fell to me, as a doctoral student of Johnson's in the late 1940s. Guided by a multitude of observations on stutterers' fluency in the voluminous literature on stuttering, I conducted personal interviews with 50 adult stutterers and received responses to questionnaires from 154 more. The result was a long list of situations in which stuttering is often reduced or absent. These, I found, could be grouped into a few general conditions.

First, stuttering decreased whenever there was reduced communicative pressure. For example, most subjects reported that they could swear, sing, count, or comment on the weather and that they could speak to an infant, animal, or themselves with little or no stuttering. They had less difficulty when the listener knew what they wanted to say; a stutterer could often pronounce his name easily once he had written or spelled it for the listener. They could usually say isolated words or talk about them as words; it is revealing to hear a stutterer say with perfect fluency, "I can never say the word Philadelphia."

Second, stutterers were more fluent whenever their attention was distracted from their speech. Stuttering tended to disappear when they were carried away by enthusiasm, when they were taken off guard, or in emergency situations. One stutterer said that if a professor called on him when he was absorbed in taking notes, he would sometimes talk without stuttering for a considerable time, until it "dawned" on him that he was speaking fluently, and then he would begin to stutter. Another subject who had been trained in administering first aid encountered a man lying unconscious on the sidewalk in the midst of a small crowd of bystanders. He took charge and gave instructions in perfectly normal speech. Several subjects were veterans of World War II and told of speaking fluently whenever they were in serious danger. Some subjects told of acting parts in plays without stuttering or of avoiding speech difficulty by assuming an unaccustomed air or acting out of character in any way. Any number could speak fluently in a dialect, when imitating another person's speech, or when disguising their speech in other ways. Some found conversing with strangers an easy situation because strangers did not expect them to stutter. This fact is well-known to any speech pathologist who has enjoyed conversing with a perfectly fluent fellow passenger on a plane or train, only to hear him suddenly break into a stutter when the conversation turns to what each does for a living. Conversely, stuttering is apt to be most severe when attention is focused on speech. When asked to repeat what they have said because the listener hasn't understood, stutterers are almost sure to block. They usually have great difficulty on the telephone, which reduces them to a voice. Oral recitation in a foreign language class is likely to be one of their most difficult and fearful situations.

Third, some of the conditions under which subjects reported little or no stuttering were simply situations in which the cues for stuttering were absent. People who speak two languages sometimes stutter in only one; it may be their first or second language. As children, some stutter only at school or only at home. Some stutter only in oral reading. The cues for stuttering may be linguistic, situational, or environmental. Individuals have been known to stutter only in elevators. Many subjects told of having spoken fluently for a time when enrolling in new schools or entering the armed services. One subject had spoken with hardly any stuttering for four months while in an airborne unit in the Army. When he returned to civilian life he noticed that he stuttered much less whenever he wore his hunting boots. He said they had the same "feel" as the paratrooper boots he had worn in the Army. Another stutterer had endured a nomadic existence because of his speech. In his thirties, trained and experienced in his vocation, he at times stuttered so severely as to be almost speechless. When that happened, he would pack up his tools and move to another town. In a strange environment, with new associates, he would speak fluently for a while, but gradually the stuttering would return with increasing severity, until one day he would gather his belongings and be off again to a new location.

If we add to these three conditions bodily relaxation and hypnotic and other kinds of suggestion, we have probably accounted for essentially all conditions under which stuttering is reduced or eliminated. When I wrote the conclusions of my study, I had no difficulty showing that my findings were in good accord with a concept of stuttering as an anticipatory avoidance reaction. Stutterers seemed to become fluent whenever the social penalties for stuttering were lessened or whenever they were less likely to anticipate stuttering. As an overarching generalization, I argued that stuttering is reduced whenever there is less anxiety about stuttering. I would not assert that today. Johnson's thesis eventually led to studies of the relationship between frequency of stuttering and physiological measures of anxiety like heart rate and electrical conductance of the skin. A relationship certainly appeared, but it was far from perfect and sometimes was scarcely evident at all. But the anticipatory struggle hypothesis, as it has been advanced in many forms for almost two hundred years, has less to do with anxiety than with a misguided belief in the difficulty of speech. Naturally, occasions when that belief holds the stutterer in its grip are also likely to be occasions for anxiety about stuttering, and so it may seem as though the blocks result directly from anxiety. But there is nothing to prevent us from hypothesizing that when a stutterer, faced with a word he perceives as difficult, tenses his speech muscles, holds his breath, and attacks the word with effort, hesitation, and false starts, he may be doing so for no other reason than a mistaken assumption that this is the only possible way to say such a difficult word. Other theories account more simply for facts like the familial incidence of stuttering, but the anticipatory struggle hypothesis seems to account with the least strain for the conditions under which the disorder varies.

It was mainly Johnson's thinking and research that served to maintain an important place in the twentieth century for the point of view that stuttering is wholly learned behavior based on little more than a belief in the difficulty of speech. While the diagnosogenic theory was still popular, Johnson's view of the nature of the stuttering block was widely accepted. Many years later, the nature of the stuttering block was still a matter of doubt and controversy. There was little question in the minds of most workers that the stutterer's beliefs and anticipations work powerfully to precipitate moments of stuttering. Some believed it was the whole problem; an increasing number rejected that view.

CHAPTER NINE

Learning Theories

Wendell Johnson's insistence that stuttering was learned behavior set the stage for an unusual development. For many years experimental psychologists had been conducting laboratory studies in an effort to discover the basic laws that govern learning and learned behavior in animals such as rats and pigeons. The University of Iowa was one of the busy centers of this activity. Psychology and speech pathology were closely related academic programs at Iowa and graduate students in psychology often studied under Johnson. In the 1950s, two of these students, George Wischner and Joseph G. Sheehan, attempted to interpret stuttering behavior in terms of the phenomena of animal learning and the theories that psychologists had advanced to account for them. The formulations that Wischner and Sheehan offered were highly abstract, so much so that they might have appeared to some to be rather far removed from the realities of stuttering. But they were impressive. And in a certain sense they were the most practical of theories. If we could fully understand how stuttering was learned and maintained, we might well be able to use that understanding to help stutterers to unlearn it. The theories of Wischner and Sheehan drew considerable interest and acclaim for as long as stuttering was widely thought to be wholly learned behavior, that is to say for a period of about twenty years.

Stuttering as an Instrumental Avoidance Act

What George Wischner attempted to do in essence was to take Wendell Johnson's hypothesis that stuttering was an anxious, anticipatory avoidance reaction, reformulate it in the terminology of the learning theory of the day, and perform laboratory experiments to see if it accorded with observation.

For reasons that will soon become clear, a prominent part was played in Wischner's thinking by a stuttering phenomenon called the adaptation effect. In 1937, Johnson and Knott had reported that when subjects read the same passage aloud several times, most of them stuttered less and less with each successive reading. The stuttering rarely diminished to zero; typically, it was reduced by about half, and this generally occurred by about the fifth reading. For the sake of understanding Wischner's thinking, one of the most important features of the adaptation effect was that it followed what is technically known as a negatively accelerated growth curve. That is, the decrease in stuttering was most marked at the beginning and progressively less in successive readings, as shown in Figure 9–1.

Like other students of psychology at the time, Wischner was thoroughly conversant with the learning theory of Clark L. Hull. Hull was the leading behaviorist of his day, occupying the place that later fell to B. F. Skinner. His theory attempted to explain the facts that were known about the common type of learning that was called instrumental act learning and later came to be known as operant conditioning. The classic laboratory example of instrumental act learning is afforded by the so-called Skinner box. This is an enclosure so designed that if an animal inside depresses a bar, a pellet of food falls into a cup. In the heightened random activity that is motivated by hunger, a rat placed in the box will eventually press the bar and gobble the pellet. If the experiment is repeated on a series of occasions and a measure is taken of the time it takes for the animal to press the bar, it will be noted that the interval becomes shorter and shorter until the time comes that the rat scurries directly to the bar and with its nose in the food cup, depresses the bar in a businesslike fashion. The principle involved has been known to psychologists since early in the twentieth century. It is called reinforcement. In ordinary terms the behavior that is rewarded gets learned.

Now, suppose we stop reinforcing the response. The rat presses the bar and nothing happens. If we do this repeatedly, the time it takes for the rat to press the bar becomes longer and longer until finally the animal fails to perform the response except by chance. This is called experimental extinction. A learned response that is not reinforced dies out. It does not have to be reinforced on every occasion, but it must be reinforced once in a while to be maintained.

If we put the rat through a daily series of experimental extinction trials, we note that at the beginning of each day the response has regained some of its strength overnight. Over time, there is a general de-

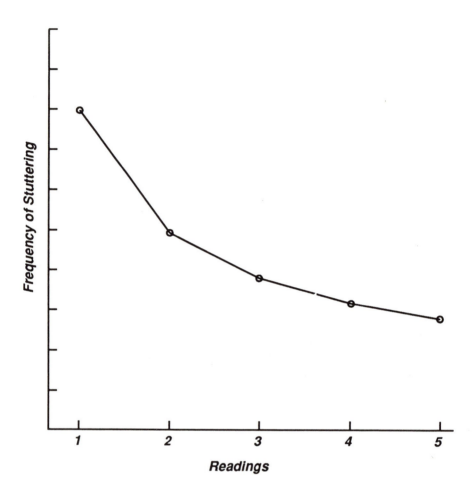

FIGURE 9-1. *The adaptation effect. When stutterers read the same material aloud successively, the frequency of stuttering tends to decrease from reading to reading, though at a decreasing rate. The figure shows a typical average curve of adaptation for a group of stutterers.*

cline in the learning, but the learning recovers somewhat during intervals of rest. This is known as spontaneous recovery.

Finally, there is a learned response that was known in Hull's day as an instrumental avoidance act. By the same principle of reinforcement that operates when the rat learned to press the bar, an animal can learn to make a response that enables it to avoid punishment, for example standing in the left half of a compartment rather than the right in order to avoid electric shock.

It was these facts that the Yale psychologist, Clark Hull, theorized about in the 1940s. Hull's main concern was with the strength of a learned response. This is simply the proclivity of the animal to perform the response—its probability of occurring in a given set of circumstances—measured, say, in the time it takes for the animal to make it. Why this should be a matter of concern is quite clear. We can assume that an animal has learned a repertoire of several possible responses to a given situation. In danger it can fight or flee, for example, or play possum. If we know the relative strength of these responses, we can predict the animal's behavior. The central tenet of Hull's theory was that the strength of a response depends jointly on two things. One is the degree to which the response has been learned, a hypothetical something that Hull called habit strength. The other is the animal's motivation to perform the response, a hypothetical drive state that could be defined and measured, say in terms of the number of hours of deprivation of food. It should be intuitively clear why response strength is a joint product of habit strength and drive. If the animal's hunger is great, it will soon press the bar even if the response has not yet been well learned. If the response has been well learned, the rat will press the bar quite soon even if it is only mildly hungry.

In a theory of learning, the most basic questions ultimately center about that hypothetical entity within the organism that Hull termed habit strength. He stated that habit strength depends on reinforcement. That had been said before. What was new was Hull's definition of reinforcement. He defined it as the reduction of a drive—hunger, thirst, sex, anxiety. He also suggested a way of measuring precisely how that unseen thing he called habit strength was related to reinforcement. If the strength of a response depends jointly on habit strength and drive, then all we need to do to observe changes in habit strength is to hold drive constant and measure response strength, which is easily observable. So Hull placed his rats in the Skinner box for trial after trial with exactly the same number of hours of deprivation of food and plotted increments of habit strength against the number of reinforcements. The result was a curve of learning that rose steeply at first and then gradually leveled off. In the same way, Hull studied the experimental extinction of a learned response. He plotted a curve that showed precisely how the strength of a habit fell off as the animals were given successive trials without reinforcement. And here we must imagine George Wischner sitting in class and learning about Hull's research. The curve of experimental extinction proved to be a negatively accelerated growth curve like the curve of adaptation of stuttering in Figure 9–1.

Negatively accelerated growth curves are a dime a dozen in the sciences. Still, Wischner was intrigued. Was it possible that what was called the adaptation effect was really the experimental extinction of stuttering? If so, here was laboratory evidence that stuttering was learned behavior. It raised the question whether other learning phenomena could be demonstrated in experiments on stuttering. Wischner chose this problem for his doctoral dissertation. And he succeeded to a reasonable extent in finding what he was looking for. For example, experimental extinction is subject to a certain amount of spontaneous recovery between trials, as we have seen. Sure enough, when Wischner tested subjects for the adaptation effect on the same reading passage on successive days, their stuttering kept returning to nearly its original level of severity each time. Another example involved an effect that the Russian physiologist Pavlov had observed many years earlier in the famous experiment in which he had conditioned dogs to salivate at the sound of a bell by associating the sound with food. Pavlov found that if an unusual sound occurred in the laboratory while the conditioning was going on, the dog's conditioned response was temporarily inhibited. This suggested to Wischner the familiar distraction effect in stuttering; there are any number of conditions under which stutterers speak fluently when their attention is diverted from their speech by distracting stimuli. Pavlov had also reported that when he proceeded to extinguish the dog's conditioned response by presenting the bell repeatedly without food, a distracting noise temporarily restored the response. This suggested another experiment to Wischner. After stutterers had read a passage aloud several times, he introduced a sudden loud noise. True to expectation, the noise caused a temporary halt in the downward course of adaptation.

Any theory that seeks to explain a response as learned behavior must confront the question, what is the reinforcement that serves to maintain the response? Wischner made a bold proposal that was in keeping with Clark Hull's definition of reinforcement as the reduction of a drive state. He suggested that stuttering was reinforced by the reduction of anxiety. He reasoned that as the stutterer anticipates the attempt on a feared word, anxiety steadily increases. Immediately after the block, then, anxiety inevitably diminishes. True enough, there is often social penalty for stuttering, but Wischner argued that the reinforcement came first, and so, in accordance with known laws of learning, it was stronger than the punishment.

Wischner theorized that stuttering was a learned, anxiety-motivated avoidance response. The laboratory model for stuttering, he believed, was the instrumental avoidance act that psychologists had repeatedly demonstrated with animal subjects. An example was the running behavior of a rat in a revolving squirrel cage that has been wired to give the animal an electric shock through its feet. The moment the animal sets the cage in motion by running, the current is automatically turned off. As a result, the rat quickly learns to avoid the shock by running. Wischner pointed out that instrumental avoidance acts had been found to possess a notable characteristic—they are difficult to extinguish. Take away the food pellets in the Skinner box, and the rat will stop pressing the bar. But how do you teach a rat in the squirrel cage to stop running? You can turn off the current and remove the wires, but in order for the animal to learn that the cage is no longer electrified, it has to stand still. This is just what the rat does not dare to do. In the rat's blind running behavior Wischner saw a revealing model of the stutterer's dilemma. If stutterers approached their supposedly "difficult" words without struggle and avoidance, they would say them normally, but this they feared to do, and so they almost never learned that the grid is not live. It was the familiar anticipatory struggle idea to which Johnson had given new life in his anticipatory avoidance hypothesis and which Wischner was now viewing from what seemed to be a promising new vantage point.

If Wischner's formulations ever held out any hope that a cure for stuttering would be at hand when experimental psychologists found an effective way of extinguishing instrumental avoidance behavior in animals, this hope was never fulfilled. As for the adaptation effect, which had originally inspired Wischner to think about stuttering in terms of learning theory, research much later seemed to show that, so far from demonstrating experimental extinction, it is probably due simply to the reader's increasing familiarity with the passage. That is, it probably bears a relationship to the reduction in stumbling and hesitating that we all experience after rehearsing a passage aloud several times. Nevertheless, the interest that Wischner's work aroused among speech pathologists in the 1950s undoubtedly went a long way to prepare the field for the wide acceptance of behavior therapies based on conditioning a decade later.

Stuttering as Approach-Avoidance Conflict

The persuasiveness of Johnson's view that stuttering is learned avoidance behavior had another outcome in a theory that was advanced in 1953 by Joseph G. Sheehan. Sheehan's theory also owed something to the assertion of the psychoanalyst Otto Fenichel that stuttering results from a conflict between the wish to speak and the wish to keep silent. But his most direct inspiration came from the research of Neal E. Miller, a behaviorist and a student of Clark Hull. Miller was among those who at an early date sought to apply learning theory to a better understanding of human problems. An important element of such problems is conflict. In the 1940s Miller was trying to identify the basic laws of conflict behavior by studying an animal model of conflict in the laboratory. He first taught

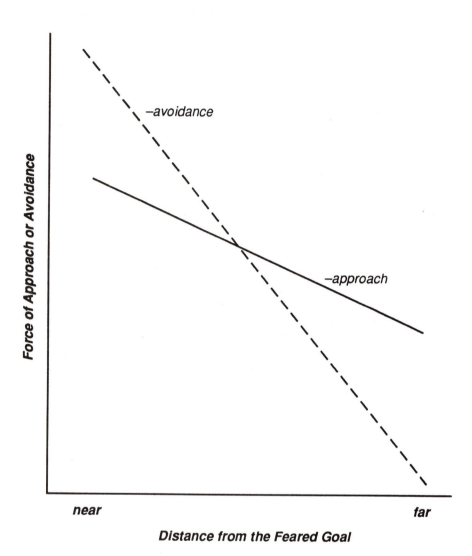

near   far

Distance from the Feared Goal

FIGURE 9-2.   *Gradients showing the changing force of the approach drive of experimental rats with distance from food and the changing force of their avoidance drive with distance from electric shock, as determined by Neal Miller. When the rats were faced with both food and shock, they became fixated at the point where the gradients crossed. Joseph Sheehan saw a model of stuttering in the conflict behavior of Miller's rats.*

rats to run down a runway toward food. By attaching the animals to a restraint that allowed him to measure the amount of force they exerted against it, he determined that the closer they came to the goal, the greater became their drive to reach it. He represented this observation by means of a sloping line that he termed the gradient of approach (see Figure 9–2). He then taught the animals to flee from an element that delivered an electric shock and plotted a gradient of avoidance. It was now possible to introduce conflict by placing the food and the source of shock together at one end of the runway and the rat at the other, making sure that the rat's drives to approach the food and avoid the shock were relatively equal. Miller had noted that the gradient of avoidance was steeper than the gradient of approach. (This simply means that the rat's drive to escape the shock declined more rapidly as it fled than its drive to reach the food increased as it approached.) This difference in the slope of the approach and avoidance gradients proved to be of critical importance. It meant that when the two drives were roughly equal, the gradients would cross. Miller predicted the behavior that would result from this crossing. At the far end of the runway from the feared goal, the drive to approach is higher than the avoidance drive, and so the rat would run toward the food. At a point on the runway where the gradients cross, the conflicting drives are equal, but Miller predicted that the rat would be propelled by its momentum into the sector where avoidance is greater than approach and so would turn and run the other way. Again its momentum, now reduced, would propel the rat a little way past the point where the gradients crossed. In this way, Miller predicted that the animal would oscillate back and forth between increasingly narrower limits and finally become fixated, unable to move forward or back. Miller ran the experiment and this is precisely what the rats did.

To Joseph Sheehan, oscillation and fixation seemed to describe stutterers' repetitions and prolongations so aptly that they suggested an explanation of stuttering. Sheehan theorized that the disorder results from conflicting drives of approach and avoidance with regard to speech. When the avoidance drive is stronger than the approach drive, Sheehan said, the stutterer is silent. When approach exceeds avoidance, as when stutterers are strongly impelled to speak by enthusiasm or in emergencies, they are fluent. But when approach and avoidance are in relative equilibrium, so that the gradients cross, they stutter. To explain why stutterers wished to avoid speech, Sheehan suggested that a variety of different reasons could operate, including word and situation fears, guilt or anxiety about the emotional content of intended utterances, an unwholesome relationship with the listener, and other psychological factors. The theory was an eclectic one that drew upon a broad array of possible causes. From the standpoint of treatment, the theory implied that the stutterer had to make sure that the approach to speech remained far enough above the avoidance drive that the gradients did not cross. Since it was difficult to envision a means of increasing the stutterer's approach to speech, Sheehan inferred that therapy needed to reduce their avoidance drive. His theory therefore provided a new rationale for one of the principal features of Iowa therapy, and throughout his career Sheehan concentrated his efforts as a clinician on teaching stutterers to give up the habit of avoiding speech.

The approach-avoidance conflict theory seemed to many workers to offer an elegant explanation of stuttering and it retained its broad appeal for many years. Like Wischner's theory, it helped to create a receptive climate for behavior therapy in the 1960s.

CHAPTER TEN

Drug Therapy

In the 1950s, a unique effort to treat stuttering medically raised some hopes for a time. It was caused by the appearance of tranquilizing drugs. Their effectiveness in reducing anxiety was soon established beyond question. With most speech pathologists assuming a direct link between stuttering and speech anxiety and with psychiatrists and others believing that stuttering is related to social and interpersonal anxiety, it was not long before tranquilizers were being given experimentally to stutterers. The research continued well into the 1960s and was done in Great Britain, France, Italy, and Japan, as well as in the United States. Many of the studies were relatively casual clinical observations. A number were carefully controlled, "double-blind" investigations in which half the subjects received sugar pills in place of the drug and neither the stutterers nor the investigator knew who had taken the drug until the end of the study.

The results were disappointing. Some improvement was occasionally noted in some subjects, but mainly in the tension and complexity of the stutterings rather than their number. Tranquilizers never came into significant use in the treatment of stuttering and the research eventually stopped. There is little doubt that stuttering is often accompanied by anxiety and often varies with it. But it doesn't follow that reducing the anxiety will eradicate the stuttering. Perhaps this fact reflects the organic factor that many believe is involved in some way in stuttering. More likely, it means that once fully convinced that Piscataway is a hard word to say, a stutterer will treat the word with the exaggerated effort and caution that a "hard" word deserves, regardless of the presence or absence of anxiety. Of course, when anxiety is high, words are more likely to be scrutinized for difficulty and so the struggle reactions are more apt to be called into play. As a result, stuttering often increases with anxiety, but may occur without it.

Only one drug was ever found to have a distinct and consistent effect on stuttering and it was not a tranquilizer. Haloperidol ameliorates the symptoms of several neurologic disorders, especially Gilles de la Tourette's disease, which is characterized by tics of the head, face, and extremities, and involuntary vocalizations. In the 1960s and 70s, a series of studies established that the drug reduces stuttering in a considerable number of subjects. Unfortunately, haloperidol has side effects, particularly drowsiness. When offered the chance, few subjects wished to continue taking the medication.

The reason for haloperidol's effect on stuttering is not known. The chemical is thought to block receptors for dopamine, a neurotransmitter in the brain. On the assumption that it is this action which reduces stuttering, David Burns and his colleagues at the University of Pennsylvania wondered if they could bring about increased stuttering by administering apomorphine, which appears to stimulate dopamine receptors. The drug did not have the anticipated effect. In fact, it seemed to reduce stuttering somewhat, an outcome which the investigators admitted was puzzling.

CHAPTER ELEVEN

Stuttering as a Perceptual Defect

The baffling nature of stuttering has continually lent itself to maverick departures from the accepted thinking of the time. In the mid-1950s, when it was becoming well established that stuttering is learned behavior, a hypothesis that had little to do with learning began to gain prominence in some circles. This was the view that stuttering results from an aberration in the way stutterers hear their own voices. The source of this unusual theory was the discovery of two new phenomena, the delayed auditory feedback effect and the white noise effect.

One day in or around 1950, an electronic engineer with the Signal Corps at Fort Monmouth, Bernard S. Lee, was trying out a new, state-of-the-art tape recorder by recording his own voice. Included in the equipment was a set of headphones through which the operator could listen to a recording as it was being made. By error, Lee had plugged the headphones into the wrong jack. Through a peculiarity in the design of the device, this caused him to hear his recorded speech with a slight delay in transmission, so that everything he heard in the headphones was what he had said a fraction of a second before. Under these conditions Lee, who is a normal speaker, found to his surprise that he was involuntarily repeating the first syllables of words. He was so intrigued by this effect, that he wrote an article entitled "Artificial Stutter" and sent it to the Journal of Speech and Hearing Disorders, where it was published in 1951. Engineer that he was, he attempted to explain the phenomenon in terms of the theory of automatic control mechanisms. "The unsatisfied monitor of the speech circuit," he wrote, causes the loop to "continue for an extra turn or two" until the missing feedback returns. In ordinary language, if you say it and you don't hear it, you think you haven't said it, so you say it again. Lengthier but no better explanations have been offered for the delayed auditory feedback effect.

It happened that speech scientists at the time were looking closely at automatic control mechanisms as models of the apparatus by which we so automatically produce our speech.[1] Partly for this reason, the Lee effect piqued their interest and it soon became the subject of a great deal of research. Among other things, it was discovered that not all individuals reacted to the delayed auditory feedback by repeating syllables. A more common effect was a slowing down of speech by prolongation of syllables, presumably as the speaker waited for the anticipated feedback. Eventually, delayed auditory feedback found a practical application in the testing of patients suspected of faking a hearing loss. In addition, Lee's discovery led to a new speculation about the cause of stuttering. Before long, the notion that stutterers are afflicted with a built-in delay in their auditory feedback began to be broached as a credible theory. On its face, the theory that stuttering is analogous to the Lee effect in normal speakers was far-fetched, and it might never have acquired much importance if it had not been for another discovery.

In 1955 two papers independently reported an unusual phenomenon, namely that when stutterers are exposed to loud white noise in both ears, most of them speak fluently. White noise is sound contain-

---

1. Automatic control theory, or servo theory, is concerned with machines that control themselves by the principle of feedback. A simple example is the ordinary home heating unit which is controlled by a thermostat. A portion of the output of the unit is fed back to the control mechanism, which senses it and turns the unit on or off depending on how the actual output matches the intended one. The device is thus regulated by its own performance. Feedback clearly involves the internal handling of information. The enormous capability of the electronic computer for handling information has made possible a vast array of automated functions from the guidance of aircraft to the regulation of the output of factories. Servo theory has also been invoked to explain various automatic processes in biology and the social sciences. And because we regulate our speech in part by auditory feedback, it was natural for speech scientists to look to servo theory for help in understanding the normal process of speech production. In 1954, Grant Fairbanks, an experimental phonetician, depicted the speech mechanism as a servosystem in order to account for the automaticity of speech. Some years later, Edward D. Mysak offered a theory of stuttering according to which stuttering was a failure of the automaticity of speech due to a breakdown in any of various parts of the servosystem. The theory unfortunately did not lead anywhere because it was difficult to conceive of any way of testing it.

ing a broad range of audible frequencies.[2] It is the sound of water run-ning or the wind in the trees, having the peculiar property of making other sounds difficult to hear. Many stutterers have observed that they can speak fluently near ocean surf or a passing train. The studies demon-strated the effect scientifically and it probably came as new knowledge to most speech pathologists. One paper was a report of an investigation by a student of Wendell Johnson's, Mary Lou Sternberg Shane. The other was by Colin Cherry, a British scientist, and his co-workers Bruce McA. Sayers and Pauline M. Marland. Both articles speculated that the cause of the phenomenon was the subjects' inability to hear their own speech. Shane suggested that they spoke fluently because they were freed from the anxiety-producing cues in their speech. Cherry and his collaborators boldly proposed a more unusual hypothesis. Stuttering, they said, was not a motor but a perceptual disorder that was due to "instability of the feedback loop" by which speakers monitor their vocalization. They de-clined to accept the suggestion that stuttering was analogous to the Lee effect, but others were quick to point out that if stutterers suffered from delayed auditory feedback, their fluency in white noise could easily be explained on the assumption that the noise prevented them from hearing the defective feedback.

One result of all this theorizing was that researchers now turned their attention to something they had hardly ever investigated before, the stutterer's hearing mechanism. Although they explored various aspects of audition in stutterers, the main question, whether stutterers' percep-tion of sound is delayed, proved difficult to answer. A few ingenious ex-periments were performed, with results that were interesting, if some-what equivocal. Why they were never followed up is not clear, but it may have been in part because of the results of some experimentation on the white noise effect.

The argument that white noise liberated stutterers from defective auditory feedback assumed that their fluency resulted from their failure to hear their own speech. An alternative was the obvious possibility that the noise simply served as a distraction. Efforts to settle this issue pro-duced inconclusive results until Samuel Sutton and Richard A. Chase performed an experiment in 1961. Making use of a noise generator that could be turned on or off automatically by the subject's voice as it was picked up by a microphone, they tested stutterers with continuous noise,

2. Sound involves vibration in a medium such as air. Audible vibrations range in frequency, or rate, from about 20 to 20,000 per second. Most of the sounds of daily experience combine multiple frequencies of vibration. In tones, as in music, the frequencies are in an orderly numerical relationship. By contrast, noise contains a random assortment of frequencies. White noise combines many vibrations of widely varying frequency.

with noise occurring only during vocalization, and with noise that was limited to the voiceless intervals between words and phrases. The stutterers spoke with equal fluency under all three conditions. At this writing we are still in doubt about why most stutterers speak normally in white noise, but it is evidently not because of any difficulty they have in hearing their own voices.

The flurry of interest in the idea that stuttering is analogous to the speech disruptions of normal speakers under delayed auditory feedback gradually abated. It was never a widely held view. But the research it gave rise to was not fruitless. Studies were done on such complex aspects of hearing as sound localization, perception of distorted speech, and other auditory functions that are mediated by higher centers of the brain. This ultimately proved to be one of the pathways that led to the discovery of some subtle peculiarities of brain functioning that some stutterers appear to possess. But before we take up this thread, we must discuss a momentous development in stuttering therapy.

CHAPTER TWELVE

Behavior Therapy

In the 1960s, while auditory research was slowly rekindling a long-dormant interest in the stutterer's neurophysiology, there took place one of the most abrupt changes of direction in the treatment of stuttering that has ever occurred in the United States. For about thirty years almost all speech clinicians had been teaching stutterers to modify their blocks and to cultivate an objective attitude in accordance with the program of therapy that Bryngelson, Johnson, and Van Riper had originated at the University of Iowa. That therapy had been designed to avoid the drawbacks of the old methods based on the use of artificial speech patterns. The Iowa mode of therapy overcame the drawbacks fairly well. Stutterers spoke naturally and spontaneously. Many learned to stutter less severely and to accept what stuttering they did with a healthier attitude. Although relapse frequently occurred, it generally had a far less crushing impact than before, partly because the immediate goal of therapy was not total fluency to begin with. By the 1960s, many speech clinicians belonged to a generation that had largely forgotten the disadvantages of the old methods. Many were hardly aware of those methods at all. What they did know was that the approach they were faithfully using was by no means ideal. Its main disadvantage was that the stutterers rarely ended up with speech that was free from stuttering. As long as there was no alternative that offered anything better, most clinicians accepted this as a matter of course. Reputable speech pathologists did not speak of a cure; the word marked one as unprofessional. But without knowing or acknowledging it, the field had gradually become ready for a new departure that promised something in the nature of a cure. It came in the form of behavior therapy.

Behavior therapy originated in the field of clinical psychology. Among a generation of young psychologists there were many who were disheartened by the results of conventional psychotherapies in which patients were helped to gain "insight" into the causes of their emotional conflicts by talking about their early home relationships. The disenchantment was brought to a head in 1952 when the British psychologist, Hans J. Eysenck published the results of a study in which emotionally troubled individuals seemed to show about the same amount of improvement over time regardless of whether or not they had been receiving psychotherapy. At the same time, experimental psychologists were demonstrating remarkable ability to modify the behavior of animals by conditioning techniques. Inevitably, it was suggested that human beings with emotional problems might be helped by these techniques, provided we viewed their complaints in the light of observable behavior, rather than some unseen neurotic conflict. Both kinds of conditioning, operant and classical, were soon being used to treat people. Controversy developed about their effectiveness, but in a few years behavior therapy, or behavior modification, gained a recognized place in clinical psychology. It did not take long for speech pathologists to react to this development. Speech, after all, was behavior too, and so were aberrations of speech. In the 1960s, behavior therapy began to influence almost every aspect of the treatment of speech and language disorders. In the case of stuttering, the new approach began with operant conditioning.

Operant Conditioning

By the late 1950s, B. F. Skinner had succeeded Clark Hull as the doyen of American behavioral psychologists. Skinner's operant conditioning was the same phenomenon that Hull had called instrumental act learning, but unlike Hull, Skinner was not interested in theorizing about how it happened. He felt that we were still too far from understanding the brain to speculate about hypothetical constructs inside it like drive or habit strength. Skinner was concerned only with the prediction and control of behavior, and at this he became a past master. In demonstrations before an audience, he is known to have conditioned a pigeon to perform a complicated ritual of turnings, peckings, and other movements in a matter of minutes.

Skinner's method made use of a remarkably small number of observable elements: the "discriminative stimulus" that set the occasion for the response (a pigeon could be conditioned to peck at a spot if a green light was on, not if a red); the response that was targeted for conditioning; and a consequence that was contingent on the animal's making of the response. The consequence consisted of either reinforcement or punishment. Reinforcement was defined simply as a consequence that increased the frequency of the response. It could be positive, like a pellet of food, or negative, like the cessation of an electric shock. Punishment was defined as a consequence that decreased the frequency of the response. The schedule on which reinforcements were given was important. Reinforcement could be administered continuously on every instance of the response, or intermittently. Continuous reinforcement made the animal learn faster, but rendered the response vulnerable to rapid extinction when reinforcement stopped. With intermittent reinforcement on a random schedule, conditioning was slower, but more resistant to extinction. So a good plan was to reinforce continuously until the response was well learned and then switch to intermittent reinforcement. A response that the animal was not likely to make spontaneously often enough to afford the experimenter the opportunity to reinforce it could be "shaped" by "successive approximations." For example, a dog could be rapidly trained to touch a doorknob with its nose by rewarding it first for approaching the door, then for facing it, then for raising its nose toward the doorknob, and so on.

Skinner had a keen interest in applying operant conditioning to human behavior. He even wrote of an ideal society in which favorable social conduct was shaped by conditioning. By the 1960s, clinical psychologists were using Skinner's methodology in a host of ways. In institutions for the mentally retarded, desirable behavior was being reinforced with tokens that inmates could exchange for candy and the like. Speechless autistic children were being conditioned to utter words. Psychologists were using reinforcement and punishment to combat overeating, excessive smoking, and various other kinds of maladaptive or antisocial behavior.

The first person to experiment with operant conditioning on stutterers was not a speech pathologist, but a psychologist trained in operant methodology, Israel Goldiamond. In 1958, together with two co-workers, Bruce Flanagan and Nathan H. Azrin, he administered loud blasts of tone to both ears of three adult subjects each time they blocked in oral reading. As a result, they read without stuttering. When the earphones were removed, the blocks returned, but the experimenters had found what they were looking for. They announced that stuttering was operant behavior; that is, it was behavior that could be modified by its consequences. It was a momentous statement, pregnant with possibilities for speech pathology, and it created a stir in the field. True enough, there was something puzzling about a demonstration that stuttering could be punished away, because it was a matter of common clinical experience that stuttering was often increased by social penalties; stutterers reported this and clinicians saw it. Could we deny the evidence of our senses? Yet, here was a scientific experiment that seemed to show just the opposite.

Any number of speech pathologists were prepared to dismiss the evidence of their clinical experience if it prevented them from embracing the hopeful premise that stuttering was operant behavior.

In 1963, George H. Shames and Carl E. Sherrick tried to show how stuttering could develop through operant conditioning. Transposing Wendell Johnson's diagnosogenic theory into operant conditioning terms, they explained that the effort to avoid normal disfluencies could arise and be maintained by "positive and negative reinforcements on complex, multiple schedules." As an alternative, they suggested that parents may create stuttering by inadvertently reinforcing normal disfluency. For example, children often tend to be disfluent in the effort to gain the ear of an inattentive listener or when demanding or asking for something. In both instances the disfluency is often followed by a reinforcement—the listener's attention or the thing being demanded.

In the meantime the findings of Goldiamond and his co-workers had gone without confirmation, but in 1966 Richard R. Martin and Gerald M. Siegel at the University of Minnesota did a careful replication of their study with three subjects on successive occasions, using electric shock applied to the wrist in place of loud tone. With one stutterer, the shock was made contingent on the subject's habit of tongue protrusion or prolongation of the sound *s*; with another, on nose wrinkling; and with the third, on all instances of stuttering. In all three cases, the targeted response disappeared in moments and continued absent as long as the electrodes remained strapped to the wrist. On their removal, the response quickly returned. In one case, a plain nylon strap placed around the subject's wrist during a single shock session was enough to do away with the stuttering in subsequent sessions. In another case, a blue light that had been associated with the shock produced the same effect.

After the Martin and Siegel study, "operant conditioning" experiments proliferated. Convinced that stuttering was operant behavior, researchers began to look for ways to use the method without giving painful shocks or potentially injurious blasts of tone. The first thing they thought of trying was less aversive forms of "punishment." Surprisingly, they found that simply saying "no" or "wrong" had the same effect as electric shock. So did time-out, a procedure in which the subject was required to stop talking for ten seconds after every block. And so did response-cost, in which subjects were given a sum of money, but saw it reduced by a dime each time they stuttered. Both verbal punishment and time-out soon began to be used in therapy. Martin and his co-workers trained clinicians to administer time-out to stutterers in the public schools. They also reported the use of a variation of the technique with two children aged three and four. During a few months of weekly sessions, each child was permitted to visit Suzybelle, a beautifully dressed doll in an illuminated glass case who conversed with you and told stories, except that any time you stuttered she stopped talking, her light would go out, and for ten seconds it was impossible to get her attention. Both children improved markedly in speech and a check a year later revealed only a few stutterings in both cases.

Of course, if stuttering was really operant behavior, the best way to extinguish it would have been by removing the reinforcement that presumably served to maintain it. But nobody knew how to do that, because nobody had any inkling about how stuttering kept getting reinforced. But clinicians did manage to find an alternative to punishment when they began to reinforce fluency. According to one published report, three school-age children were rewarded after every five or ten-second interval during which they spoke without stuttering. After a few brief sessions they were observed to be speaking fluently both in and outside of the speech clinic. In time, many workers combined reinforcement and punishment. At the Prince Henry Hospital in Sydney, Australia, Roger J. Ingham and Gavin Andrews designed a three-week token economy for adult stutterers. In hourly rating sessions throughout the day, they counted the stutterers' blocks. When the blocks decreased, the stutterer received tokens; whenever stutterings increased, tokens were taken away. The tokens were the only means by which the stutterer could buy meals, reading materials, cigarettes, and the like. Ingham and Andrews claimed that the procedure rarely resulted in a stutterer going hungry, but in time they did supplement the procedure with other techniques for helping stutterers to speak fluently.

Operant conditioning did not endure for long as the mainstay of behavior therapy for stuttering. One reason was that the benefits were too often temporary. Probably a more compelling reason was that clinicians found simpler techniques that satisfied the yearning for quick and easy results that behavior therapy has released from its long suppression. And perhaps some part was also played by the doubts that eventually arose about whether stuttering was operant behavior at all, in the sense that B. F. Skinner had applied the term to the simple bar-pressing response of a hungry rat. For example, research showed that the "punishments" that reduced stuttering often had little or no aversive quality. In one study in which subjects were questioned, most interpreted time-out from speaking merely as a chance to relax. In another study, neither the use of loud noise nor the word "wrong" produced any psychogalvanic skin reflex, normally a sensitive indicator of emotional stress, even though the stuttering was reduced. Furthermore, if stuttering were operant behavior, it would be expected to increase if rewarded, yet various attempts to reinforce stuttering produced inconsistent results. A particularly severe blow was delivered to the theory in 1970 when

Eugene B. Cooper and his associates at the University of Alabama showed that presentation of the word "right" following stuttering blocks rendered subjects just as fluent as the word "wrong." So did the word "tree." The effect that for so long was called operant conditioning or punishment is evidentally a powerful one, but the reason for it has continued to be in doubt. Some believe it is simply an example of distraction.

Attempts to punish stuttering and reinforce fluency were still in use by some practitioners as this book was being written. And operant conditioning has left its mark on the treatment of stuttering in the form of programmed therapy. Many clinicians program the treatment process to proceed in small steps with target responses carefully specified at every step, a procedure that developed directly from operant conditioning.

Systematic Desensitization

Before we come to the approach that became the principal tool of behavior therapy for stuttering, it is necessary to describe the other kind of conditioning that was borrowed for this purpose. This was the kind of conditioning that Pavlov had made famous in his experiments with dogs many decades earlier. The behavior therapy that is based on Pavlovian, or classical, conditioning has become known as systematic desensitization.

Classical conditioning deals with involuntary, reflex responses like the eye blink, the knee jerk, or salivation. Suppose we devise a way of measuring a dog's salivation. We now ring a bell. It produces no increase in salivation; the bell is a neutral stimulus. Next, we place food powder in the dog's mouth and note a distinct salivation response. No conditioning is involved; it is a purely reflex response. But now we ring a bell and follow it immediately with food powder. If we do this several times, we discover that the bell alone is sufficient to induce some salivation. Salivation has become a conditioned response. In operant conditioning, which involves mainly voluntary responses, the important relationship is between a response and its consequence. In classical conditioning, the dog salivates whether it is rewarded or not. The relationship is between two stimuli. Psychologists aptly describe Pavlovian conditioning as stimulus substitution. By association, the stimulus bell acquires some of the power of the stimulus food.

The importance of classical conditioning for behavior therapy is that this is the way most psychologists believe that anxiety is learned. Suppose a child is bitten by a dog. As a result, the child's heart beats faster, its hair stands on end, adrenalin is secreted into the child's bloodstream, there are changes in blood distribution that result in pallor, and many other physiological events occur. Collectively, these changes are spoken of as autonomic arousal. In this case, they are not a learned reaction, but a reflex response to a noxious stimulus. But the next day the child may react with much the same symptoms of arousal merely on seeing a dog. The child is experiencing anxiety. Anxiety, psychologists say, is the conditioned form of the physiological reaction to stress. The sight of the dog, once a neutral stimulus, has acquired some of the effect of the stressful stimulus because it was associated with it.

Psychologists are often called upon to help people who have irrational fears of certain well-defined objects: spiders, thunderstorms, crowds, high places, the boss, and so forth. In 1958, Joseph Wolpe suggested a way of deconditioning such fears. Wolpe noted that certain responses are incompatible with fear. Examples are eating, relaxation, assertive behavior, and vigorous physical activity. His idea was to condition to the feared object a response that was incompatible with fear. For example, a child with a fear of dogs might be fed repeatedly in the presence of a dog. The dog might then elicit physiological responses associated with eating that would overcome the autonomic arousal responses of anxiety. An obvious problem with this procedure is that it could work the other way too; the fear might prevent the child from eating. Wolpe's solution was to arrange the presentations of the feared stimulus in a hierarchical order of increasing fearfulness. The dog might at first be tied up at a great distance from the child and by degrees brought closer.

As a convenient response incompatible with fear, Wolpe's choice fell on bodily relaxation, which can be taught by well-known methods. But he was faced with yet another problem. You can tie up a dog at a distance from a child, but you can't tie up the boss or a thunderstorm. After experimenting briefly with presentations of the stimulus in hypnosis, Wolpe discovered that it was enough for the patient to imagine the thunderstorm as it came closer or the boss in conditions of increasing formidability. So he adopted the procedure of vividly describing the scene as the patient sat with eyes closed in a state of relaxation. Wolpe wrote a book demonstrating his success with this technique and the method was soon applied widely as a form of behavior therapy.

Anxiety is such a prominent part of the typical adult stutterer's problem, that stuttering seemed to lend itself readily to treatment by systematic desensitization, and Wolpe himself was the first to treat a stutterer by this method, reporting excellent results. But it was Gene J. Brutten and Donald J. Shoemaker who developed this form of stuttering therapy at the University of Southern Illinois. Brutten and Shoemaker advanced a theory of stuttering in which anxiety played the central role. They pointed out that fear makes for disintegration of fine motor coordinations. They suggested that stuttering is a disintegration of speech that is brought about directly by anxiety. Their theory was that as children stutterers were repeatedly under the necessity to speak in a stressful environment; consequently they were conditioned to experience fear, and motoric disintegration, when speaking. To decondition stutterers' fears, they had them draw up a list of their feared speaking situations arranged in order of fearfulness. After training the stutterer to relax, they began work on the least fearful situation in the hierarchy. With the subject in a state of maximum relaxation, they narrated the situation in vivid detail. The stutterers then had to imagine themselves reliving the situation. If they felt any anxiety in doing so, they were instructed to relax and the process was repeated. When they had experienced the entire situation in imagination without fear, they went on to be desensitized to the next situation in the hierarchy.

Brutten and Shoemaker made no immoderate claims for their therapy, but reported encouraging results. Although systematic desensitization never came into wide use with stutterers, many clinicians have had it in their bag of techniques and a few have employed it regularly.

Artificial Speech Patterns

Conditioning was not the principal form of behavior therapy for stuttering for long. What conditioning did was to release speech pathologists from the obligation to adhere to a long-established method of treatment whose effect on the symptoms themselves was usually limited and slow in coming. Now Iowa therapy seemed to many to be merely an effort to help stutterers learn to live with it. Suddenly it was reputable to think about helping people to rid themselves of stuttering altogether. A spirit of experimentation with new methods sprang into being. In this climate an old attempt to solve the problem of stuttering seemed new and promising. Once again, the power of almost any change in the stutterer's pattern of speech to bring about immediate and total fluency proved to be an irresistible lure. Within a few years, most speech clinicians were using this approach in some form and reporting gratifying results. Many seemed unaware that such techniques had ever been extensively used before. This was especially true of the relatively young, who were present in large numbers in the rapidly growing field and of some few in other professions who were practicing behavior therapy with stutterers. One psychiatrist believed he was pioneering a new treatment for stuttering. There was little hesitancy about referring to the use of artificial speech patterns as behavior therapy. To those in professions such as psychiatry and clinical psychology, this treatment for stuttering was behavioral because it was far removed from the "insight" psychotherapy that they thought of as the conventional approach to the disorder. For speech pathologists, the artificial speech patterns were behavioral because they contrasted with work on the stutterer's attitudes. They argued that it was unnecessary to work on attitudes; take away the stuttering, they said, and there would be no occasion for anxiety or shame.

The use of artificial speech patterns was soon so common that the issue dividing speech pathologists who treated stutterers with behavior therapy from those who still used Iowa therapy became whether to teach stutterers to talk differently or to teach them to stutter differently. By the 1970s, the talk-differently side were in the majority.

For the most part, the speech patterns that stutterers were trained to adopt were confined to a small number. One was metronome-timed speech, in which each syllable or word was timed to a rhythmic beat. At the University of Pennsylvania, the psychiatrist and behavior therapist John P. Brady designed a miniature electronic metronome that was worn behind the ear like a hearing aid and produced a tick-tock of variable rate. To mitigate the strangeness of the speech pattern somewhat, he taught stutterers to time first each syllable, then each word, and finally each phrase to the metronome. In Newcastle-upon-Tyne in England, Gavin Andrews and Mary Harris had stutterers speak rhythmically without the use of a metronome, in what they called syllable-timed speech.

More widely adopted than rhythmic speech was a pattern called gentle onsets of phonation. Introduced by Ronald L. Webster at Hollins College in Roanoke, Virginia, it called for each voiced sound to be initiated at a barely audible level and gradually raised to normal intensity. Webster's systematic program of therapy became well-known and attracted stutterers from all parts of the country. One of his clients was Annie Glenn, the wife of John Glenn, the astronaut and senator from Ohio. Some time after her therapy, she addressed the American Speech and Hearing Association at one of its annual meetings and in a speech full of praise for speech pathologists, she indicated that although her stuttering was not completely gone, her life had been changed by the help she had received.

In another approach called airflow, stutterers were instructed to precede each utterance with a passive outflow of breath. Airflow was popularized by Martin Schwartz in a book entitled *Stuttering Solved.* The title offended many speech pathologists, but the technique proved attractive to a considerable number of them.

Finally, there was syllable prolongation or, as it has often been called, "prolonged speech." This required stutterers to slow down their rate of speech by drawing out each syllable and to eliminate the breaks in vocalization between syllables. Described by one of its eminent practitioners, William H. Perkins, as a slow drone, it soon became the dominant form of therapy for stutterers in the United States and, like gentle onsets and airflow, is in prevalent use at this writing. Its use had a curious beginning. It will be recalled from the last chapter that a delay in the auditory feedback of speech was discovered in the 1950s to cause most normal speakers to prolong their syllables and many of them to stutter. Before long, a streak of morbid curiosity prompted some workers to wonder what would happen if they placed actual stutterers under delayed auditory feedback. The effect turned out to be astonishing. Most of them spoke fluently, exhibiting neither their usual stuttering blocks nor the repetitions that the delayed feedback often causes. This is really not so mysterious. It is apparently the slow rate of speech, a very common effect of this condition, that does away with both kinds of disruptions. At all events, by the end of the 1950s, devices for delaying stutterers' perception of their speech by a fraction of a second had occasionally been used in therapy. The first reports came from Europe, notably West Germany, where speech pathology had a tradition dating back to the nineteenth century. But what gave this form of treatment the prominence it acquired in the United States was its independent discovery by Israel Goldiamond.

After Goldiamond and his associates had established that stuttering could be eliminated by loud blasts of tone, he continued to perform experiments on stuttering as operant behavior. Searching for a form of punishment less noxious than blasts of tone, he tried brief intervals of delayed auditory feedback on the assumption that it was aversive, and it worked just as well. He then reasoned that if stuttering was operant behavior, it should be possible to reinforce as well as punish it. His plan was to see if he could increase the frequency of stuttering by placing the stutterer under continuous delayed feedback and briefly turning it off whenever the subject stuttered. But when he turned it on, something unexpected happened; the subjects fell into a slow pattern of syllable prolongation and did not stutter. It occurred to Goldiamond that he was in possession of a potential treatment for stuttering. By varying the rate of exposure of reading material on a screen, he trained stutterers to use a more normal rate of speech and he gradually faded out the delayed auditory feedback by decreasing its intensity. In 1965, he reported a high rate of success in treating stutterers by this method.

Goldiamond's work gave delayed auditory feedback unusual cachet as a treatment for stuttering. Enthusiasm about operant conditioning was at its height, and the use of delayed auditory feedback to establish slow speech now became associated with operant conditioning in the minds of many clinicians. For a time, it was not unusual to hear it referred to by that name. At the University of Southern California, William

Perkins and his associate, Richard F. Curlee, developed an improvement over Goldiamond's method. Delayed auditory feedback had been found to slow down the rate of speech most effectively at a delay time of about a quarter of a second. Curlee and Perkins started stutterers at a quarter of a second's delay and then decreased the delay in short steps. At each step, the rate of speech increased. In this way, the stutterer was weaned from the auditory feedback device and at the same time made to speak at a more normal rate. Many other clinicians eventually adopted this technique. By the 1970s, syllable prolongation, both with and without the aid of delayed auditory feedback, had become one of the most commonly employed therapies for stuttering.[1]

Fervid Optimism and Sober Reappraisal

As soon as the use of artificial patterns of speech became the major form of therapy for stuttering, a new spirit of optimism pervaded the treatment of stutterers. For the first time in thirty years, the total elimination of stuttering in large numbers of cases began to be reported in enthusiastic terms. In the 1970s, it was not uncommon to hear zealous young speech clinicians assert that a remedy for stuttering had finally been found. It was claimed that behavior modification or "operant conditioning" eradicated stuttering, in contrast to "traditional Van Riper therapy," which only helped stutterers to live with it. In some cases, the claims for behavior therapy were convincingly backed up by tape recordings in which individuals were heard to stutter severely before treatment and to speak with impressive fluency afterward. Needless to say, the news media pounced upon these developments, and, in newspaper reports, magazine articles, and television segments, it was announced that new cures for stuttering had been found.

Of course, many clinicians were still doing Iowa therapy. Some remembered the disapproval with which techniques that taught stutterers to talk differently had been regarded in earlier years, and they were star-

---

1. In the innovative climate that developed in the treatment of stuttering, the term behavior therapy came to be applied to various other methods. Some workers reported success from a form of biofeedback that made it easy for stutterers to learn to relax tense speech muscles; as they reduced the tension, there was a change in the pitch of a tone. Another device delivered white noise to both the stutterer's ears. It was hardly a cure, and experience with portable noise generators showed that most stutterers found the inconvenience of using them to outweigh their advantages, but for some it was a relief that they could get in no other way. The apparatus, in a commercially available form called the Edinburgh masker, has drawn unqualified praise from more than one grateful stutterer.

tled to hear the innovations of Johnson and Van Riper dismissed as traditional. Van Riper, now close to retirement, commented wearily that each
new generation seems to have to learn for itself the futility of the old
methods. Joseph Sheehan, not so forbearing, inveighed against the rehabilitation of these methods with biting sarcasm. A selection of headings
from one of his writings will indicate the tone: "The 'Experimenters' Are
Always Successful; But Are the Stutterers?"; "Only the Claims Are New,
Not the Methods"; "The 'Laetrile Effect' in the Treatment of Stuttering";
"On the Trail of the Rapturous Testimonial."

To many speech pathologists who were aware of their past, the new
departure did seem to recall Santayana's famous dictum that a people
who forget their history are doomed to relive it. Yet history never repeats
itself exactly, and in this case at least one distinction between then and
now turned out to be of the utmost importance. In the past, when stutterers were taught techniques for changing the way they spoke, there
were no scientific studies of the outcome of therapy. Now the journals
fairly teemed with them. This was an inevitable consequence of the new
turn of events. When the behavior therapists borrowed conditioning
techniques from the animal psychologists, they also borrowed the psychologists' experimental methods. So when speech pathologists borrowed behavior therapy, a rigorous scientific methodology that demanded objective verification of results came with it. It was this difference that eventually resulted in a more restrained assessment of the talk-
differently approach to stuttering therapy. For a brief interval the studies
seemed to fulfill the experimenters' most earnest hopes and results were
sometimes reported in extravagant terms. But soon the realization grew
that studies of the outcome of therapy are an extremely difficult kind of
research, fraught with opportunities for error and self-delusion.

A common pitfall in the evaluation of clinical progress is due to the
tendency of stutterers to stutter less with their clinicians as the relationship grows increasingly intimate. It is impossible to say how often
speech therapists have been lulled into a gratifying sense of accomplish-
ment before they became aware that their client was stuttering as much
as ever outside the clinic. For this reason, evidence was soon demanded
of researchers that the fluency they had established had carried over into
the stutterer's daily world. As a result, it became clear that this carryover
by no means occurred as a matter of course. Clinicians had to confront
the task of extending therapy in various ways into outside situations.
Systematic attempts to effect "transfer" became a routine aspect of treatment.

Before long, relapse, that ancient nemesis of the talk-differently
therapies, returned to dog stutterers and clinicians so persistently that it
became unthinkable to do a study of clinical outcome without providing

for a follow-up evaluation after an interval of time following the end of therapy. But after how long an interval of time? Few researchers were prepared to follow up their cases for more than six months, despite clinical experience suggesting that relapse often took place after longer periods. Even at that, the studies made it apparent that in most cases there was some recurrence of stuttering within a few months. And the short follow-up interval was not the only problem. The follow-up assessments were usually done by the same person who had administered the treatment and in the same environment. Research showed that this was apt to produce spuriously favorable evaluations of outcome. Valid assessments could only be done in new surroundings by someone unknown to the stutterer.[2] There was even some evidence that they had to be done without the subjects' knowledge that they were being tested. Otherwise, some stutterers mustered enough fluency to perform better than they usually did.

Not all subjects relapsed, and those that did did not all revert to their former levels of severity, even on long-term follow-up evaluations, so that often there was a net gain. But the perception of difficulty in maintaining lasting fluency became so acute that in 1979 an international conference on the subject of relapse was held in Banff, Canada. It became commonplace to hear that the problem was not the difficulty of making stutterers fluent, but of keeping them that way. The term eggshell fluency entered the professional vocabulary. Speech clinicians turned their attention to what they called maintenance, and this now came to be viewed as a necessary adjunct to treatment programs. In most cases maintenance was carried out by continuing to give the stutterer post-therapy booster sessions of treatment at increasing intervals of time.

---

2. This was illustrated by the experience of one of my students who underwent a course of therapy consisting of gentle onsets of phonation. Fluent for a time, he soon relapsed, but found himself perfectly fluent again on re-evaluation. He wrote, "The follow-up consists of returning to the clinic approximately one month after treatment. You are greeted and tested by the same clinician you worked very closely with for three months and with whom you have developed a rather personal, relaxed, and comfortable relationship. You are then tested in a room previously used for treatment... In that room (or very nearby) for three months, for two hours a day, three days a week, you did not utter a single stutter. The point is that regardless of how your stuttering may be on the outside, after being re-immersed in a supportive, non-threatening context that brings to mind nothing but fluency, it is not surprising that very little stuttering goes on." It is interesting to note that if a before-and-after tape recording had been made of this person's speech under these conditions, it would obviously have told a very misleading story.

When research on the outcome of behavior therapy began, it seemed obvious that the way to measure the severity of the subjects' difficulty was by counting their stuttering blocks. Eventually this seemingly objective procedure began to be viewed as simplistic. One reason was that it ignored what Sheehan ridiculed as the "voice-from-the-tomb" quality of the artificial speech patterns that stutterers were being taught. From the start, clinicians had seen the need to modify these patterns by training stutterers to use more normal rate, inflections, and phrasing, but so much strangeness often remained that in time many workers insisted that a valid appraisal of the stutterer's progress had to include a measure of the "naturalness" of speech. The counting of stuttering blocks also failed to take into account the fact that many stutterers who had undergone these therapies were fluent only by dint of conscious and deliberate employment of their artificial speech patterns; they were in the irksome position of needing to continually "monitor" their speech. Some speech pathologists reported that their successful clients generally thought of themselves, not as normal speakers, but as stutterers who could speak fluently. With this self-concept as a stutterer often went considerable anxiety in speaking situations. The belief steadily grew that a valid assessment of results had to take into account self-concepts and attitudes as well as mere frequency of blocks. As usual, Sheehan, a stutterer himself, put the case against the counting of stutterings strongly:

> *A stutterer may feel miserable at the strain and vigilance required to keep an artificial pattern going. But the resulting monotone might dramatically lower the frequency count. Conversely, a stutterer might relax his suppressive vigilance enough to feel much freer and more open, even though the frequency count might be reported as higher by an objective observer. Which one feels better about himself? Who is ahead in a genuine therapeutic sense?*

When Sheehan died prematurely in 1983, the treatment of stuttering lost a lone voice of passionate dissent. But by then the exhilaration of the early 1970s over the promise of behavior therapy had already given way to a more subdued outlook. At the Banff conference, Richard Martin had delivered the conclusions of his comprehensive review of the outcome research of the 1960s and 1970s: about one-third of stutterers seemed to gain lasting fluency, about a third relapsed significantly, and about a third either dropped out of treatment or were not available for follow-up evaluation.[3] It was clear that many stutterers had benefited. But all thoughtful workers knew that they had to find ways to do better.

3. It is important to keep in mind that the subjects of the studies Martin reviewed were of all ages. There is evidence and much clinical impression that the success rate is considerably higher in the case of children than it is in the case of adults.

In the meantime, Iowa therapy had not been totally forgotten. Although Van Riper's followers had largely dwindled to a middle-aged few, his name still inspired reverence and his book, *The Treatment of Stuttering*, which appeared in 1973, contained his finest writing. In the 1980s, professional opinion gradually came to be dominated by the point of view that an effective program of treatment had to combine the best features of behavior therapy and Iowa therapy. In the majority of cases this meant teaching stutterers how to achieve immediate fluency through artificial modes of speech together with work aimed at their beliefs, fears, and avoidances. Others suggested that stutterers learn artificial fluency for occasions that threatened severe social penalties for stuttering and an acceptable type of stuttering for ordinary use. A very few workers, to their credit, even thought that an informed choice between the two forms of therapy should be left for the stutterer to make.

This is where matters stood at the writing of this book. To some it may seem that in the end those of us who deplored what we saw as an attempt to rehabilitate old, discredited methods were vindicated. But this episode was a sobering experience for many of us as well, because it demonstrated that the old methods had more potential for genuine help than we had been taught to believe. It was not that Johnson and Van Riper knowingly misled us. But they were keenly aware of the serious drawbacks of those methods and were convinced that we could do better. From their zeal and conviction we received an oversimplified message. They knew better. Many years ago, in the course of a conversation with Van Riper in which he was excoriating the old techniques, I said to him, "I'll bet one in a thousand stutterers was helped by those methods." "Oh, many more than one in a thousand," he replied, "many more," and seemed surprised that I didn't know it.

CHAPTER THIRTEEN

The Search for Brain Differences

In the 1970s, a change in outlook on the nature of stuttering suddenly began to manifest itself. For about thirty years, notwithstanding a brief flurry of interest in the stutterer's auditory feedback mechanism, the prevailing belief of speech pathologists was that stuttering is wholly learned. Opinion had been shaped by Johnson's diagnosogenic and anticipatory avoidance theories, by psychological learning theories, and by a Zeitgeist that was somewhat obsessed with nurture, as against nature, in the molding of human behavior. But by the end of the 1970s, many speech pathologists had become convinced that there are subtle organic influences that contribute to the origin of the disorder.

The Wada Test

The event that set this change in motion was the publication in 1966 of a report by a Philadelphia neurosurgeon, R. K. Jones, in a British medical journal. The report concerned four patients, three males aged 13, 27, and 50 and a 36-year-old woman. All had operable lesions of recent origin in one hemisphere of the brain, caused chiefly by the rupture of blood vessels. All four had something else in common—severe stuttering, though this was evidently not related to the brain pathology since they had all stuttered since childhood. As a routine procedure prior to surgery, Dr. Jones gave each patient the Wada test. The Wada test consists of the injection of sodium amytal into the carotid arteries. The left and right carotid arteries lie on each side of the neck. Each one sends blood to one cerebral hemisphere. The purpose of the Wada test is to determine if the hemisphere to be operated on contains the patient's language centers, in which case the surgeon must be careful to avoid giving the patient aphasia—problems in the use and comprehension of language. Most people develop language centers in one hemisphere, usually the left. Some make more use of the right hemisphere and in a few cases language resides in both. Before surgeons had the Wada test, it was difficult for them to know for sure which half of a patient's brain was dominant for language. In administering the test, the surgeon has the patient continue to speak while each carotid artery is injected in turn. The effect of the sodium amytal is to block cerebral activity temporarily. If injection of the left carotid artery causes the patient to involuntarily stop talking, there is clearly a language center in the left hemisphere.

It was the outcome of the Wada test and surgery on his four stuttering patients that prompted Jones to take to his pen. In all four cases, the Wada test showed language activity in both hemispheres. In all four cases the stuttering disappeared immediately after the lesion was removed. And following the surgery, in all four cases the Wada test showed normal representation of language in only one hemisphere. At the writing of his report, all had continued to talk normally for as long as Jones had followed them up—three years, 27 months, 18 months, and 15 months.

There is obviously something puzzling here. The simple inference that a brain defect of these patients had resulted in a stutter which disappeared when the pathology was gone is flatly contradicted by the fact that the speech difficulty was present long before the onset of the pathology in each case. We might speculate that the stuttering was due to a long-standing bilateral representation of language in the brain which somehow corrected itself as a serendipitous result of the surgery. Still, it is difficult to conceive, as Gavin Andrews and his co-workers pointed out, that normal unilateral representation of language could have asserted itself so quickly after the operation. Despite these perplexities, Jones's report created a stir among speech pathologists. To a field that still had some memory of the Orton-Travis theory of cerebral dominance, these findings were intriguing. To be sure, the Orton-Travis theory was concerned with the timing of nerve impulses to the speech muscles, whereas the Wada test is concerned with cerebral dominance for the formulation of language. Also, the Orton-Travis theory offered a plausible explanation of the symptoms of stuttering, whereas the connection between stuttering and a lack of cerebral dominance for language is vague. But any difference that set stutterers as a group apart from nonstutterers was a prize that researchers had sought unsuccessfully for forty years, and if this one was reliable, it could not be allowed to elude their grasp.

Speech pathologists waited expectantly for the results of further Wada testing of stutterers. Unfortunately, the Wada test has a risk of mortality comparable to that of some surgery. It took a few years before subjects who were not facing imminent brain surgery could be found to take it. In 1971, Eugene L. Walle, a professor of speech pathology at the Catholic University of America in Washington, D.C., obtained three volunteers from an adult stutterers' self-help group affiliated with the university. The sodium amytal injections were administered by Alfred J. Luessenhop, a neurosurgeon at Georgetown University Hospital. The results failed to confirm Jones's observations. All three stutterers showed normal left cerebral dominance for language.

In the hope of forestalling unnecessary Wada testing of stutterers by others, Walle hastened to submit a brief preliminary report to the Journal of Speech and Hearing Disorders, but by that time Gavin Andrews and his associates at the Prince Henry Hospital in Sydney, Australia, had already tested three additional adult stutterers. All had left cerebral dominance for language. The Australian researchers also administered the Wada test to a 35-year-old man with the adult-onset neurological speech disorder that resembles ordinary stuttering and is often called acquired or neurogenic stuttering. The problem had appeared suddenly when he was 31 years of age after a head injury with aphasia. That subject failed to show unilateral cerebral dominance for language.

Dichotic Listening

The failure to confirm Jones's findings with subjects who had not sustained brain injury did little to stem the revival of interest in stutterers' cerebral dominance. In the late 1960s, neurologists and others had begun to make use of a new test of hemispheric dominance for language called the *Dichotic Word Test*. Through headphones, pairs of words are presented to the subject simultaneously, one to each ear. The subjects are then asked to repeat as many of the words as they can recall. Most normal individuals remember more words heard with the right ear than with the left. With environmental noises, on the contrary, the left ear usually does better. The right ear advantage of most subjects for words presumably reflects the dominant role that the left hemisphere of the brain plays in most individuals in the perception of language. With no risk to subjects, the *Dichotic Word Test* appears to show the extent to which they use each half of the brain for perceiving, recognizing, and interpreting the sounds of speech. In 1969, Frederic K. W. Curry of the Michael Reese Hospital in Chicago and Hugo H. Gregory of

Northwestern University reported the first of a long series of studies of dichotic listening in stutterers by various workers. Curry had been doing research on dichotic listening in normal subjects. Gregory, a speech pathologist, had done his doctoral dissertation on some auditory brain functions of stutterers such as sound localization and perception of distorted speech. His doctoral study, an outgrowth of the short-lived concern with the stutterer's auditory feedback system, had disclosed nothing that differentiated stutterers from normal speakers. But when Jones's arresting report was followed by the appearance of the *Dichotic Word Test*, Gregory recognized another promising opportunity for research on the auditory functions of the stutterer's brain.

Curry and Gregory tested 20 stutterers and 20 normal speakers. Fifteen of the 20 nonstutterers recalled more words with the right ear, a proportion that was consistent with previous results on ordinary subjects. Of the 20 stutterers, only 9 exhibited a right-ear advantage. What was more, the difference between the scores for the two ears was on the average more than twice as great for the control subjects as for the stutterers. There was no difference between the two groups in ear preference for environmental noises. In sum, the results suggested that stutterers were not only more apt to use the right hemisphere for speech perception, but also tended to have weaker brain dominance, whether right or left.

Researchers took immediate notice. In November of the following year two further studies of dichotic listening in stutterers were reported at the convention of the American Speech and Hearing Association. Both confirmed Curry and Gregory's findings. In one, stutterers demonstrated a left-ear advantage for words. In the other, they showed no consistent ear preference. The nonstutterers showed the usual right-ear advantage in both studies. But in 1972 some conflicting results were presented by P. T. Quinn of the Prince Henry Hospital in Sydney. Quinn gave the *Dichotic Word Test* to 60 stutterers and 60 nonstutterers. The two groups turned out to have an equal degree of ear dominance as shown by the difference in score for the left and right ear, although 12 stutterers and only two nonstutterers showed a left-ear advantage.

More studies now followed in rapid succession, four in 1975 alone. Some confirmed Curry and Gregory's findings; others gave more support to Quinn's. By 1989, more than 20 investigations of dichotic listening in stutterers had been done, and they were about equally divided between those that showed evidence of weak or right hemisphere dominance and those that did not. By then, it had begun to seem futile to do any more studies. It was a situation reminiscent of an earlier era of physiological investigation of stuttering that was bedeviled by conflicting and inconclusive outcomes. But there were some who thought they saw a pattern in this seeming inconsistency. About half the studies had used meaningful words; the other half had employed nonsense syllables, mainly for convenience in synchronizing their presentation to both ears. As early as 1976, Walter H. Moore Jr. of the University of California at Long Beach pointed out that stutterers performed atypically on the *Dichotic Word Test* whenever meaningful verbal stimuli were used. When one carefully reviews all of the investigations that have been reported to date, in the main this proves to be so, despite a few apparent exceptions. It is also true that even in the studies with generally negative findings, there are often more stutterers than nonstutterers who demonstrate a left-ear advantage.

It would seem that the dichotic listening research has produced enough reason for continued interest in the subject. Yet it raises perplexing questions. Whatever their outcome, the studies leave little doubt that there are any number of individual stutterers with ordinary right-ear preferences. So atypical cerebral dominance for perceiving words is not a necessary condition for stuttering. Then just what is the nature of the relationship, if there is one? On the whole, this research offers enough encouragement to the skeptical that fewer workers might have taken the question of cerebral dominance in stutterers seriously if it had not been for evidence that came from another approach to the question.

Brain Waves

The propagation of nerve impulses along the nerves of the body is in part an electrical phenomenon. In the region of the head there is naturally a concentration of this electrical activity. Like much other electricity, it comes in waves of varying amplitudes and frequencies. These waves of voltage were first recorded by Hans Berger in 1929 by means of an instrument called an electroencephalograph. They are of interest to physiologists and clinical neurologists because they are responsive to various states of the body. The predominant electrical activity of the brain, the so-called alpha wave, comes in a frequency of ten oscillations per second. In excitement, concentration, or attention, the alpha wave is replaced by a rapid, irregular wave of low intensity. Slow waves, of one to three cycles per second, are prominent during sleep, anesthesia, coma, or localized injury to the brain. Epilepsy has a characteristic wave by which it has been diagnosed in some patients even before they had their first convulsion.

The brain waves of stutterers have generally been found to be grossly normal. For years researchers tried to find subtle differences between the waves of stutterers and normal speakers, with inconclusive results. When interest in stutterers' cerebral dominance for speech revived in the 1970s, a search began for new ways to use the electroencephalograph to investigate their brain activity. John R. Knott had done the earliest work on stutterers' brain waves together with Lee Travis in the old days at Iowa.[1] In 1974, Knott and Gerald N. Zimmermann reported a study of the so-called contingent negative variation in stutterers. This is a slow voltage change that appears following a signal to the subject to prepare to perform a response. It is the neural correlate of readiness or attention. Zimmermann and Knott found that 4 of 5 normal speakers showed a greater voltage shift in the left hemisphere than the right when signaled to prepare to say a word that had been flashed on a TV screen. Of 9 stutterers, only 2 exhibited this apparent indication of left cerebral dominance for speech.

Two subsequent studies of the contingent negative variation in stutterers failed to confirm Zimmermann and Knott's findings, but in 1975, a different attack was described in a paper that listed Travis, now approaching eighty, as one of its four authors. The researchers measured the amount of electrical activity that was evoked by the word "fire" when it was displayed on a screen in the sentence "Fire is hot" and in the sentence "Fire the gun." For 10 normal speakers, the average difference in the responses to the two words was greater in the left hemisphere than in the right. For 9 stutterers, the average difference was greater in the right. A few years later Travis issued a brief account of the cerebral dominance theory of stuttering in which he made it clear that he had never renounced it. Before he died, in 1987 at the age of 91, the search for evidence of atypical cerebral dominance in stutterers was in full swing again.

Most of the subsequent brain wave research was done by Walter Moore and his students at the University of California at Santa Barbara. Moore simply measured the amount of alpha activity in each hemisphere. The alpha wave is the ongoing electrical rhythm of the brain that is present during our waking hours when the brain is idling. Whenever the brain concentrates, the alpha activity is reduced. When it concentrates on speech, there is more alpha suppression in the left hemisphere of most individuals than the right, as would be expected. In 1977, Moore and Mary K. Lang studied the alpha wave in 10 stutterers and 10 nonstutterers just before each of five consecutive oral readings of a passage. Nine of the 10 control subjects demonstrated the expected suppression of the wave in the left hemisphere. By contrast, 8 stutterers had less alpha in

---

1. Travis built the first electroencephalograph in the United States in collaboration with an electronic engineer.

the right. Moore and Lang concluded that stutterers appear to process linguistic information in the right hemisphere of the brain.

By 1986, Moore and his co-workers had published four more studies in corroboration of this inference. In one, subjects heard a passage from the Congressional Record about which they were told they would be asked questions. In others, they listened to a series of words with the expectation of having to recall as many as possible afterwards. In each case, stutterers as a group showed less alpha on the right than the left hemisphere, whereas controls exhibited the reverse. It remained only for independent studies by other workers to confirm Moore's findings. But with the perversity that has marked so much of the research on the stutterer's physical constitution from the start, two attempts that have been made so far to replicate Moore's investigations both failed to produce the looked for confirmation. One of these yielded anomalous results, inasmuch as neither the stutterers nor the normal speakers had appreciably more alpha activity in one hemisphere than the other.

All of this research was confined strictly to subjects' silent processing of speech. This was necessary. To have had them speak would have permitted the occurrence of stuttering, and when phenomena are observed during stuttering, it is impossible to determine whether they are causes, results, or aspects of the problem. Even if the subject seems to be speaking fluently, the observations may in part reflect the subject's anticipations of stuttering or even blocks too mild and fleeting to be perceived as stuttering.[2] But the strategy of studying stutterers' silent processing of speech has its limitations too. Any abnormality we note while stutterers are merely comprehending speech can only be related very indirectly to their speech difficulty. So some curiosity about the stutterer's alpha waves during speech is justified. In 1983, Einer Boberg and his associates at the University of Alberta recorded stutterers' brain waves while the subjects were engaged in defining words and counting backward by sevens. Just as in Moore's studies, the stutterers failed to show the normal suppression of the alpha wave in the left hemisphere. But the Canadian study produced a startling additional finding. After they were tested, the

2. During the 1970s and 1980s, a great amount of futile effort was expended on the study of recorded segments of stutterers' speech that were judged by observers to be fluent. Analysis of spectrograms (voice prints) usually revealed a certain hesitancy or sluggishness in the subjects' "fluent" articulation that some workers assumed to reflect an underlying neurologic cause of stuttering. We had put the stutterer's "fluency" under a kind of microscope only to find more disfluency. Whether that disfluency is "stuttering" too mild to be perceptible or whether it is something else is no more answerable than the question whether Shakespeare's plays were written by Shakespeare or someone else with the same name. As an effort to reveal an underlying cause of stuttering, this research was a dead end.

stutterers underwent a three-week program of speech therapy in which they were taught to speak fluently by using syllable prolongation and easy onsets of phonation. Retested following treatment, their alpha waves now showed the normal hemispheric relationship—less activity in the left than the right. The following year, Moore made the same observation in a study of a single subject. Just what this means is hard to say, but a skeptic could hardly have been blamed for doubting that these alpha wave findings were indicative of some ingrained neurophysiological trait. The investigation of stutterers' cerebral dominance did not end here, however.

Visual Tests of Brain Dominance

For several thousands of years, language has had a visual form for those who could read and write. As with spoken language, the left cerebral hemisphere is dominant for written language in the majority of people. This fact can be demonstrated. Each hemisphere of the brain contains a center for vision. It is not a simple matter of one hemisphere for each eye, however. Instead, each hemisphere "sees" one half of the visual field— the roughly oval area that is visible to the limit of our peripheral vision when we look at a fixed point. The left hemisphere sees the right half of the visual field and the right hemisphere sees the left. By means of a device called a tachistoscope, it is possible to present visual stimuli to each half separately. Experiments that are parallel to dichotic listening studies have demonstrated that if pairs of words are shown simultaneously to the two halves of the visual field, the majority of ordinary subjects tend to have a more ready perception of words seen on the right.

In 1976, Walter Moore presented pairs of words simultaneously to the two half fields of a group of stutterers with instructions to say which word they saw first. Unlike their controls, the stutterers failed to show a significant right-half field advantage. Of the 15 stutterers, 8 showed a left-half field preference, whereas this was true of only 3 of the 15 control subjects.

Some years later, two researchers at the University of Ulm in Germany, Claudia Victor and Helge S. Johanssen, employed a different method in an investigation of 42 stutterers and 42 normal speakers. They exposed nonsense syllables to the left and right visual fields so briefly that subjects were able to recognize them only about half the time. The subjects' task was to identify as many syllables as possible. Although the majority of subjects in both groups turned in either a normal or equivocal performance, 11 stutterers correctly identified more syllables in the left half of the visual field, as compared with only 4 normal speakers who did so. Victor and Johanssen concluded that "at least in some stutterers" there is a deviant dominance for speech.

In 1983, C. Rebekah Hand and William O. Haynes at Auburn University introduced still another procedure. They presented nonsense words and real words to each half field of subjects separately. The subjects' task was to signal as fast as possible each time they recognized a real word. The stutterers' reaction times were faster when the words appeared in the left visual half field than when they appeared in the right. The nonstutterers reacted somewhat faster to words in the right half field, but the difference in their case was too small to be considered unequivocal.

Later in the 1980s, Michael P. Rastatter and his students at Bowling Green State University conducted a number of studies of subjects' reaction times in reading words or naming letters or pictures presented to the left or right visual fields. With regard to the hypothesis that stutterers are more likely than others to use the right hemisphere for speech, the results of these studies were at best conflicting and inconclusive.

Interference Studies

There is still another way in which it has been thought possible to demonstrate the dominance of the left half of the brain for language in most normal individuals. Each hemisphere controls voluntary movements on the opposite side of the body. It has been observed that if normal right-handed subjects engage in a verbal task while tapping rapidly with a finger, the verbal activity will interfere more with tapping with the right hand than with the left. Presumably there is a limit on how much one cerebral hemisphere can do at any time; when the left half of the brain is busy with language activity, its capacity for producing a motor response with the right hand is diminished. In 1982, this experiment was reported for the first time with stutterers. Harvey M. Sussman at the University of Texas had subjects tap as fast as possible while reading aloud. He found as expected that right-handed normal speakers showed a reduction in the rate of tapping only with the right hand. In stutterers and left-handed normal speakers, oral reading interfered equally with tapping in both hands. The results suggested that stutterers lack a distinct cerebral dominance for language.

Sussman's findings were promptly challenged by two further studies by others. One showed that while a speech task did indeed interfere with tapping with both hands of stutterers, so did a nonspeech vocal activity, namely imitating the sound of a siren. The other study found no difference between stutterers and nonstutterers, except that stutterers were slower than nonstutterers with either hand.

Reaction Time

While all this research on the cerebral dominance of stutterers was going on, many researchers were pursuing a line of investigation that had little obvious connection with cerebral dominance and was producing far more consistent results. In 1976, Martin R. Adams and Paul Hayden at Purdue University reported that when subjects were instructed to say the vowel "ah" as quickly as possible after hearing a tone, stutterers took more time to do it than nonstutterers. The same difference was evident when they were asked to terminate the vowel as quickly as possible. The difference, to be sure, was very small—under a fifth of a second on the average. It would not have been detectable without the use of accurate recording devices. So it could hardly be related to stuttering in any simple or direct way. Yet, it was too large to be regarded plausibly as merely a chance difference, and when the same result was found by several other workers within the next few years, it set in motion a massive research effort. At this writing, over 40 studies have been published, and with few exceptions they have confirmed the observation that stutterers as a group have vocal reaction times that lag behind those of normal speakers by anywhere from less than a tenth to three tenths of a second. There is, in fact, hardly any more convincingly attested finding in the whole range of scientific comparisons of the two groups, though some reports have made it clear that by no means are all stutterers slower than all nonstutterers.

In most of these studies, the investigators were bent, not only on verifying the phenomenon, but on shedding some light on what it meant. One obvious possibility was that the slight delay in initiating a vowel was an effect of stuttering itself, even though stutterers rarely have difficulty saying isolated speech sounds. This explanation was ruled out when it was discovered that slow reaction times appeared even when stutterers were instructed merely to clear their throats or produce a sound on inspiration. It seemed to some that stutterers might be suffering from a faulty larynx or a faulty way of using the larynx to produce voice. This view gained support from research showing that various muscles of the larynx functioned in abnormal ways during stuttering blocks, some of them attempting to bring the vocal cords together for phonation while others were trying to separate them, and all in a state of excessive tension. For a brief period, there was some interest in the surmise that the larynx was of primary importance in stuttering, in the sense that blockages in that organ gave rise to the various other symptoms of the disorder. This led inevitably to the question whether stutterers are slow in initiating movements of other speech structures such as the lips and jaw, and some research findings, as yet small in amount, have suggested that they may be.

More convincing evidence that it is not the larynx that is primarily at fault was the observation that it is possible to stutter without a larynx. In cases of laryngeal cancer, it is often necessary to remove the larynx surgically, an operation that leaves the patient without the ability to produce voice. Most of these patients can be helped to regain speech in several ways. Some learn to belch voluntarily while making speech movements, a method known as esophageal speech. In many cases, surgeons can modify structures within the throat to assume the function of vocal cords. Finally, the patient may resort to the use of an electrolarynx, a device that, when pressed against the throat, sends sound vibrations to the speaker's oral cavity, making speech movements audible. What happens when stutterers are forced to adopt such modes of speech? We now have confirmation from a number of independent sources that some of these persons continue to stutter. Stuttering, like speech itself, is not instigated by the lips, tongue, or larynx, but by the brain. It may be worth noting that blockages and repetitions that some observers regard as stuttering are sometimes seen even in the manual signing of the congenitally deaf.

Much of the research on the stutterer's vocal reaction time has been aimed at pinpointing the aspect of brain activity that is involved in the delay. Initiating voice as fast as possible in response to a signal requires a sequence of separate acts. Subjects must first place themselves in a state of readiness to respond. Next, they must perceive the signal. Then they must make some muscular adjustments in the larynx that will prepare the vocal cords to vibrate in response to the outgoing breath stream. Finally, the subject must activate the respiratory muscles of the chest and abdomen to produce an outward flow of air. The first of these segments to be scrutinized was the perception of the tone that signaled the stutterer to respond. A number of studies showed that stutterer's slow reaction times persisted when the signal was a light, so the trouble was evidently not in their auditory perception. Neither did the problem seem to reside to any great extent in the stutterer's readiness to respond. Ben C. Watson and Peter J. Alfonso at the University of Connecticut investigated that possibility by giving subjects a warning just before the signal to say the vowel. It did little to help the stutterers react as quickly as the control subjects, although the difference was not so pronounced among the mild stutterers. It seems, then, that the delay is in the act of responding itself. Robert A. Prosek and his colleagues at the Walter Reed Army Medical Center in Washington, D.C. simultaneously recorded both the onset of voice in their subjects and the beginning of muscular activity in the larynx. Stutterers were slow in initiating voice, but not in laryngeal activity. Apparently, it was not the response of the larynx that lagged, but something else, perhaps the start of airflow. Klaas Bakker and Gene J. Brutten at Southern Illinois University achieved a similar division of the response. They measured the time interval between the signal to respond and the start of laryngeal adjustments preparatory to initiating voice. This is the "premotor" interval during which the brain perceives the stimulus and plans the response. By subtracting the premotor interval from the total vocal reaction time, they obtained a measure of the laryngeal adjustment time. Their results showed that the stutterers took longer than the control subjects in both the premotor and the laryngeal adjustment periods.

In short, many stutterers take minutely longer than many nonstutterers to do the things that it takes to get the voice going, and it is questionable whether further research to find a single faulty link in this activity will be useful. On the other hand, a few questions that remain may prove to have some illuminating answers. We do not yet have a convincing answer to the question whether stutterers' slow reaction times extend to movements of speech structures such as the tongue, jaw, and lips. There is also the possibility that stutterers as a group are slow in all of their motor responses. A series of studies has been done on their finger movements, so far with inconsistent results. Another question is whether the difference between stutterers and nonstutterers in reaction time is to be found in children as well as adults. If not, it presumably develops as a reaction to stuttering. Here too, findings have been conflicting and inconclusive. Finally there is the question that was raised by Walter L. Cullinan and Mark T. Springer in their study at the University of Oklahoma in 1980. It is well established that defective articulation of speech sounds and delayed language development are common among stuttering children. In an investigation of 20 stuttering children, Cullinan and Springer found that slow vocal reaction times were largely confined to 11 who had articulation or language problems. They suggested that stutterers' slow reaction times might be related to the high incidence of other speech difficulties among them.

Conclusion

This chapter has surely told many readers more than they wanted to know about the results of research on the stutterer's brain functions. Yet it must be clear that it would have been impossible to state what we know about this vitally important question in briefer form without crudely oversimplifying it. Already, some of the popular information media are proclaiming that stuttering is a "medical" problem. Such a description of stuttering is grossly incautious. Without doubt, we have more than a little reason for suspecting that organic factors have an important part to play in stuttering. But there is a great deal that we do not understand about what these factors may be and how they may contribute to the development of the disorder. Research on cerebral dominance for language in stutterers has yielded some interesting results by various methodological approaches, but in each of these lines of investigation there are conflicting findings. It is also notable that where stutterers as a group have been found to differ from nonstutterers, some stuttering subjects have exhibited perfectly ordinary hemispheric relationships. Some studies have found that stutterers process speech in the right hemisphere; others that they do so equally in both. And in neither case do we have an adequate explanation of how the alleged anomaly is related to stuttering—whether causally or in some indirect way; and if causally, how. The possibility that the anomaly may disappear after a few weeks of speech therapy is surprising and unsettling. Finally, how deviant cerebral dominance can relate to the fact that stutterers as a group have slightly slow vocal reaction times is a mystery.

Can evidence so riddled with uncertainty outweigh the observations that in the past convinced so many workers that stuttering is purely a learned disorder—for example, its tendency to disappear when stutterers forget that they are stutterers or to occur in response to nothing more than the anticipation of stuttering? The answer is yes, because there is an additional fact that compels us to take very seriously the probability that organic differences between stutterers and nonstutterers exist. It is the fact that stuttering has a strong tendency to run in families and the evidence that this is at least in part due to genes.

CHAPTER FOURTEEN

Stuttering and Heredity

Quite suddenly in the 1970s, almost all speech pathologists came to believe what a few had maintained all along—that genes play a part in the causation of stuttering. This change came about primarily because new light was shed on the occurrence of stuttering in the families of stutterers by a Yale geneticist, and also because of accumulating evidence concerning stuttering in twins.

The Familial Incidence of Stuttering

That stuttering often runs in families was one of the earliest facts that were observed when scientific attention was first focused on the disorder by European physicians in the 19th and early 20th centuries. In the 1930s, investigators began to make systematic counts of the number of stutterers reporting a history of stuttering in their families, and it was soon evident that between one-third and two-thirds make such reports, as compared with only 5 to 18 percent of normal speakers. Allowing for the probability that stutterers are more likely than others to have learned of stuttering relatives or ancestors, it seems clear that the familial incidence of the problem is quite high. Long ago, this fact suggested to some workers the simple and natural explanation that a predisposition to stuttering is part of a stutterer's genetic make-up. This seemed to them all the more plausible when imitation was ruled out as a significant factor by evidence that there frequently had been no personal contact between stuttering children and their stuttering relatives. Yet the genetic explanation for many decades failed to gain general acceptance. There was a good reason. If a trait is hereditary, it is transmitted in certain well-known ways—recessive, dominant, sex-linked recessive, and so forth. It was pointed out as early as 1945 that the distribution of stuttering relatives in the families of stutterers is not consistent with any known mode of transmission. For example, a simple recessive trait appears less often in the parents of an affected individual than in the siblings; this is not the case in stuttering. A sex-linked recessive trait like hemophilia is rarely transmitted from fathers to sons, yet it is common for male stutterers to have stuttering fathers. Dominant inheritance is ruled out by the relatively low incidence of stuttering.

So the high familial incidence was widely blamed on the transmission of home environments that tended to make children stutter, and this view accorded well with an intellectual climate that for many years gave extraordinary weight to environmental explanations of many things that go wrong in the course of children's development. It was not until later that geneticists recognized that some human traits that run in families do not exhibit the classical Mendelian patterns of inheritance because they are caused jointly by genes and environmental influences. One geneticist who was interested in traits of this kind was Kenneth K. Kidd of the Department of Human Genetics at Yale University. It was known that such traits may be due to a single gene (monogenic) or to several or many genes (polygenic). Kidd had devised a method of determining whether the trait was monogenic or polygenic, based on analysis of the distribution of the trait in the families of affected individuals. The method yielded two sets of predictions of the frequencies of the trait among mothers, fathers, sisters, and brothers of affected persons, one set on the assumption that the trait was monogenic, the other on the assumption that it was polygenic. The aim was to determine which assumption gave the better predictions. A feature of the analysis was that it was applicable only to traits whose incidence in the two sexes differed and to traits that were continuously variable, like stature or intelligence. In order to apply his method, Kidd accordingly began to search for human traits that appeared frequently in the same family, did not exhibit Mendelian patterns of transmission, had a sex ratio, and were continuously variable. Naturally, he found stuttering. The only requirement that stuttering failed to meet was that it be continuously variable; people seem to be either stutterers or nonstutterers. But geneticists had surmounted similar obstacles in the past by invoking the concept of "threshold." Kidd made the assumption that the predisposition to stutter was a continuously variable trait that people could have in different degrees and that manifested itself outwardly in stuttering when it reached a threshold amount.

Satisfied that stuttering met all criteria, Kidd and his co-workers worked out predictions, on the monogenic and polygenic assumptions, about the percentages of stutterers' mothers, fathers, sisters, and brothers who would be stutterers. They then compared the predictions with actual percentages that had been obtained in two previous studies of familial stuttering by other workers. The observed values turned out to be exceedingly close to the predicted ones. The monogenic assumption yielded particularly accurate predictions, but the polygenic hypothesis could not be ruled out. Kidd and his co-workers concluded that there was probably a "major genetic component" in stuttering. The component interacted with environmental factors. Both contributed to the liability that revealed itself overtly when it reached a certain threshold level. The threshold was higher in females than in males.

Kidd pointed out that these findings did not constitute proof of a hereditary factor in stuttering. Rigorous proof, he cautioned, could be obtained only by two methods. One would be by "genetic linkage" studies in which stuttering was shown almost always to be transmitted together with a known genetic trait, indicating their close proximity on a chromosome. The other would be by studies showing that stutterers who were adopted at birth had a significantly large number of stuttering relatives in their biological families. Nevertheless, the papers that Kidd and his associates published on their findings between 1973 and 1981 were enough to convince the great majority of speech pathologists. No doubt, the field was ripe for this conversion. By the 1970s, we were in a new intellectual climate in which the role of genes in human problems was being taken more seriously than ever before.

The Sex Ratio

Boys who stutter outnumber stuttering girls by about three to one.[1] Because boys and girls differ in both heredity and social environment, both have been invoked to explain the sex ratio. To Robert West, the sex ratio was one of the features of stuttering that marked it as an inherited organic disorder. Wendell Johnson was just as sure that the sex ratio reflected a difference in the pressures for fluent speech that parents imposed on boys and girls. It is evident that if we understood the contribution that heredity makes to the sex ratio, we would know what it contributes to the origin of stuttering itself.

Only two attempts have been made to draw the answer directly from observational data. One was reported in 1966 by Jon Eisenson of Queens College in New York. On a trip to Israel he had visited a kibbutz

---

1. The ratio is probably lower in early childhood and higher in adulthood, meaning that with advancing age either boys begin to stutter with increasingly greater frequency than girls or that girls recover with increasingly greater frequency than boys.

that was structured on the classical model in which children were cared for by nurses and teachers during most of the day. Among the ideals to which these surrogate parents were devoted was that of treating the two sexes exactly alike. Accepting that the social environments of these boys and girls were in fact highly alike, Eisenson inferred that there should be no sex difference in the prevalence of stuttering if the ratio was culturally determined. When he made inquiries, however, the sex ratio emerged robustly. Of fifteen kibbutz children who were known to stutter, twelve were boys. Eisenson concluded that the sex ratio has an organic basis.

The other study was published a year later and concerned the sex ratio among Americans of African descent. Some sociologists had suggested that the lower socioeconomic strata of African-American society in the south tended to have a matriarchal structure, with women often bearing more responsibility for the support of their families than men. This was imputed to greater earning power on the part of women in this group and to the lingering repercussions of slavery, which often dismembered families and left women to care for children alone. Ronald Goldman of the Vanderbilt University Medical Center reasoned that if the general preponderance of male stutterers results from greater pressures of some kind upon boys in a patriarchal society, the sex ratio might take an unusual turn in a group alleged to be to some degree matriarchal. In a survey of school systems in Tennessee in which 694 stutterers were identified, it developed that among the white children the sex ratio was 4.9 to 1, whereas among the black children it was only 2.4 to 1. From among the black children, Goldman then selected two groups of stutterers, 38 who came from what he defined as "patriarchal" homes and 77 from "matriarchal" families, a distinction he based on whether or not there was a "stable and consistent male figure" in the home. In the patriarchal group the sex ratio was 3.5 to 1. In the matriarchal group it was 1.1 to 1. Goldman concluded that the sex ratio in stuttering is due to cultural patterns.

The findings of Eisenson and Goldman obviously leave us in doubt as to whether the sex ratio is due to heredity, environment, or both. So does the work of Kenneth Kidd. On the assumption that stuttering is caused by interacting social and genetic factors, Kidd raised the question of the role that sex plays in the development of the disorder. Like others, he discounted sex-linked inheritance as incompatible with the facts, but found that stuttering met all the criteria for sex-limited transmission. In sex-limited or sex-modified inheritance, a trait is transmitted as an ordinary dominant or recessive character, but the gene is expressed differently in males and females. A boy and girl might both have inherited a gene that predisposes children to stutter, but the girl may be less susceptible to the influence of the gene because of some other factor that is peculiar to females. To use Kidd's term, the girl may have a higher "threshold" for stuttering. This reasoning helps to explain a fact that at first sight may be baffling. Kidd found that female stutterers tended to have more stuttering relatives than male stutterers. Andrews and Harris had made the same observation ten years before and had explained it by a simple analogy. As in stuttering, there is a sex ratio in human stature; on the average, men are taller than women. Now, consider a man and a woman who are both exactly six feet tall. Which of these two is more likely to come from a family of very tall individuals? Quite clearly, the woman. Unlike the man, she is unusually tall for her sex, so she must be the product of a particularly favorable heredity for tallness. Similar reasoning can be applied to stuttering. Kidd inferred that, because the female threshold for stuttering is higher than that of the male, whatever genetic and environmental influences make for the disorder, a girl would have to be subject to more of them before she crossed the threshold.

Unfortunately, there is nothing in the familial data to indicate the source of those hypothetical male and female thresholds, and it is precisely there that the key to the sex ratio lies. Kidd pointed out that the difference in the thresholds might be due to factors as diverse as sex roles in society or neurological development. It can be argued that boys are more likely than girls to experience speech pressures. On the whole, girls are not expected to be as self-assertive as boys. When under pressure, perhaps a girl is therefore more likely to seek refuge in silence, whereas the boy may feel compelled to speak up. On the other hand, it may well be nothing more than the somewhat faster maturation of girls in speech and language that determines their lesser vulnerability to the causes of stuttering. There is surely something significant about the well-established fact that many stutterers begin to speak somewhat late and have slightly immature speech and language in their early years. Finally, a bold hypothesis was advanced in 1985 by the neurologist Norman Geschwind in collaboration with Albert M. Galaburda. They pointed out that the male hormone testosterone tends to retard the rate of neuronal development in the fetus. In addition, the left hemisphere of the brain takes longer to develop than the right, and is therefore exposed for a longer time to the effects of the hormone. Since the male fetus has higher levels of testosterone than the female, Geschwind and Galaburda theorized that boys are more vulnerable than girls to defects of the left-hemisphere functions of language and hand preference. For this reason, they asserted, speech and language disorders, reading disabilities, and stuttering are more common among boys. Their hypothesis also implied that stutterers should be more prone to reading difficulties and left-handedness, which is contrary to most of the evidence. Nevertheless, Geschwind and Galaburda's speculations are provocative.

It is apparent that nothing we have learned about the sex ratio so far tells us conclusively about the part that heredity plays in stuttering. All we can say is that the sex ratio is easy enough to reconcile with a partially genetic origin of the disorder.

Stuttering in Twins

By the 1980s, additional evidence of the influence of heredity on stuttering had come from studies of twins. The reader will recall from Chapter 5 that an early investigation done in 1945 by students of Robert West had found that identical twins, who have identical genes, were usually concordant for stuttering; when one member of the pair stuttered, the other one did too, in almost all cases. By contrast, fraternal twins, who are genetically no more alike than ordinary siblings, were found with few exceptions to be discordant for stuttering. This evidence seemed conclusive to West. A number of years later, however, Wendell Johnson countered with a study by his student, Odny I. Graf. Through questionnaires addressed to schools, Graf identified 16 twin pairs in which one or both members stuttered. Among seven pairs which she described as "probably identical,"[2] she found only one that was concordant for stuttering.

The issue remained in doubt for many years as further evidence accumulated slowly. But in 1959 Richard Luchsinger reported from Zurich on 44 cases of stuttering in twins from his own clinical files and those of several other European speech pathologists. There was very high concordance for stuttering among the identical pairs and total discordance among the fraternal ones. Then, in 1976 three Italian workers, Godai, Tatarelli, and Bonanni, presented similar findings on 31 pairs from the twin register in the Mendel Institute in Rome. Still more confirmation came from a study of 29 pairs in Australia by Pauline M. Howie in 1981. By then, there could no longer be any doubt. If we pool these reports, we have information about 60 identical and 100 fraternal pairs. Of the identical pairs, 43 are concordant for stuttering and 17 discordant. By contrast, only 9 of the fraternal pairs are concordant and 91 are discordant.

The figures demonstrate beyond question that if one member of a pair of identical twins stutters, the other will also be found to stutter in the great majority of cases. Yet they also reveal a striking number of exceptions. Now if identical twins differ in a trait, it can only be because of

---

2. Due to the nature of her study, Graf was unable to obtain conclusive evidence of identity such as a single placenta at birth or identical fingerprints.

a difference in environment. So these exceptions constitute one of the best pieces of evidence we have that environment plays a part in causing stuttering. The exceptions do not of course cast doubt on the contribution that genes make to the disorder. But not everyone was convinced that the high concordance of identical twins for stuttering was valid evidence of any genetic inheritance in the first place. And indeed it does not constitute proof. The reason is that the environments of identical twins are likely to be more similar than those of fraternal twins. As Bernard C. Meyer stated the argument long ago, the fact that identical twins closely resemble each other makes it likely that they will be reacted to alike and "insures a more intimate sharing of infantile and childhood experiences and environmental influences than obtains in the case of two children whose identity is clearly unlike the other from the start."

So the only way to make the argument from concordance in identical twins really convincing is to demonstrate concordance in twins who were separated at birth and reared in different environments. Needless to say, people who stutter, who are members of an identical twin pair, and who were separated from their co-twin at birth are extremely rare, and information about them was long in coming. When it finally came to light on a small number of individuals, it was surprising.

Susan Farber is a psychologist. In 1981, she published a book, *Identical Twins Reared Apart: A Reanalysis*. The book was based on a search of the psychological literature from 1923 to 1973 for reports of identical twins who were separated at birth or soon afterward and studied when they were rejoined years later. Farber's interest was in sorting out the relative contributions of heredity and environment to any and all physical and behavioral traits. Many of the reports she found were accounts of single cases. They were not all equally reliable, so she established a set of criteria for reliability and on that basis selected 95 cases that formed the subject of her book. The similarities between identical twins reared apart are notorious, and Farber's cases were no exception. They tended to talk alike, laugh alike, and gesture alike. They generally had similar tastes in books, music, and clothing. The husband of one of the twins reported that when she was tired, she had a habit of rocking herself and rubbing her nose; the other husband reported the same behavior. One pair even had the same nickname—Pussy. Farber devoted one chapter of her book to speech characteristics. Here too, seemingly remarkable similarities emerged with regard to talkativeness, hoarseness, and vocal pitch. Among speech traits one exception stood out, and that was stuttering. Among Farber's 95 case reports there were five which made mention of stuttering. In all five cases only one member of the pair stuttered. Farber concluded that among the reported speech characteristics "Only stuttering seems environmentally related."

In a footnote Farber mentions an additional pair of twins, not included among her 95 cases, that was concordant for stuttering. This was a Japanese pair, described in 1941 by Yoshimasu. Takao and Kazuo had been separated at birth and rejoined at age 32. Takao had been imprisoned for theft and embezzlement. Kazuo had become a Christian minister. Both of them stuttered. That even one pair of twins who had been raised apart both stuttered seems more than coincidence. And in any case, Farber's five discordant cases do not cast serious doubt on the prevailing view that stuttering is a joint product of genes and environment. It is entirely possible that, in each of these five cases, both members had inherited a constitutional predisposition to stuttering that was manifested in only one. It is even possible that the normal speaking twin had had a brief episode of stuttering that was later forgotten. What Farber's cases do show is the powerful effect of environment. If the twins were born equally predisposed to stutter, it was environment that determined which of them would manifest the disorder. Alternatively, if both twins stuttered in early childhood, it was because of a difference in environment that one of them spontaneously recovered and the other did not.

Adoption Research

When all is said and done, the findings we have reviewed, though strongly suggestive of a hereditary factor in stuttering, do not constitute proof. In some minds, Farber's discordant twins might even justify skepticism in this regard. As Kidd has cautioned, only genetic linkage or adoption studies could afford absolute proof. Of such research, regrettably, all we have is my own inconclusive attempt at an adoption study. In any large group of stutterers who were adopted at birth, we could expect to find about one-third to two-thirds having a family history of stuttering, simply because that many stutterers do. But where are the stuttering relatives to be found? If they are in the birth family, the transmission of stuttering is clearly biological; if in the adoptive family, it is clearly social. Information about the birth families of adopted children is not easily accessible, but if we had sufficient knowledge about stutterers' adoptive families, we could deduce all that we needed to know. Since the 1950s, when I began interviewing parents of stuttering children at the Brooklyn College Speech and Hearing Center, I have collected data on the families of stutterers who were adopted at birth or soon afterward. Unfortunately for science, such cases are not common, and at this writing I have information on only 13 cases. This is too small a sample from which to draw reliable inferences, but if this is kept in mind, it will do no harm to report what I have found so far. If the inheritance of stuttering were wholly biological, and this were a representative sample of adopted stutterers, we would expect at most one or two children to have stuttering relatives in their adoptive families, this being the highest number we would expect to find in any ordinary group of nonstutterers. On the other hand, if the transmission were wholly social, we would expect from four to eight or so to have such relatives. The actual number of my cases with stutterers in their adoptive families is four. This is about as ambiguous as such a number could possibly be. As far as these results show, the reason for the high familial incidence of stuttering may be genetic, social, or both.

Anecdotal evidence is the kind of evidence that social scientists generally scorn, yet occasionally one stumbles upon an example that is difficult to thrust aside. Some years ago I made the acquaintance of a neuropsychologist who had a personal interest in the subject of stuttering because she stuttered herself. She told me that she had been adopted at birth. In adulthood she resolved to find out who her parents were. When she finally succeeded in making contact with her biological family, she discovered that her mother was a stutterer too.

CHAPTER FIFTEEN

The Inception
of Stuttering

The title of this chapter must immediately put readers on their guard. There is, of course, little agreement on precisely how stuttering begins. In this chapter I am simply asserting an author's license to tell the truth as he sees it. What follows is based on some of my own research, the way in which I read the research of others, and also to a large extent on my clinical observations.

The Environmental Factor

Most speech pathologists today are agreed that stuttering is a product of both heredity and environment. The last chapter surveyed the reasons we have for believing in the contribution of genes. The evidence for the influence of environment is equally strong. There is, in the first place, the work of Kenneth Kidd. His accurate predictions about the occurrence of stuttering among stutterers' relatives assumed an interaction of genes with environmental factors. Second, despite the high concordance of identical twins for stuttering, there are many cases in which only one member stutters; the difference can only be due to a difference in environment.[1] Third, when identical twins are reared apart, evidence based

1. However, we must not fail to take the intrauterine environment into account. Some years ago, I had a graduate student whose two grown children, a doctor and a lawyer, were identical twins. She told me that the doctor had stuttered since early childhood, whereas the lawyer had always spoken well. When I asked her what had been different about their early environments, she said the doctor had been a breech delivery. The lawyer had a normal birth. The doctor

as yet on a small number of cases suggests that most of them may be discordant for stuttering. In addition, Andrews and his co-workers have shown that the concordance for stuttering is greater among fraternal twins than among ordinary siblings. On the basis of pooled data from several studies, they estimated that the fraternal co-twin of a stutterer had a 32 percent chance of being a stutterer, whereas the risk was only 18 percent for the ordinary sibling. Since fraternal twins are no more similar genetically than ordinary siblings, their higher concordance can only be due to a more similar environment.

If more proof of the importance of environment were needed, it might be found in a curious observation. When we examine old school records and search the memories of elderly workers in the speech and hearing field, we find evidence that when speech pathology began as a profession in the 1930s, there were greater numbers of stutterers than there are today and their speech difficulties tended to be more severe. The reason is not known. Perhaps the decline in stuttering has something to do with a permissive trend in child-rearing practices that was due ultimately to the influence of Freud. Van Riper has suggested that it is related to the growth of professional speech therapy. Johnson thought it was caused by the dissemination of his diagnosogenic theory. My own view is that there is something naively egocentric in the notion that an event that has happened only once in human experience has happened in our lifetime. It seems far more reasonable to me to imagine that there have always been gradual changes in the incidence of stuttering from era to era in step with changes in patterns of social behavior. At any rate, whatever caused the incidence of stuttering to decline in recent decades, it was almost certainly associated with something that was happening in children's environments—in their homes in most cases and sometimes in their classrooms at school, because these are the places where stuttering is generally first noticed.

What we urgently need to know is the nature of that environmental factor. Now, if we could observe children's environments while their first signs of stuttering were developing, this would certainly yield a clue. As it happens, we do have such a clue. Strange as it may seem, one of the places in which episodes of stuttering occasionally develop is the speech clinic. Many speech clinicians of experience have seen this happen and it

---

was a fearful child from the start. It was difficult to toilet train him because he was afraid of falling into the hole in the potty. He screamed when he was having his hair cut. In his first few weeks at school his mother had to sit beside him in the classroom. The lawyer had none of these problems and was a confident child from the beginning. It is well known that babies who endure difficult births often show signs of tension, anxiety, and irritability as children. In turn, parents tend to react differently to troubled children.

has even been reported in professional journals. In a typical case, a child between the ages of three and seven is brought to the clinic because of retarded language development; the child has begun to speak late and has failed to master vocabulary, grammatically complex sentences, and articulation of speech sounds on his or her age level. After weeks or months of remediation with slow improvement, the child begins to make rapid gains in speech and language. It is precisely at this point that in some cases the clinician becomes aware that the child is stuttering. Frequently, the parents have not noticed any stuttering at home. These episodes of stuttering are generally transient. The clinician reduces some of the demands on the child and, whether for this or other reasons, the child in most cases stops stuttering.

That it is the pressure of remedial work that makes these children stutter gains corroboration from a study by Ruth Merits-Patterson and Charles G. Reed. These workers recorded the speech repetitions of three groups of nonstutterers: children receiving treatment for delayed language development, children with delayed language who were not getting any help, and children with normal language. The children who were undergoing treatment had more repetitions than either of the other two groups. The other two groups did not differ from each other.

Once suspicion falls on the role of language pressures, several facts take on special significance. Most stuttering develops between the ages of two and five, just the time when children are undertaking the arduous task of learning the rules of adult language with many errors and false starts. Some children become stutterers after this stage, but no stuttering appears beforehand, when children's utterances are limited to single words; stuttering emerges with syntax, the arrangement of words in phrases and sentences. An unusually large number of stutterers begin to speak somewhat late and encounter early difficulties in learning to articulate speech sounds. At every stage, stuttering increases in frequency with the length and grammatical complexity of utterances.

If stuttering can be precipitated by speech remediation, it is not hard to believe that it is often triggered by speech pressures in the home and school. Van Riper and others have cited cases in which stuttering arose in the course of excessive attempts by parents to hasten their children's speech and language development. This has also been my own experience. When I arrived at Brooklyn College in 1948 as a young instructor in the Department of Speech, one of my responsibilities was overseeing the work of a community speech clinic where for the next twenty years I conducted the initial interview with a continual stream of young stutterers and their parents. As a student of Wendell Johnson, I expected to find indications that these parents had mistaken their children's normal disfluencies for stuttering. Instead I soon began to receive the impression that stuttering had often been first noticed after the parents had become worried about other aspects of the children's speech. A recurring report was that the child had begun to stutter following the parents' efforts to improve the child's articulation of speech sounds. Infantile articulation is very common in young children and so are parents' attempts to help children overcome it, so we must avoid being misled by what may be mere coincidence. But there were too many accounts that seemed to leave little allowance for chance. One example was the following. The mother of a five-year-old stutterer began the interview with a confession that she herself had caused the child's speech difficulty. The boy, their only child, was late in beginning to speak, and as he approached the age of three, the parents were beside themselves with worry. At age three he finally began to speak. For a time the parents were relieved, but then they observed with dismay that the child "wasn't saying all of his sounds right." Few children do when first beginning to talk, but the parents had been so sensitized by their previous anxiety that they devoted themselves to correcting the child's articulation. The mother singled out two sounds, the "l" and the "g", and every day she sat down with the boy to work on them. Instead of allowing the boy to listen to the sound and imitate it, the normal procedure with a young child, she directed him to watch her "mouth" as she said it and to do exactly as she did. It would be difficult to think of a more effective way to make speech laborious for a child. She had done this for a time when, to their horror, the parents noticed that the child was beginning to repeat the first sounds of words. According to the mother, the words on which they first observed stuttering were words beginning with "l" or "g".

Of course any number of children who stutter have begun to speak early and have normal or superior language and articulation. A child may labor under excessive communicative pressures mainly because of a parent's perfectionism about speech. This is the view that Wendell Johnson's writings made well-known. Johnson's portrayal of stutterers' parents gave rise to a series of investigations of their attitudes and child-training policies, and researchers did find a tendency for many of them to be more critical or anxious than ordinary parents and to impose high standards of behavior. But the differences between the two groups were relatively small and some findings were conflicting. It was clear that there are many individual exceptions to this view of stutterers' parents, and this accords closely with clinical experience. Many parents of stutterers do seem dominating, anxious, overprotective, or demanding. "I would like him to be perfect," one mother said. One child was recalled to have asked his father, "Daddy, why is it everything I do is wrong?" Some mothers freely described themselves as overprotective or perfectionistic. One mother said, "Since my childhood I liked people to speak well. If a girl had grammatical errors or anything like that in her speech, I didn't want her as a friend. My great fear was that my child wouldn't talk well." In another case, a teenage boy could not play with his friends because they complained that his father would be there to help him run with the ball.

Examples of overanxious or demanding parents could be multiplied. On the other hand, many were not demanding at all. I encountered many parents of stutterers who made positive impressions of wisdom, warmth, and emotional stability. In some of these cases, it was possible to detect more subtle sources of communicative pressure. Some children had received too much praise for their speech. The parent ruefully stated that the child spoke "beautifully" before beginning to stutter or could recite twenty nursery rhymes and say "tyrannosaurus rex" by the age of two, and it was evident that the child had been on display because of his precocious speech. Other children simply had unattainable adult models in the form of parents who spoke very rapidly or used an adult vocabulary when speaking to the child. One boy was brought for examination by his father, a rabbi whose articulate, flowing speech must have been a source of great family pride and was in stark contrast to the labored hesitancy of the child.

Pressures that involve language and articulation are not the only communicative pressures that are associated with the development of stuttering. Sometimes the child has been badgered to talk more slowly. Occasionally the trouble seems to stem from the oral reading situation in the early grades at school. It is revealing that there are adults who stutter severely when reading aloud although they have no difficulty when speaking spontaneously in all situations. All too often stuttering that starts in the classroom spreads to the home and becomes the child's habitual way of speaking. Some insight into the way stuttering may originate in school was provided by a mother who asserted that her eight-year-old boy had begun to stutter the year before, in the second grade, in the classroom of a teacher who had a reputation for terrorizing the children by her scoldings. The boy, who happened to be an unusually sensitive, insecure child, would sometimes come home crying and would refuse to tell his mother why, but she would find out from his friends that the teacher had scolded him that day. According to the mother, the teacher placed great emphasis on speed in oral reading and had laid down the rule that there was to be no pausing except at periods.

Finally there were cases, by no means rare, which seemed to disclose no unusual pressures to speak better or provocations in the form of persistent speech failures. Possibly in these instances I was not seeing deeply enough, or perhaps they were cases in which a genetic predisposition to stutter was of such magnitude that it would have manifested it-self in practically any environment.

Stuttering as Tension and Fragmentation

It would seem that the environmental factor that precipitates stuttering is to be found in any condition that imbues children with a sense of failure at speaking or with a conviction that speech is a difficult task. If so, what does that imply about the nature of that moment of speech interruption that we call a stuttering block? The conditions that precipitate stuttering appear to be calculated to make children exercise undue effort and cau-tion in their attempts at speech. The concept of the stuttering block that seems to me to accord best with such conditions is the one that I have termed in this book the anticipatory struggle hypothesis. This is a conve-nient name for an idea that has been expressed in many different ways since it was first advanced by certain 19th-century European physicians. Stutterers were "speech doubters" according to one early writer. Later, the problem was blamed on faulty autosuggestion or on a tendency to produce speech movements with conscious deliberation rather than au-tomatically. To Wendell Johnson stuttering was an "anxious, anticipa-tory, hypertonic avoidance reaction." Van Riper embodied the idea in his observation that stutterers virtually condemn themselves to blockage on a feared word before they attempt it by establishing a focus of tension in their articulators, by preparing to say the word as a fixed articulatory posture instead of a movement, and by silently forming their articulators for the first sound of the word in advance. All of these statements em-phasize an aspect of the same general perception of stuttering as the er-ror of speaking with effort and hesitation due to a belief in the difficulty of speech. A particularly useful way to distill the essence of these formu-lations is to say that all of the surface features of stuttering are reducible to two underlying tendencies, that of producing utterances with abnor-mal muscular tension and that of fragmenting them. Stuttering, in short, is speech transformed by tension and fragmentation.

Excessive tension of the speech musculatures is part and parcel of stuttering in all of its forms and probably in some degree even in the ear-liest stages of its development. Stuttering is a struggle reaction. Without tension there can be no stuttering. To the observer this tension is most conspicuous in two of stuttering's surface features: prolongation of a sound and a hard, explosive attack on a sound. Prolongations only occur on so-called continuant sounds, for example "m" or "s", that are capable of being prolonged. Hard attacks only occur on "stop" consonants such as "t" or "b" which are incapable of being prolonged. So it is a reasonable guess that the two symptoms are merely surface manifestations of the same underlying activity: transform a continuant sound by excessive tension and you get a prolongation; transform a stop consonant by tension and the result is a hard attack.

Fragmentation is a reaction to which we all resort when faced with the demand for precision in performing a difficult motor task. We break the task into parts and perform the parts one by one. We may even repeat the first part of the activity until we feel ready to attempt the whole thing all at once, like the dart thrower who begins by rehearsing the first part of the throw. In the same way, the stutterer tries to cope with the perceived difficulty of feared words. The result is most evident in the other surface features of stuttering: broken words, pauses, and especially repetitions of the initial sounds or syllables of words. From this point of view, the stutterer repeating the "m" of "Mississippi" is doing so because of a lack of the conviction a speaker needs to say the whole word all at once. Like tension, fragmentation is at work to some degree behind all of the features of stuttering. Normal speech involves a continual movement of the speech organs. Fragmentation is present whenever normal movement stops.

The usefulness of this conception of stuttering lies in the insight it gives us into some of the most basic phenomena of the disorder. If we stop to wonder about them, the stutterer's repetitions may seem paradoxical. When the stutterer says, "My name is N-N-N-Nathaniel," we are apt to conclude that he is having trouble with the sound "n" and the stutterer himself may say as much. Yet he has said "n" perfectly four times. He has in fact demonstrated an imposing ability to say "n". The solution to the paradox is, of course, that he is not having trouble with "n" at all, but with the name "Nathaniel," and he is repeating "n" because that is his way of fragmenting the name. The insight that the concept of fragmentation affords is that when stutterers seem to be repeating sounds, they are not doing that at all; they are repeatedly stopping themselves from going on to say the rest of the word.

The same concept goes far to explain the locations of stuttering blocks. Over 90 percent of stutterings are heard on the first sound or syllable of a word. The rest occur on a sound or syllable within a polysyllabic word, as in "Nov-v-vember" or "Novem-vem-vember." Stuttering essentially never occurs on the last sound of a word.[2] This is a strict rule.

---

2. In the rare cases in which repetition of the final sounds or syllables of words has been reported, it is probable that this is not a primary feature of stuttering, but a postponement device due to anticipation of difficulty on the next word.

Stutterers do not say "November-ber" or "Novemberrrrr." There are very few strict rules to be found in stuttering behavior. Almost all generalizations about the conditions under which stuttering occurs or the way in which it is distributed in the speech sequence have many exceptions. So when we encounter a strict rule, we can infer that it holds the key to something significant; if we could state the reason for the rule, we would be saying something of basic importance about stuttering.

Now the absence of stuttering from the ends of words can only mean that there is no reason for stuttering at the end of a word. And that is easily explained on the assumption that what speakers are doing when they stutter is fragmenting words—breaking off and repeating or prolonging the first part of the word, or occasionally a syllable within a word, in the belief that the whole thing is too difficult to accomplish all at once. In short, the problem of stuttering in its developed form is for the most part a difficulty with words, as opposed to other speech segments such as sounds or phrases or sentences. This is corroborated by an entirely independent fact. As we saw in Chapter 8, the factors that influence the locations of stuttering blocks in the speech sequence are all attributes of words: their length, their grammatical function, their location in the sentence, their initial sound, and their information value.

Now it may not seem so remarkable that developed stuttering is mainly difficulty with words, but this inference has some far-reaching implications. In particular, it casts an unusual light on the earliest symptoms of stuttering, because incipient stuttering does not seem to involve difficulty with words at all; it appears to center about whole syntactic units—that is, phrases and sentences.

Early Stuttering

It is axiomatic that if we wish to explain the origin of something, we have to start with a good idea of what it is. Now stuttering is usually reported to begin in early childhood; yet most of our accumulated knowledge about the problem is about the form in which it is observed in older children and adults. Of the vast number of investigations that have been conducted on stuttering, only a minuscule percentage has been done with preschool children as subjects. There has been doubt and controversy on even the very description of early stuttering. All that most speech pathologists are agreed on is that the incipient form of the disorder is different in some respects from that of fully developed stuttering. An early attempt at this differentiation was made by Charles S. Bluemel in 1932. Bluemel saw the development of stuttering as a two-stage process. About the first stage, which he called "primary" stuttering, he made some acute observations. He said it most commonly consisted of repetitions of the first word of a sentence. He also noted sound and syllable repetitions, especially on the initial word. Bluemel described these symptoms as devoid of physical effort, devices for concealing or controlling stuttering, or signs of awareness of any difficulty with speech. He observed that at this stage stuttering may disappear and return repeatedly for months or several years. Despite the accuracy of many of his observations, Bluemel's simplistic division of stutterers into "primary" and "secondary" was eventually rejected by most speech pathologists. Effort and secondary symptoms are to be found in the speech of some of the youngest stutterers, as Bluemel himself conceded. So are signs of frustrated awareness. Conversely, some older children with otherwise advanced cases of stuttering seem to experience fear only sporadically if at all.

In the 1940s, Wendell Johnson added enormously to the uncertainty over the nature of early stuttering by declaring that much of what had been labeled early stuttering was really normal disfluency. As a result, the question of how to identify early stuttering was still perplexing speech pathologists 50 years later, but few seemed disposed to accept Johnson's assertion that stuttering began only when a child manifested effort, avoidance, and a self-concept as a stutterer. As a faithful student of Johnson's at the beginning of my career, I tried with little success for about two years to convince parents of young children that what they thought was stuttering was really normal, before I defected to their side. But if the way these children were talking was not exactly normal, neither was it quite like the stuttering of most older children and adults. It was not until ten years later, when I was able to look back on my examinations of several hundred cases of early stuttering, that I formed what I believe is a valid picture of the problem in its incipient phase.

As Bluemel had noted, in most of my cases the stuttering was episodic; it had appeared for weeks or months at a time between intervals of normal speech that were sometimes many months in duration. This intermittent recovery from stuttering is consistent with our knowledge that so many cases of stuttering in preschool children are transient. The children were generally said to stutter when excited or when they had a lot to say. They were probably not totally unaware of the interruptions in their speech. About half of them, at all events, had been observed by their parents to react in some way to their stuttering blocks, for example by saying "I can't talk," laughing, crying, or hitting themselves on the face. One child of two sometimes lay down on the floor, kicked his heels, and said to his mother, "Talk a me," which meant "Talk for me." But reactions of this kind tended to occur only sporadically, at moments when the children were severely blocked. At other times, and generally during the clinical interview, most of these children spoke freely despite their stuttering and could have been thought oblivious to it. In short, when they reacted emotionally to their stuttering, it was merely to the momentary frustration of being unable to speak. They gave little evidence of that negative concept of themselves that children later reveal when they say "I stutter," "I don't talk good," or "Take me to a doctor." One boy of three, on the occasion that he was first heard to stutter, turned to his mother and said, "I can't say goodnight to my daddy." By contrast, an older child, a girl of seven, asked her mother, "Will I stutter after I get married too?"

What was most arresting about these children was the stuttering itself. In a great many respects its features were similar to those of stuttering at any stage. Repetitions and prolongations of sounds, strenuous effort, and even secondary mannerisms such as eye closure and head movements were prominent in the behavior of some of the youngest children I examined. But there were also some features that set the stuttering of these children apart. First, they did a great deal of repeating of whole words. In some cases the entire stuttering pattern consisted of whole-word repetition. Whereas an older stutterer would say, "I have t-t-two sssssisters," these children might say,"I-I-I-I have two-two-two sisters." Now a normal speaking child will often repeat a word once like-like this. But these children were more apt to repeat it like-like-like-like this and to exhibit such repetitions with considerably greater frequency than ordinary children do. As a result they were sufficiently impeded in speech to be regarded as stutterers by the parents, relatives, friends, and neighbors. Second, their stuttering usually occurred on the first word of an utterance. Studies of older children and adults have shown that they too stutter more often on the first word of a sentence than on words in other positions, but in these children the effect was far more pronounced; in some cases the child's stuttering was essentially confined to the first words of utterances. And third, the children often stuttered on pronouns and grammatical "function" words such as conjunctions and prepositions, in contrast to older stutterers, who do most of their stuttering on the "content" words—nouns, verbs, adjectives, and adverbs.

It was these three peculiarities of early stuttering that eventually opened a window for me on what children are doing when they first begin to be regarded as stutterers. The first two peculiarities had been observed by Bluemel. I decided to do a formal study of the third, the tendency of these children to stutter on pronouns and function words. In 1967, together with my student Barbara F. Gantwerk, I reported findings on the grammatical factor in the stuttering of 13 preschool children. The children stuttered indiscriminately on most parts of speech. Unlike older stutterers, they showed no tendency to have particular difficulty on content words. Instead there was an unusually large amount of stuttering on pronouns and conjunctions. Inspection of the transcripts of the children's speech showed that the excessive stuttering on pronouns and conjunctions had a very simple explanation. Most of the stuttering had occurred on the first words of utterances, and these were very often pronouns such as "he", "she", "I" or conjunctions like "and", "but", or "so." In short, there was no true grammatical factor; the grammatical functions of words simply did not influence the distribution of stutterings in these children's speech. I did not grasp the significance of that fact until much later.

Barbara Gantwerk and I had established the reason for the high frequency of stuttering on pronouns and conjunctions, but there was still the question of why early stuttering occurred so often on the first words of utterances and why it so often took the form of repetitions of whole words. I had to wait some years for the answer. By the 1970s advances in the field of linguistics had led to the growth of a new scientific discipline called developmental psycholinguistics. It was concerned with the study of how children learn language, and in the 1970s the emphasis was on the development of syntax and grammar. As a result, the so-called constituent phrase structure of language became a familiar fact to all who had a scientific interest in the way children acquire language. Large syntactic structures were made up of smaller ones. A sentence was composed of a noun phrase like "a rolling stone" and a verb phrase like "gathers no moss." The verb phrase in turn might contain a constituent noun phrase like "no moss" or perhaps a prepositional or adverbial phrase. One April day in 1974 I was suddenly struck by the realization that a word repetition like "A rolling stone gathers no moss-moss" sounds outlandish. We never hear anything like it either in stuttering or in normal disfluency. Word repetitions may occur at the beginnings of sentences, but never at the end. I had heard children repeat prepositions such as "in" within utterances, so word repetitions could evidently occur at the beginnings of phrases within sentences. But could they occur at the ends of such units? Evidently not, because we are not accustomed to hear anything like "A rolling stone-stone gathers no moss."

As the meaning of these observations began to sink in, I became eager to examine some stuttered speech to see if they were valid. I had on hand a tape recording consisting of six brief samples of early stuttering that I was in the habit of playing for my students. During the spring break I carefully transcribed them, noting all the stutterings, and confirmed what had escaped my attention in listening to early stuttering for over twenty years. Every word that a child repeated was the first word of a syntactic unit. Most were the first words of sentences or clauses:

HE-HE-HE-HE HIS FATHER'S (pause) NAME (pause, gasp)
IS (gasp) STEVIE TOO.
'CAUSE-'CAUSE-'CAUSE-'CAUSE I'LL GET SICK.
AND-AND-AND-AND IRA'S COUSIN CAME TOO.

Some were the first words of noun phrases within sentences:

I DON'T EAT ICE... (gasp) ICE... (gasp) ICE... (gasp)
ICE-CREAM CONES.

Some began verb phrases:

AND YOU WON'T FEEL-FEEL-FEEL GOOD, YOU WON'T.

In not a single instance was the last word of a sentence, clause, or phrase repeated. I had found a rarity in stuttering, another strict rule. Like the rule that sound or syllable repetitions do not occur at the ends of words, it conveyed a message. The absence of word repetitions from the ends of syntactic units could only mean that when word repetitions appear in a child's stuttering pattern, the child is fragmenting syntactic units. The child who says "And-and-and-and Ira's cousin came too" is obviously having no difficulty saying "and." He is troubled by the problem of producing the whole syntactic structure. And a perfectly natural way of coping with this difficulty is to say the first word and repeat it until he feels able to produce the unit as a whole.

All three of the peculiar features of early stuttering were now accounted for, including the repetition of whole words and their unusually frequent occurrence at the beginnings of utterances. That Easter week I enjoyed the scientist's supreme reward. I was in possession of a significant bit of information that was unknown to the rest of humankind.

It should be mentioned that not all young stutterers exhibit the features that are typical of early stuttering. One of the six children in that tape recording was a case in point. At age four Jacob was repeating not words but sounds in a way that was indistinguishable from fully developed stuttering. He was fragmenting words. It would have been instructive to know if he had previously fragmented syntactic structures. In the other five cases, the stuttering was dominated by word repetition. One of the utterances of Joseph, age three, provided a particularly revealing example. Asked what squirrels eat, he replied "Dirty nuts." Pressed for an explanation, he said:

'CAUSE-'CAUSE-'CAUSE-'CAUSE SQUIRRELS SQUIRRELS L-LIKE-LIKE-LIKE-LIKE-L-L-L-LIKE- LIKE (takes a breath) DIR-DIR-DIR-DIR-DIR-DIR-DIRTY NUTS.

When I first transcribed this utterance, my immediate reaction was that it conflicted with the inferences I had drawn. The child seemed to be aimlessly engaging in repetition. The utterance brought to mind Van Riper's observation that when incipient stutterers exhibit repetitions, they sometimes seem to be merely playing with speech. But when I examined the transcription more closely, this is what I saw. Joseph first fragments the clause by repeating the first word, "'cause." This exposes the sentence "Squirrels like dirty nuts." He proceeds to fragment that by repeating "squirrels." This confronts him with the verb phrase "likes dirty nuts." Fragmenting that, he next encounters the noun phrase "dirty nuts," which he fragments by repeating the first syllable. There now remains only the word "nuts." Of all the words in the utterance, this is the only one that he does not repeat, either in whole or part. Joseph only fragments syntactic structures and "nuts" is not the first word of a syntactic structure.

As the foregoing example shows, word repetitions may occur in combination with sound repetitions as in "l-like-like-like-like-l-l-l-l-like-like." In such cases sound repetitions appear to function as part of the fragmentation of a syntactic unit. On the other hand, the fragment that the child may choose to repeat may sometimes be larger than a word. For example, Joseph said:

> MY-*MY MOTHER-MY MOTHER* SAY "DON'T-DON'T EAT DIR-DIRTY-DIRTY NUTS!"

And three-year-old Rachel, who refused to repeat after me "I like to eat ice-cream cones," explained with great effort:

> I EA... I EA... I EA... I EAT IT FROM A DISH.

The inference that stuttering begins as a fragmentation of syntactic units has received some confirmation from an independent source. Recall once more that the factors that influence the location of stutterings in the speech sequence in older children and adults are chiefly attributes of words (such as their length, initial sound, and grammatical function) and that this fact accords with the assumption that fully developed stuttering is largely difficulty with words. If the incipient stutterer's difficulty is with whole syntactic structures, it follows that early stuttering should not be influenced by features of words. This actually seems to be the case, although the evidence is as yet somewhat scanty. In 1974, the only source of such evidence was the study of some years before in which Barbara Gantwerk and I had found that the grammatical factor was not at work in early stuttering. I had no suspicion then that we had touched the edge of something considerably larger than the grammatical factor. In 1981, in collaboration with my colleague Marcia Grossman, I studied the distribution of stutterings in the speech of five preschool subjects. Word length had no effect. Only one child did more stuttering on initial consonants than initial vowels. And there was no preponderance of stuttering on content words; once again more stuttering occurred on pronouns and conjunctions because these stood at the beginnings of sentences and clauses. In the same year Meryl J. Wall, C. Woodruff Starkweather, and Katherine S. Harris noted the absence of the initial consonant-vowel factor in a study of nine preschool stutterers. It is by now a plausible inference that no factors related to words play a part in early stuttering.

The view that early stuttering involves difficulty with whole utterances or their constituent phrases fits well with our knowledge that stuttering usually develops in the language learning years and that many children have difficulty with or are pressured about speech or language before they become stutterers. But this view also leaves us with some difficult questions. What kind of trouble is the child anticipating when repeating the first word of an utterance? Is it difficulty with language itself—the retrieving of vocabulary and the evoking of grammar and syntax? Or is it more like the trouble that older stutterers anticipate with words—that of rendering the language units into speech by appropriate articulatory gestures? I am without an answer to this question. Likewise, if stuttering usually begins with the fragmentation of syntactic structures, what causes the transition within a few years to the fragmentation of words? Here it is possible to make some reasonable guesses. All of us are highly conscious of words. Any normal adult members of a human society, no matter how lacking in education, can offer an example of a word in their language. But this is not true of young children. Investigations of children's knowledge about language have shown that most children do not develop the concept of a word before about age five. Given a simple sentence, for example, they are unable to answer the question, "What is the first word?" In one study a child, when asked for an example of a long word, suggested "train." It is self evident, then, that before a certain age children cannot formulate any expectations of speech difficulty in terms of words. As they get somewhat older, two influences operate to give stuttering its developed form. Children tend to become increasingly concerned about stuttering as a speech difficulty and they become increasingly aware of words as such. As a result they begin to have anticipations of stuttering and to focus these anticipations on individual words.

Stuttering as an Extreme Degree of Normal Disfluency

I have dwelt on the features of early stuttering that distinguish it from the developed form of the disorder. But most speech pathologists have been more concerned about how to differentiate it from normal childhood disfluency. Incipient stuttering does often bear a distinct resemblance to the speech interruptions of many normal speaking children, and ever since Wendell Johnson called attention to these normal interruptions in his diagnosogenic theory, they have created a dilemma for both clinicians and researchers.

Clinicians to whom it seems common sense that they must be able to tell whether a child is exhibiting stuttering or merely normal disfluency have been hard put to it to find adequate criteria for doing so. To be sure, many children brought to a speech clinic with stuttering as the complaint undergo such a severe physical ordeal when they attempt to speak that there can be little doubt in the minds of the clinician or the parents. But this may not always be the case. Attempts have sometimes been made to separate disfluencies by kind into so-called "stutter-type" and "normal" disfluencies. Examples of the first are repetitions and prolongations of sounds or syllables, whereas interjections like "uh" and repetitions of whole phrases have been dubbed "normal." When such criteria are imposed without regard to the quantity of these disfluencies in the child's speech, however, they are of little use. Any number of ordinary children sometimes repeat or prolong sounds or syllables, while listeners even identify interjections such as "uh" as stuttering when they are frequent enough, as a study by M. N. Hegde and David E. Hartman has shown. The effort to distinguish stutterers from normal speakers by type of disfluency fails particularly badly in the case of whole word repetitions. These are so common in the speech of normal children that some workers go so far as to classify them with normal disfluency types. Yet research has shown that stutterers repeat whole words about four times as often as other children do and tend to repeat the word more times during a given instance of repetition. And clinical observations reveal that they often do so together with signs of frustration and struggle, and that they are perceived as stutterers by parents, friends, neighbors, and relatives even when the word repetitions are essentially the only conspicuous aspect of their disfluency. Despairing of descriptive criteria for separating early stuttering categorically from normal disfluency, some workers have imagined that it might be possible to do so by the application of sensitive laboratory instrumentation for recording subjects' sound waves or speech movements, but little has come of this hope so far.

Normal disfluency has created an equally troublesome problem for researchers. In view of Johnson's theory that stuttering arises from the confusion of normal disfluency with stuttering, an important question would seem to be the nature of the symptoms at the "onset" of the disorder. Researchers would like to have answers to such questions as what form the symptoms take at onset, under what conditions they vary in frequency, how they are distributed in the speech sequence, and so on. However, in order to conduct the relevant studies, one must first define what is meant by stuttering at its onset. But in order to define it, we must assume the answers to some of the questions we are asking. On the face of it, there is no solution to this paradox, because definitions are not scientifically verifiable as true or false, but can only be established by mutual consent.

As in logic or mathematics, when we are faced with a paradox it is because of faulty assumptions in our reasoning. I think the faulty assumption in this case becomes apparent when we recall that there are two distinct ways in which the abnormal may be related to the normal. Some abnormalities are of the either-or kind, like a broken bone, a gallstone, or hepatitis; either you have them or you don't. But others merge with the normal by fine degrees, like mental retardation, high blood pressure, emotional maladjustment, or hearing loss. We differentiate them from the normal by drawing an arbitrary line where it seems reasonable, and when cases are close to the line on one side or the other, we do not exercise ourselves unduly about whether they are "normal" or "abnormal." Does stuttering belong with the categorical or the dimensional abnormalities? To the vast majority of people it probably seems common sense that a child is either a stutterer or not. When Johnson brought normal disfluency to the attention of speech pathologists, it became possible for the first time to view early stuttering as a disorder that differs only in degree from the interruptions that are to be heard in the speech of ordinary children. But old habits proved very strong. And Johnson himself viewed stuttering as categorically different from normal disfluency, because he believed that stuttering began as an effort to avoid normal disfluency. Between the avoidance of something and the thing being avoided there is a difference of kind, not degree, and so Johnson repeatedly stated that a "sharp distinction" had to be made between stuttering and normal disfluency.

Eventually it was Johnson's own research that provided the most conclusive evidence that the sharp distinction he spoke of could not be made. In 1959, in collaboration with a dozen assistants, he published the massive collection of data from interviews with stutterers' and nonstutterers' parents that he called *The Onset of Stuttering*. One chapter of the book was devoted to an analysis of the children's disfluencies based on tape recorded samples of the speech of 89 stutterers and 89 nonstutterers ranging in age from two to eight years. The results showed that although the stutterers exceeded the control group in the frequency of many types of disfluency, there were no disfluencies, whether repetitions of sounds, syllables, words, or phrases, prolongations of sounds, or "complete blocks," that did not appear in the recordings of some of the nonstutterers. Johnson drew the inference that there is "no natural line of demarcation" between the disfluencies of stutterers and those of nonstutterers. He might easily have concluded that stuttering and normal disfluency in young children are different degrees of the same thing. Remarkably, he did not. He was so committed to the assumption that the two were categorically distinct, that he concluded instead that stuttering could not be defined merely as a feature of a child's speech. Stuttering, he wrote, could only be defined as a "problem" that arose for a listener.

When I first made the suggestion that there is a continuity between stuttering in young children and certain forms of early childhood disfluency, I received a letter from Johnson in which he said, "...it seems to me that you come close to saying that what might possibly be referred to as 'normal nonfluency' is really stuttering" and added a wish that we had "a shady tree, a log, and a long afternoon." Indeed Johnson divined what I was saying quite accurately, and the fact that he thought it an absurdity is revealing of his adherence to the notion that something was either "stuttering" or "normal." If most children do mildly and occasionally what "stuttering" children do more severely a great deal of the time, then in a significant sense most children stutter. It may be useful to reserve the term "stutter" for the more severe degrees of the behavior, but whether we do or not, the point is that the "stutterer" and the normally disfluent child may be doing much the same thing for the same reason. The speech pressures and failures that so often seem to precipitate stuttering in its clinical form are common in some degree to the experience of a great many children. It should not occasion great surprise if many normal children who are engaged in the arduous task of acquiring language exhibit tensions and fragmentations in their speech. In a few, the pressures or failures may be so severe and chronic, or an inherited predisposition to succumb to them may be of such magnitude, that the tensions and fragmentations come to be perceived as abnormal.

If this is so, the question of how to distinguish stuttering from normal disfluency does not need to trouble speech clinicians greatly. The question cannot have an absolute answer, and even arbitrary criteria such as the frequency of disfluencies of various types in the child's speech are likely to be futile in view of the tendency of early stuttering to vary erratically from day to day. The questions that matter are whether the child is frustrated by its speech interruptions and whether they alarm the parents and are noticed unfavorably by others. Moreover, researchers who would like to describe the symptoms of stuttering at its "onset" need not be concerned about their inability to define what they wish to study without assuming the answers to some of their questions. If normal tensions and fragmentations merge by fine degrees with incipient stuttering, the concept of an onset of stuttering as an event that occurs abruptly at a certain moment of a certain day disappears together with any questions we may have about it.

CHAPTER SIXTEEN

The Treatment of Early Stuttering

We have seen that stuttering at its inception is generally an evanescent phenomenon, difficult to distinguish categorically from normal childhood speech interruptions, and highly subject to spontaneous recovery. From a therapeutic point of view, the problem has therefore most often been considered to be the prevention of the more chronic and serious forms of the disorder. This has meant above all guarding against the development of that self concept as a defective speaker that underlies the anticipations, fears, and avoidances of chronic stutterers. For this reason the clinician's chief concern must be with the child's reputation as a speaker in the child's family environment. It should occasion no surprise, then, that the most commonly adopted approach to the problem for many years has been parent counseling.

An important source of the prevailing clinical attitude toward early stuttering is to be found in the 1932 paper by the British-born Denver psychiatrist Charles S. Bluemel in which he distinguished what he called "primary" stuttering from the developed form of the disorder. In that paper, as we have seen, Bluemel suggested that primary stuttering was a transient phenomenon of childhood that would soon disappear if it were not for the efforts parents make to help the child get over it. He argued that by repeatedly urging the child to "stop and start over," "talk slowly," or "think" before they speak, parents often make the child tense and anxious about the primary stuttering. In these cases, he said, the child develops the secondary stage of stuttering marked by anticipation, effort, shame, and devices for avoiding or minimizing stuttering.

Bluemel's observation came just at the moment when speech pathology was beginning its rapid evolution into a scientific discipline

150

and profession in the United States, and his thinking had a lasting influence. In 1939 Van Riper, in the first edition of his widely used textbook, "Speech Correction: Principles and Methods," wrote, "...the way to treat a young stutterer in the primary stage is to let him alone and treat his parents and teachers." A few years later the idea of treating the child's parents received strong reinforcement from Wendell Johnson. Giving Bluemel's thinking a sharp twist, Johnson asserted that "primary stuttering" was in essence normal disfluency, and that it was excessive parental help for it that put children in danger of becoming stutterers. He popularized the notion that most parents who alleged that their young children were stuttering needed to be counseled to regard them as doing only a bit more of what normal speaking children do.

With the passage of time some change in the treatment of young children has been discernible. Johnson's theory has lost much of its former luster from lack of evidence; and the almost certain knowledge that heredity plays a part in stuttering has relieved parents of much of the onus of blame for the disorder. With the advent of behavior therapy for stuttering, Johnson has sometimes been taken to task for fostering clinicians' reluctance to work directly with very young stutterers, and some have advocated teaching children as young as three or four to imitate a slow rate of speech with prolongation of syllables. A few have even applied operant conditioning by giving children rewards for fluent speech and mild punishments, such as withdrawal of attention, for stuttering. Nevertheless, parent counseling, particularly along lines suggested by Van Riper, remains the most trodden path to the treatment of early stuttering. To the best of our knowledge, stuttering is caused by the interplay of an inherited predisposition with certain environmental factors. At the moment there is little we can do about the predisposition. But with stuttering of such recent origin, there is hope that we can still exert an influence on the problem through the child's home environment. We must not forget that the majority of children who stutter in their preschool years get over it after some months or years despite whatever inborn predisposition they may have. It is a plausible assumption that how a stuttering child is managed at home may have a great deal to do with whether stuttering is a transient episode or persists into adulthood as a chronic problem.

Parent Counseling

Generally speaking, the speech pathologist's endeavor in working with parents is to relax communicative pressures and to nurture the child's conviction that speech is easy and pleasurable. If the parents have been making excessive efforts to improve the child's speech or hasten its language development, they are of course advised to desist. But in many cases the pressures are more subtle. For example, parents may unwittingly make demands on children to speak faster than they are able simply through the rapidity of their own rate of speech. Children tend to start life with an overpowering compulsion to imitate adults. It is part of the unproven lore of the speech clinic that one of the most effective ways of causing incipient stuttering to vanish is to train the parents to talk to the child at a slow rate of speech. This is very different from urging the child to talk slowly, and far preferable. Most children who are talked to in a slow, deliberate way unconsciously fall in with that manner of speaking.

Communicative pressure may also result from the parents' style of interacting with a child. Some parents habitually bombard the child with questions, interrupt the child, or hurry the child by their impatient reactions to the slow and halting utterance that is characteristic of early childhood speech. For this reason some clinicians make a practice of studying or even videotaping the parent and child in a play situation. Such observations may result in useful suggestions for changes in the parent's behavior. The clinician may then play with the child while the parent watches. As the clinician makes simple, quiet comments on their activity, the child will generally respond simply, quietly, and fluently in kind.

By the time parents bring a child to the speech pathologist, the most severe pressure that the child endures may consist of parental reactions to the child's speech difficulty. Much of the advice the parent receives may be aimed at putting a stop to their anxious efforts to help the child avoid stuttering. There may be irritation or anger. There may be patient insistence that the child take a deep breath, stop and start over, and the like. Parents may promise children a bicycle for their birthday if they stop stuttering, praise them extravagantly for speaking fluently, or continually supply words for them. It may be true that children often overcome their difficulty in spite of such measures, or perhaps sometimes even because of them, but so many older stutterers with severe, chronic problems remember being subjected to these measures, that they have come to be regarded as generally useless and probably too often counterproductive. Not only should parents avoid using them, but they may also need to school themselves to control the reactions they unconsciously display by facial expression, posture, or tone of voice when the child stutters. But this does not mean that they should always "ignore" the stuttering, advice they all too often receive from unqualified sources. From earliest infancy, children learn to expect help and empathy from their parents, even with trivial problems as when their wagon gets stuck.

When a child in the throes of severe stuttering meets with a total absence of any response, the message may be, not that stuttering isn't worrisome, but that it is unspeakable. Far better is an empathetic "That was a hard one" when the child has had an unusually severe block. And on those rare occasions when a child may seem terribly frustrated and upset in the attempt on a particularly difficult utterance, it may not be inappropriate for parents to say it for the child, provided they offer this assistance in the casual way that they do when the child's wagon gets stuck.

When parents impose communicative pressures on a child, these pressures sometimes occur in a setting of excessively high standards with regard to the child's behavior in general. From the beginning, clinicians have often advised parents to relax demands on the child with respect to politeness, cleanliness, obedience, eating habits, and the like. In part, this approach was prompted by the theory that stuttering resulted directly from maladjustive tensions in the home. But when Wendell Johnson popularized the view that stuttering was caused by unrealistic demands for fluency, he too attached great importance to the need for parents to allow the child as much freedom as possible from high expectations and restrictive demands and to treat the child as a child rather than as a small adult. This aspect of parent counseling probably looms less large than formerly in current practice because of more qualified conceptions of the parents' role in the causation of stuttering and the virtual abandonment by speech pathologists of the theory of an emotional origin of the disorder. Nevertheless, more than a few parents of stutterers do appear to be unusually dominating or perfectionistic, and many speech clinicians advocate the reduction of parental pressures with regard to the child's general behavior where this seems appropriate.

The view that such advice may be effective in treating early stuttering is epitomized in a story that Lee Edward Travis once told at a convention. A mother had brought her small son to Travis because the boy was stuttering severely. In the course of the interview it developed that the mother was rigidly controlling almost every aspect of the child's daily routine down to the smallest detail. Whether it was what and when he ate, with what or whom he played, when he napped, had his bath, or went to bed at night, all went according to a strict schedule without the slightest deviation. Travis's advice to the mother was that she "call off all the dogs." She was to allow the child to eat what he wanted whenever he was hungry, to go to bed when he was sleepy, to play as his fancy took him, and to allow him every freedom subject only to the requirements of physical safety and the approval of the child's pediatrician. The mother was horror-stricken. But she was so distraught over the boy's stuttering that she was willing to try anything, and so she agreed to follow Travis's advice. Two weeks later she called Travis on the telephone to report with relief and gratitude that the boy had stopped stuttering. "Now," she said as she was about to hang up, "can I go back to treating him normally?" Travis, who was elderly and wise, replied, "All right, go back to treating him normally." Two weeks later she telephoned again with the disheartening news that the boy was stuttering. On Travis's advice she resolved to apply the same treatment that had worked before. Two weeks later she reported that the boy was speaking fluently again and wanted to know whether she could finally treat him normally. On the last of several similar phone calls she confided to Travis a suspicion that she might not have been treating the boy normally in the first place.

Travis's story is of course hardly a typical one. For the most part the pressures that parent counseling seeks to alleviate are communicative pressures. And that is only one of its aims. The other is to imbue the child with an expectation of success at speaking to counteract the growth of that habitual anticipation of failure that underlies developed stuttering. There are a number of measures that parents can take with this end in view. Early stuttering is generally intermittent. Van Riper suggested that during fluent intervals the child should be encouraged to talk as much as possible, while for "bad" days the parent should have in reserve some absorbing activity to keep the child engaged in solitary play. Parents are often advised to spend part of each day in speech activities that give the child pleasure and fluency. Examples are talking in time to rhythmic movement, talking for a doll or puppet, or reciting nursery rhymes. Reading a familiar story to a child quietly at bedtime usually evokes plenty of fluent speech as the child joins in the narration.

Finally, it is often possible to guide parents to eliminate some of the conditions that provoke the child's stuttering. For the most part these are the same conditions under which most ordinary children are disfluent. When parents make careful observations, they generally find that the child stutters most when excited or when having a lot to say as when telling a long story. Other common examples are: when trying to gain the attention of an unresponsive listener; when competing with older children for the opportunity to talk, for example at the dinner table; when hurried to make the school bus in the morning; during battles over aspects of the child's routine; when confessing guilt; or in anticipation of some upsetting event like a father's prolonged absence on a business trip. Johnson even cited the case of a child who stuttered severely when he awoke one morning to discover that his parents had rearranged the living-room furniture. Some of these situations can be avoided. A parent can get up earlier to get the child ready for the bus; can lend a patient ear to the child's prattle; or can see to it that the child gets a chance to contribute to the dinner-table conversation. It is of course impossible to protect a child from every eventuality that is capable of precipitating stuttering. But that is not necessary. All that is vitally important is that the child have enough experience of fluency to fortify against a feeling of failure as a speaker. A child who stutters now and then but speaks fluently a good part of the time is probably in little danger of becoming a life-long stutterer.

Early stuttering is widely regarded as being very easy to treat. Reports of clinical success are abundant. No doubt, some of this success has owed more to the nature of the problem than to the therapy. Between the ages of two and six, transient episodes of stuttering are exceedingly common.

The Treatment of School-Age Children

By about age seven or so, stuttering has usually acquired some advanced features that distinguish it from the incipient disorder. It no longer comes and goes in the form of episodes. The child has a distinct self-concept as a defective speaker. And there is now far more repetition or prolongation of the initial sounds of words than repetition of words themselves; the stuttering has apparently progressed from difficulty with syntactic structures to difficulty with words. Something is now called for besides parent counseling alone, and schoolchildren have been treated by speech clinicians for many years, at times with modified forms of Iowa therapy and more often in recent years with behavior therapy.

Despite the changes that have occurred in the problem, it is usually still in a fairly rudimentary stage. These children evince few emotional reactions to stuttering besides frustration. They tell you evenly, without apparent shame, "I stutter when I talk fast." Given a choice, they would much rather not. But in most cases the child does not avoid speaking and there is generally little in the way of anticipations, word fears, or word substitutions. Persistent shame and fear usually do not set in until later, though they may do so as early as age ten in some instances.[1] With many children of school age it seems realistic to imagine that the self-concept as a stutterer has a rather tenuous hold, and this is consistent with observation. There is still considerable spontaneous recovery from

1. From about age 10, stuttering children vary markedly in their sensitivity about their speech difficulty. This fact may pose a dilemma for classroom teachers who must decide whether or not to call on a stutterer to recite. Some stutterers have so much anxiety about oral recitation that forcing them to recite may make the problem worse. Others feel hurt if the teacher doesn't call on them; they want to be treated like everyone else. This is true even of some adolescents. There is no satisfactory alternative to taking the pupil aside to gain his or her point of view.

stuttering in this age range. In some cases, very little seems to be required for recovery to happen. A memorable example from my own clinical experience was the case of an eight-year-old girl who had stuttered severely for three years according to the mother, but stopped abruptly on being told that she was to be taken for speech therapy. She spoke fluently and with ease and spontaneity during the clinical interview.

In view of the tendency for many school-age children to recover from stuttering without formal help, it should not be surprising that clinicians often report high rates of success in treating them. So many different kinds of treatment have been known to produce favorable results, that the therapeutic method would seem to be less important than the child's perception that a remedy is forthcoming. Even in adulthood, stuttering is apt to succumb quickly to suggestion. In the case of adults, the effect is usually temporary; adults are too sophisticated to accept uncritically the assumption that, given this or that expedient, they will stop stuttering. To children, the kindly adult stranger who claims to be able to help them talk better is likely to seem powerful and all-knowing. In the days before speech therapy, there were occasional accounts of teachers who helped children overcome stuttering by doing little more than coach them to participate in the school's declamation or debating contest.

Many years ago, the director of the college speech and hearing center in which I have pursued my career was the renowned pioneer in U. S. speech pathology, Robert West. West was an impressive person and he was also an impressive looking one. He was large, bald, elderly at the time, with a dark, penetrating gaze and a deep, resonant voice. One day he examined a seven-year-old girl who had been brought to the center because she stuttered. The child's speech difficulty did not seem to him to require immediate attention, so he advised the mother on home management of the child's disfluency. But before they left, he drew the child aside and spoke to her alone for a few moments. He told her that girls stutter less frequently than boys, that they more often stop stuttering (there is some evidence for this), and that, all things considered, it was not likely that she would be stuttering much longer. About two weeks later the mother telephoned to report that from the moment they left the center, the child had spoken without stuttering. A year later we confirmed that she was talking normally.

I do not mean to leave the impression that there is a sure cure for stuttering in the case of every child who stutters. But there is every reason to maintain that in the majority of cases in which adequate remedial help is available, the outlook for recovery is good.

CHAPTER SEVENTEEN

The Treatment of Developed Stuttering

The accounts of Iowa therapy in Chapter 6 and behavior therapy in Chapter 12 have already acquainted the reader with the forms of treatment that have been in use for some time for older children, adolescents, and adults. The purpose of this chapter is to survey the scene at the writing of this book. By the 1990s, much of the experimentation of the 1960s and 1970s with operant and classical conditioning had been largely abandoned along with expedients such as rhythmic speech, white noise, and biofeedback. What had survived the ferment of those times were in the main a few methods that teach stutterers to gain immediate fluency by talking differently and the Iowa approach that teaches them to stutter differently and master their fear of stuttering. This chapter describes a number of treatment programs that have become widely known and emulated through the writings of their authors or through the training of other speech clinicians in their use. They are representative of many other programs like them that were in use by speech pathologists at the date of this book. Some clinicians were employing Iowa therapy, especially as Van Riper had developed it. More were teaching artificial speech patterns. Many were trying to combine features of both methodologies.

Program of Bruce P. Ryan and Barbara Van Kirk

A program intended primarily for children of school age is one that was developed by Bruce P. Ryan and Barbara Van Kirk at Monterey, California. One of the earliest programs of behavior therapy for stuttering to be disseminated widely, it depends more heavily than other well-known programs on operant conditioning. The basic principle employed is verbal reinforcement for fluency and verbal "punishment" for stuttering as the length of the child's utterances is gradually increased. Like many other highly structured programs, it is divided into distinct phases for establishment of fluency, transfer of fluency to daily life, and maintenance of fluency.

The clinician begins by determining a so-called base rate: The number of stuttered words per minute is calculated as the child reads aloud, talks continually in a monologue, and engages in conversation with the clinician. The establishment phase then begins with the child instructed to read fluently, one word at a time. Each time a word is read fluently the child is told "Good." If a word is stuttered, the child is told "Stop. Read it fluently." Once the child can read a specified number of single words in succession fluently, the number of words read at a time is gradually increased and the child progresses in small steps to sentences and continuous reading. Verbal rewards and punishments continue to be applied and precise criteria are specified for advancing to each step. When fluency in reading is established, the same procedure is repeated in monologue and conversation. For cases in which a child cannot attain fluency in this way, Ryan and Van Kirk have available an alternate program in which fluency is established with the aid of delayed auditory feedback by teaching the child to speak in a monotone with slurred articulation and prolongation of sounds.

In the transfer phase, the program is continued in a variety of settings, for example outside the door of the speech clinician's room, down the hall, in another room, the playground, the cafeteria, and, with the cooperation of teachers and parents, in the classroom and the home. Reinforcement is given at specified intervals and goals are set as before. For adults, the program includes procedures for transfer to the workplace, the telephone, and other situations.

The maintenance phase of the program is designed to help prevent relapse. The child returns for re-evaluation after two weeks following the end of therapy and then after one, three, six, and twelve months. If there is more than a specified amount of stuttering on any of these occasions, the child is recycled through the program at an appropriate point.

The entire program, including the maintenance phase, requires many months for completion.

Program of Ronald L. Webster

During running speech, we continually initiate voice by setting our vocal cords into vibration. We do this after every pause and after every voiceless consonant such as *s* or *t*. At Hollins College in Roanoke, Virginia, Ronald L. Webster has devised a treatment program in which stutterers are trained to speak with more gentle onsets of voice than we normally use. The "Precision Fluency Shaping Program," as Webster has named it, is an intensive, three-week course in which stutterers work on their vocal onsets all day and evening, a half hour at a time alternated with a half hour of rest. Although groups of stutterers are treated at a time, each stutterer is assigned an individual cubbyhole equipped with a tape recorder, a stop watch, and an instrument called a voice monitor.

In addition to the power of any novel speech pattern to produce immediate fluency, an important advantage of gentle vocal onsets is that they are physically incompatible with stuttering blocks. However, initiating voice in a new way in rapid, running speech is difficult. Consequently, stutterers spend the first three days learning to speak in a way that will make it possible for them to apply the new pattern. They markedly slow down their speaking rate, prolonging each syllable for fully two seconds with the aid of the stop watch, and eliminate any breaks between and within syllables. The result is a smooth, flowing manner of speech in slow motion.

Now the stutterer is taught to initiate the voice very softly on individual vowels and voiced consonants, increasing loudness gradually to a normal level. On voiceless consonants, the stutterer practices gentle onsets of the following vowel. Learning of these skills is facilitated by the voice monitor, which is designed to flash red when a vocal onset is too abrupt and green when it is gradual. From sounds and syllables the stutterer progresses to words of one syllable and, by the end of the second week, to two-syllable words. During the third week, more complex speech is introduced, speech is gradually speeded up to a normal rate, dependence on the voice monitor ceases, and stutterers practice their fluent speech in conversation, in speeches, on the telephone, and in speech situations outside the clinic.

Program of Martin Schwartz

Another program dedicated to the aim of immediate fluency through the use of an artificial speech pattern is that of Martin Schwartz. In the technique known as airflow, the stutterer precedes every utterance with a passive outflow of breath. Schwartz's rationale for his method is the assumption that the immediate cause of essentially all of the abnormality of stuttering is a tight spasm of the vocal cords. Although this premise is not accepted generally, it is true that the larynx is involved along with the rest of the speech mechanism in the muscular tension that is part and parcel of stuttering, that the system tends to block as a whole, and that as long as air is being allowed to escape between parted vocal cords, it is virtually impossible for a person to engage in a stuttering block. Airflow, then, has the same virtue as gentle voice onsets, in that it adds physical incompatibility with stuttering to the distractive effect of a novel way of speaking.

In Schwartz's program, stutterers are seen six hours a day for five days, after which almost all are said to be speaking fluently. They are then instructed to practice an hour a day for a year and to send tape recordings, which are returned with evaluations and suggestions.

Like most other methods of treatment which appear simple when described, airflow has some complexity in practice. Schwartz cautions that the stutterer must not force the airflow, but must relax and allow the expiration to take place spontaneously. The outflowing breath must not be interrupted, but must lead directly into the utterance. The stutterer must not place his articulators in position for the first sound before beginning airflow; attention should not be on speech until the breath begins to flow. Finally, there must be no break in airflow between inhalation and exhalation; the one must lead smoothly into the other.

Program of William H. Perkins

At the University of Southern California, William H. Perkins has experimented since the 1960s with therapy based mainly on a slow rate of speech enhanced by a number of additional techniques. In a sequence designed to establish fluency, stutterers first practice prolonging each syllable for a duration of two seconds with the aid of delayed auditory feedback when necessary. They then learn to initiate phrases in a breathy manner with the sound *h*, to produce sounds with light contacts of the articulators, to maintain a continuous flow of breath, and to blend syllables and words in a smoothly flowing pattern. Before any attempt is made to transfer fluency to daily life, attention is given to increasing the naturalness of the stutterer's speech. The rate is speeded up until it sounds normal, unstressed syllables are produced briefly as in normal speech, and the stutterer practices speaking with normal rhythm, stress, and inflection.

On the assumption that relapse is inevitable in most cases, Perkins' program prepares the stutterer for it. The stutterer deliberately induces repeated relapses by abandoning the fluency techniques or speeding up the speech rate and then practices recovery from the breakdown of fluency.

Perkins has commented that, although many stutterers achieve fluency, they are less likely to think of themselves as normal speakers than as stutterers who are able to speak fluently by using techniques. He has suggested that for many stutterers the best possible use of such techniques may be to reserve them for occasions when it is especially important to speak without stuttering.

Iowa Therapy

For clinicians who do not wish to teach stutterers to achieve immediate fluency by an artificial manner of speaking, the main alternative is the form of therapy that Bryngelson, Johnson, and Van Riper developed with the aim of overcoming the drawbacks of such methods. For the majority of these workers, it is Van Riper's methodology that has proved most useful, particularly his teaching of "fluent" stuttering by means of cancellations and pullouts. These measures were explained in Chapter 6, so there is no need to describe them here. But it is worth noting that in the most recent and fullest exposition of his program, Van Riper divided it into a sequence of four steps that is certain to have been adopted by many of his followers. He called these steps identification, desensitization, modification, and stabilization. In identification, stutterers analyze their abnormal speech behavior and develop awareness of its various features. In the desensitization phase, they practice calming themselves while stuttering and performing their blocks without shame or panic. In modification, they learn that it is possible to stutter in different ways and, with the help of cancellations and pullouts, they transform their stutterings into smooth, effortless prolongations of sound.[1] In the stabilization phase of the program, stutterers build up resistance to relapse by continuing therapy as their own clinicians; for example, they regularly

---

1. Individuals who confront the varieties of stuttering therapies for the first time sometimes claim that they can't see much difference between Van Riper's modification methods and the prolongation of all syllables that is a favorite device of those who teach artificial speech patterns. The unbridgeable difference between them appears quite clearly in their totally different advantages and disadvantages. Methods that teach stutterers to talk differently almost always result in immediate and complete fluency at the cost of the necessity to monitor speech, some unnaturalness, and vulnerability to relapse. Methods that teach people to stutter differently allow them to speak naturally and with no special attention to their speech except when they stutter, and generally do not leave them as helpless in relapse. The cost is the abandonment of any aspiration to speak with normal fluency.

do some voluntary stuttering to guard against creeping fear and avoidance.

An offshoot of the Iowa school of therapy is the program that was employed by Joseph G. Sheehan and continued after his death by his wife, Vivian Sheehan. Rejecting all talk-differently treatments as perpetuating stuttering and insuring relapse by suppressing it, Sheehan adopted avoidance-reduction and the relinquishment of a false role as a normal speaker as "almost the sole vehicle of therapy." His program calls for clients' self-acceptance as stutterers, exploration of unfavorable speech attitudes, awareness of what they are doing when they stutter, deliberate confrontation of feared situations, modification of stuttering by substituting an effortless "slide," and the use of the slide on nonfeared words to counteract the avoidance of stuttering.

Dean E. Williams has adapted Iowa therapy for use with schoolchildren. In the program he developed for the public schools of Iowa City and Cedar Rapids, children are encouraged to use descriptive language about what they do when they stutter, to distinguish between "talking hard" and "talking easy," to do the things that make it easy to talk instead of trying not to stutter, and to accept their fears as normal. The therapy is an extension of Johnson's, together with Williams' emphasis on teaching stutterers to do more of the things that normal speakers do as they move forward in speaking without holding back.

Program of Hugo H. Gregory

Hugo H. Gregory was among the first speech pathologists to attempt an amalgamation of the two major traditions of stuttering therapy. In keeping with the Iowa school, he has favored teaching stutterers to study and analyze their stuttering behavior and to modify the way they stutter by doing it less rapidly and strenuously. At the same time, he has trained stutterers to change the way they talk by using an easy, relaxed manner with smooth movements throughout speech. In addition, he advocates the use of bodily relaxation and works on general speech improvement with attention to rate, phrasing, rhythm, and stress.

Program of Theodore J. Peters and Barry Guitar

Integration of the Iowa and behavioral approaches is the central emphasis in the therapy of Peters and Guitar. On the premise that spontaneous fluency will be difficult for most adult stutterers to attain, they regard as legitimate goals both fluency that is controlled by "fluency-enhancing behaviors" and stuttering that is acceptable in the sense that it consists of mild disfluencies without fear or embarrassment. Accordingly, they teach stutterers how to achieve immediate fluency by using a slow rate of speech, gentle voice onsets, and soft articulatory contacts. And they also train them to stutter easily by employing these behaviors on stuttered words in cancellations, pullouts, and preparatory sets.

Peters and Guitar begin treatment by orienting stutterers about the problem and helping them to identify the alterable features of their behavior and attitudes. Next, they work on anxiety reduction by encouraging stutterers to discuss their difficulty openly with others, to stop avoiding difficult words and situations, and to practice voluntary stuttering. The client then learns the technique of speaking fluently and the modification of stuttering blocks and transfers both skills to everyday situations. Finally, stutterers work on maintaining their improvement by taking responsibility for their own daily assignments as the frequency of clinical sessions is gradually reduced. As long-range goals, they make their own choice between controlled fluency or acceptable stuttering.

Program of C. Woodruff Starkweather

Like Peters and Guitar, Gregory, and others, C. Woodruff Starkweather believes in equipping stutterers with both the skill of speaking fluently and of modifying their stuttering. In Iowa fashion, he counsels stutterers to revise unfavorable feelings and attitudes, to confront their feared situations, and to stutter voluntarily. Employing Van Riper's methods, stutterers in his program identify and desensitize themselves to stuttering blocks, learn to stutter in different ways, and use cancellations and pullouts to cultivate a type of stuttering that is as free as possible of tension and abnormality. But, in contrast to the Iowa approach, Starkweather also teaches stutterers to speak fluently by controlling their speaking rate. He believes that most adult stutterers should learn an effortless manner of stuttering for ordinary use and a technique for speaking fluently for special occasions.

Program of George H. Shames and Cheri L. Florance

The detailed program that Shames and Florance call "Stutter-Free Speech" aims exclusively for immediate fluency by means of an artificial manner of speaking. But it draws to a unique degree on a variety of sources including operant conditioning, counseling methods, and Iowa therapy. The fluency technique is a slow rate of speech with continuous voice or airflow. The format for each clinical meeting is that of a nondirective counseling session. This is the well-known method of Carl R. Rogers in which counselors encourage clients to talk constructively about their problems by listening nonjudgmentally and reflecting back their feelings in an accepting and clarifying way. In the Shames and Florance program, stutterers make use of this format to practice fluent speech, but it also serves as a means of helping them to come to terms with their feelings of anxiety and inadequacy about their speech and their attitudes of indecision or resistance toward speech therapy. The program has five distinct phases. Reinforcement is used continuously and criteria are specified for advancement to each phase.

In the first phase of the program, the stutterer learns a slow, fluent pattern of speech with the aid of delayed auditory feedback. Attention is given from the start to the use of natural stress and inflection.

In the second phase, the delayed auditory feedback is discontinued. As the stutterer speaks, the clinician from time to time instructs him to use his slow speech pattern and administers reinforcement for fluent utterances. The method of reinforcement is based on the so called Premack principle in behavior modification. According to this principle, a highly effective reinforcement for not smoking is a puff on a cigarette; for dieting, it is a piece of strawberry shortcake. In the Shames and Florance program the clinician applies this precept by signaling the stutterer to relax his controls and allow himself a few words of "unmonitored" speech. On another principle borrowed from behavior modification, the stutterer is gradually made responsible for his own reinforcement. The stutterer learns to instruct himself to use monitored speech, evaluates his own performance, and reinforces it with unmonitored speech.

The third phase of the program is devoted to transfer of fluent speech to situations outside the clinic. Here a method is taken from psychological counseling practice. Each outside assignment is negotiated by the stutterer and clinician as a contract that specifies that the stutterer will engage in a given duration of monitored speech at a given time with a certain listener and will reinforce fluency with a specific duration of unmonitored speech. Written down and signed by the stutterer, the clinician, and the stutterer's parent or spouse, the contract becomes a public document.

At this point stutterers are monitoring about 80 percent of their speech and reinforcing this with unmonitored speech about 20 percent of the time. As the fluency controls become habitual, the unmonitored portion tends to acquire the speech pattern and fluency of the monitored part. During the fourth phase of treatment, the proportion of unmonitored speech is gradually increased, so that all of the stutterer's speech is eventually unmonitored. This is the program's device for overcoming one of the drawbacks of therapies that demand stutterers' continual attention to the way they speak.

In the fifth phase, clinical contacts become progressively less frequent and the stutterer is finally seen just once a year for assessment over a period of five years.

To conclude this chapter, it is necessary to repeat that the treatment programs surveyed here are simply representative of the work that was being done by any number of highly qualified speech clinicians at this writing. They do not even exhaust the list of those that had been described in publications. To have included them all would have been possible only at the cost of intolerable redundancy.

CHAPTER EIGHTEEN

Self-Help Groups

Ever since Alcoholics Anonymous demonstrated the value of support groups, the self-help movement has expanded to respond to almost every imaginable category of human need. Stuttering has been no exception. Stutterers have formed their own organizations from time to time for many years. There was one called the Demosthenes Club at the University of Iowa in the 1940s. But it was in the 1970s that such groups began to grow rapidly in number, in both the United States and other countries.

In a typical case, a group of five to fifteen persons meets every two weeks in the home of one of its members. They may practice a technique they have been taught to use for speaking fluently. Or they may simply volunteer to make short speeches; this is no small achievement for most stutterers, and it is a common occurrence for a member to look on for weeks or months before getting up to speak, to enthusiastic applause. Sometimes they hear guest speakers. But by far the most important thing they engage in is the process called sharing. In informal discussions they exchange their experiences of fear, frustration, and humiliation and their feelings of inferiority and hopelessness as stutterers. To most participants in such a process, it is extremely liberating to discover that others have had their exact emotions and experiences. The result is a high level of group feeling. They tend to believe that only someone who has stuttered can ever totally understand what it is like to have a stuttering block. They feel like brothers and sisters.

By no means do all stutterers join self-help groups readily. Most would like to forget about the problem when they can and do not find the thought of mingling with other stutterers appealing. But for those who take this step, it is often a turning point in their lives.

Self-help groups are sometimes started by stutterers who have become acquainted in the same treatment program. More often they are established by regional or national self-help organizations. In the United States the principal organizations are the National Stuttering Project, the National Council on Stuttering, and Speak Easy International.

The National Stuttering Project [1]

By far the largest self-help organization of stutterers in the United States was founded in 1977 by Bob Goldman and Michael Sugarman. Goldman, the group's first director, was a 31-year-old administrative consultant with varied organizational experience. Sugarman was a 23-year-old University of California student who had contemplated suicide because of his stuttering when he was 19. The idea for a national organization of stutterers had occurred independently to both of them. They met when Sugarman learned from a California state senator's aide that Goldman had applied to the senator's office for funding for such an organization. By the summer of 1977, they had incorporated the National Stuttering Project in California, had enlisted a board of directors, and from their office—a desk, two-chairs, a telephone, and a typewriter in Goldman's den—were sending grant proposals to philanthropic foundations, news items to every newspaper in the United States, and public service announcements to radio stations throughout the country. The public service announcement read:

> *If you stutter you are not alone. 2.6 million Americans stutter. If you are a person who stutters or a parent of a child who stutters, please contact the National Stuttering Project...*

In response they received about 2,000 requests for information from individuals who wanted to know how to organize a self-help group or how to obtain help for their own or their child's stuttering. In three years the National Stuttering Project had 400 dues-paying members, had established local chapters in a number of cities across the United States, was sending literature to hundreds of stutterers, parents, and speech professionals, and was receiving mail from as far away as Australia, Kenya, and India. In 1981 the directorship, after being held briefly by Sugarman, passed to John Ahlbach, a 28-year-old San Francisco teacher who had been associated with the organization from the beginning. Ahlbach set to work with tireless fervor. By 1985, the NSP had 1,800 members. In that year, Abigail Van Buren's endorsement of the NSP in her syndicated col-

---

1. Address: 2151 Irving Street, Suite 208, San Francisco, California 94122. Phone: (415) 566-5324.

umn *Dear Abby* brought 5,000 letters. By 1991, there were 3,700 members and 58 affiliated self-help groups in 26 states.

Among other activities, the National Stuttering Project distributes information about stuttering to parents, teachers, and stutterers, develops guides for establishing a self-help group and conducting sessions, and publishes a monthly newsletter called *Letting Go*. Each year it organizes regional workshops and a national convention. What stutterers gain from these meetings is best shown by their comments in *Letting Go:*

> *I experienced a sense of worth like I'd never experienced...the affinity which makes us feel so close to each other even though most of us had never met before.*

> *There is no place on earth I have ever felt so accepted, so loved, so needed, so happy and so blessed.*

> *The most healing event I have experienced in my life.*

> *I truly feel like I've come home to my family.*

> *I was Alice crawling through the looking glass. I entered a room where, for the first time in my life, I didn't feel handicapped, where I didn't feel like a freak, and where I had absolutely nothing of importance to hide. I was with people with whom I instantly felt as one. I intimately knew them and they intimately knew me, all before we even spoke.*

The National Stuttering Project champions the causes of individuals who are discriminated against in the workplace because they stutter. It also conducts an ongoing campaign to educate the press and entertainment media, which sometimes foment hurtful misconceptions about stuttering, outright insults, or unflattering portrayals of characters who stutter. For example, a biography of the Roman emperor Claudius describes him as a "clumsy stutterer"; a character in a motion picture asserts that he was once a "lonely stutterer" who needed the love of a good woman to restore his virility. In 1986 the Boston chapter of the NSP, with vigorous support from the membership at large, protested the Massachusetts State Lottery Commission's use of Porky Pig in their radio commercials. As a result, the ad was withdrawn. No doubt many nonstutterers who perceive Porky Pig as endearing and regard stuttering as merely a somewhat eccentric mannerism would be surprised to learn that he is offensive. And when the NSP asked a Chicago television station to take Porky Pig off the air, even a few stutterers rose to the defense of the little porcine. Nevertheless, this cartoon character has probably brought mortification to countless numbers of children. As one member wrote in *Letting Go:*

> *Picture the ten-year-old kid who was very disfluent, watching the rest of the kids laughing at Porky the stutterer on the movie screen...Porky injured our lives. Mel*

Blanc, the voice for Porky, would use the same avoidance, substitution and cir-cumventing schemes that I used. And as a kid who stutters, who was the only kid who stuttered in the whole crowd, this was devastating.

In 1988, MGM released the motion picture *A Fish Called Wanda,* in which the actor Michael Palin portrayed a comic, withdrawn bumbler who stutters profusely until he is cured at the end of the film when he runs over his tormentor with a steamroller. John Ahlbach protested vehemently to the producer and others at MGM, personally handed out leaflets to patrons of a San Francisco theater in which it was being shown, and urged members of the National Stuttering Project to do the same at their local movie houses. Again not all members were in accord, but Ahlbach was well satisfied. Some of the news media had picked up the story and so more of the public had learned to see stuttering as a personal problem rather than an object of fun. In 1988 the National Stuttering Project took this educational effort as far as Congress. As a result, the 100th Congress issued a joint declaration designating the period from May 9th to May 15th as National Stuttering Awareness Week.

The National Council on Stuttering [2]

In the 1970s, local self-help groups were in existence in a number of cities. One such group, calling itself the Council of Adult Stutterers, was meeting regularly in Washington, D. C. at the Catholic University of America, where they had received speech therapy from Eugene L. Walle. In 1973, the idea of a national organization of stutterers took firm hold of one of its members, Michael J. Hartford, a 32-year-old writer of grant proposals for Georgetown University. On the advice of Dr. Walle, Hartford contacted several other local groups, including those in Albany, St. Louis, and Grand Rapids. A meeting was held in St. Louis and, in 1974, the organization now known as the National Council on Stuttering was founded in Washington, D.C. Later the group was headquartered in Michigan and Illinois, following the locations of its most dedicated members, and has been active primarily in the midwest. The organization holds annual conventions and distributes a newsletter.

2. Address: 558 Russell Road, De Kalb, Illinois 60115. Phone: (815) 756-6986.

Speak Easy International [3]

In 1977 Bob Gathman, a linotype operator of Paramus, New Jersey, began to meet regularly with four other stutterers to practice a fluency technique they had learned to use in the same remedial program. Almost immediately, Gathman sensed the broader possibilities presented by stutterers meeting together. In a few months he had recruited a group of 40 members by placing notices in libraries and newspapers. By 1992, Speak Easy International, with Bob Gathman as president and his energetic wife, Antoinette Gathman, as executive director, had grown to an organization of about 300 members with chapters in New York, New Jersey, Connecticut, and Arizona. In addition to sponsoring local chapters, Speak Easy International publishes a newsletter and holds annual symposia featuring workshops on subjects of interest to stutterers and keynote speakers, many of them speech pathologists of national repute who stutter themselves.

Self Help Abroad

The stutterers' self-help movement is a worldwide phenomenon. In 1992, there were national organizations in at least 15 countries. The German group, with more than 500 members in over 40 cities in what was West Germany, calls its newsletter *Der Kieselstein* (the pebble). The Swedish organization has been in existence since 1952 and has chapters in Sweden, Norway, and Finland. The Italian association styles itself *La Lingua Amara* (bitter speech). Japan has its *Genyukai* (Stutterers' Mutual Aid and Friendship Society). Great Britain has its *Association of Stammerers*.

In August 1986, the first international conference of stutterers took place in Kyoto at the invitation of the Japanese. Although most of the more than 300 participants were from various parts of Japan, some came from the United States, Australia, Sweden, Finland, the Netherlands, and West Germany. The symbol of the conference was a woodpecker. At the end of four days of speeches, symposia, workshops, laughter, singing, partying, and fun, the conference adopted a declaration that called on researchers, speech therapists, and stutterers around the world to broaden the communication network through publications and international conferences to the end of solving the problem of stuttering.

3. Address: 233 Concord Drive, Paramus, New Jersey 07652. Phone: (201) 262-0895.

A Second World Conference of Self-Help Groups took place in Cologne, West Germany in August 1989, and was attended by approximately 500 people from 20 countries. The scene was aptly described by Thomas Krall, a 34-year-old Düsseldorf schoolteacher who was relatively new to self help and had never attended a stutterers' convention:

> *Over 400 stutterers on one spot. Everyone I spoke to stuttered—some more, some less—and everyone had his own way of stuttering. Even severe stutterers had the courage to express themselves at the microphone in front of the whole hall. I was very much impressed by a 22-year-old woman from New Zealand. She flies halfway around the world, ventures onto the stage, stutters through an account of herself and her national organization, and walks beaming off the stage, quite well unaware as yet that these five steps onto the stage were a milestone on her way to the conquest of anxiety.*[4]

From all accounts, the most memorable event of the second international conference for most participants was the performance of a theater piece written and directed by Irving Burton, a professional actor, and performed by himself and several other members of the Speak Easy International Foundation. Entitled *Why Can't We Talk?* it satirizes a stutterer's avoidance strategies and portrays his frustrations as he attempts unsuccessfully to cope with the purchase of a railroad ticket, a job interview, a date, a ringing telephone, and other situations. Stutterers instantly recognize themselves. The play had received extraordinary ovations at annual conferences of Speak Easy for eight successive years. When it was presented in Cologne the effect was explosive. Here again is Thomas Krall:

> *The piece tore the audience right out of their seats. Unbelievable salvos of laughter—liberating, long-drawn-out, deafening laughter. It was the most beautiful evening of theater I had ever experienced, and the crown: The 66-year-old principal, he stood on the stage though he was ill, he wept after the piece, wept and said to us fellow stutterers: "This is the most beautiful evening of my life!" I could not believe it, yet afterwards I had to believe it. He was so stirred and wept for joy.*[5]

The Self-Help Viewpoint

Whether in the United States or elsewhere, members of stutterers' self-help groups tend to share certain values and perceptions that amount in the aggregate to a group ideology, although self-helpers are rarely unan-

4. From *Der Kieselstein*, November 1989, p. 24.
5. Ibid., p. 25.

imous on any issue. Most, for example, take a great deal of heart from the consensus among speech pathologists that there is probably some kind of organic component in stuttering and it is common for them to assert flatly that stuttering is "physiological." If such assertions seem to go too far, they are understandable as a triumphant counterreaction to their own and others' conception of stuttering as an emotional disorder. The knowledge that there is probably some organic basis for stuttering tends to free them from the stigma of an unfavorable home environment and from the lowered self-esteem that comes from the belief that one is afflicted by a weakness that an adequate person should be able to overcome or control.

If there is anything on which group members are unanimous it is in the belief in their self worth as individuals in spite of the fact that they stutter. Their manifesto, as it were, is: Don't think less of yourself because you stutter; you are not less intelligent, more neurotic, or inferior to others in any way because you stutter; don't hide your stuttering; assert your right to speak without fear or embarrassment even though you stutter. Members of the German organization of self-help groups wear a button that says, "Ich stottere—na und?" (I stutter—so what?). Their motto is "Besser stottern als schweigen" (It's better to stutter than to keep silent). When the Japanese "Genyukai" celebrated their first ten years of existence in 1976, they adopted a "Declaration of People Who Stutter" that reads in part:

> For too long a time we have attempted to conceal our stuttering and to close our mouths, living in grief and fear in the common misapprehension that stuttering is a defect, a disability, a disease... We invite all our fellows who stutter all over the country: stop looking down on yourself because of your disfluent speech! Devote your energies to a constructive life in society, rather than daydream of a life without stuttering!

Self-help groups encourage pride in the accomplishments of famous stutterers. Among the local chapters of the National Stuttering Project are some with such names as the Isaac Newton Club, the Lewis Carroll Club, the W. Somerset Maugham Club, the Winston Churchill Club, and the Marilyn Monroe Club. The letters that stutterers write to the editor of *Letting Go* are full of affirmations of self-acceptance like the following:

> Now that I have stopped running from stuttering...my life is rich with friendship and support...I'm not going to let this thing hold me down any longer. Life is too short.

> I know I can feel good about myself in spite of my speech.

> It has just been so much better not hiding it.

> For me, this is one of the most important aspects, just not hiding it anymore.

Trying to hide your stuttering is like trying to hide a watermelon under your T-shirt.

The value that self-help groups attach to self-acceptance as stutterers exerts a strong influence on their attitudes toward speech therapy. As might be expected, there is a noticeable leaning toward the treatment methods of the Iowa school. This leaning is by no means universal. Various therapies are endorsed and condemned in the pages of *Letting Go* in accordance with the writers' individual experiences. But Iowa therapy, with its emphasis on modification rather than avoidance of stuttering, and on stuttering without fear, is in accord with the most cherished values of the self-help movement. Van Riper and Sheehan are much revered names. By contrast, certain aspects of the behavior therapies often evoke disapproval. The behavior therapist's optimistic view that normal fluency is an attainable goal often grates. Most stutterers who are involved in self help are well aware of the difficulty of eradicating stuttering totally and permanently in adult cases and many adopt it as an article of faith that stuttering is "incurable." There is particular resentment of some behavior therapists' readiness to assume that when stutterers fail to reach the goal of normal fluency, it is because they have not worked hard enough to acquire the therapist's fluency "technique."

For many stutterers, the technique itself may be a sore point. The common stock in trade of behavior therapy is an artificial pattern of speech. To stutterers who are imbued with the attitude that their stuttering should not matter to their self-esteem, it may seem an affront to be told that it is better to talk in some unnatural manner than to stutter. Irving Burton offered a devastating parody of this type of speech therapy in the theater piece, *Why Can't We Talk?* that has earned accolades at self-help conventions. In one sketch, he plays the part of a hapless stutterer who has been trained to talk fluently by beginning each word with the vibratory disturbance variously known as a razzberry or Bronx cheer. The audience is convulsed.

Although the self-help movement often looks with a jaundiced eye on certain aspects of professional stuttering therapy, its relationships with the profession of speech pathology have with rare exceptions been excellent. The stutterers' groups have organized presentations that have been eagerly attended by speech clinicians at professional conventions and speech pathologists have frequently appeared at regional and national self-help meetings. The National Stuttering Project invites membership on the part of professionals as well as stutterers. Surprisingly, Michael Sugarman, reflecting in *Letting Go* on the early years of the organization that he helped establish, wrote: "All along we fought the attitudes of 'professionals' opposed to the NSP style of self-empowerment."

What Sugarman encountered far from represents the attitude of the vast majority of workers in the speech and hearing field. Helping stutterers to rid themselves of fear and shame has come to be recognized as a necessary aim of speech therapy, regardless of what other clinical methods are employed, and most speech therapists know that a self-help group can contribute far more to that end than anything that therapists have it in their power to do.

CHAPTER NINETEEN

Conclusion

The Search in Brief

The endeavor to find an explanation for stuttering is centuries old. In every era, the search has been shaped by what people thought they knew about aberrant behavior. Throughout antiquity and the middle ages little distinction was made between medicine and what we now call psychology. Disorders were of the body. And almost nothing was known about how we speak except that it obviously involved some activity of the oral structures, especially the tongue. So for more than a millennium physicians ruminated about the stutterer's tongue and what could be done about it. When scientific research on stuttering began in the early decades of the twentieth century, a physiological outlook on the problem was consequently dominant. Far more was now known about the physiology of speech and although much remained, and remains, to be learned about the role of the brain in speech production, it was clear that the brain was a more promising site to look for the source of stuttering than the tongue. Reflecting this outlook, the Orton-Travis theory of cerebral dominance came to the fore and for a brief period seemed to many to provide an ingenious explanation of the disorder. At the same time, Robert West offered a considerable refinement of the old organic viewpoint in his concept that stuttering resulted from an interaction of genetic predisposing factors with environmental precipitating causes. In the hope of establishing the organic component, West, Travis, and their students initiated investigations that ranged widely over neuromuscular, cardiovascular, biochemical, and other aspects of the stutterer's physiology. Neither the Orton-Travis theory nor any other organic hypothesis was confirmed by this research. In the end, on the contrary, the studies

175

served mainly to rule out the possibility that stutterers differ from others in any gross aspects of bodily constitution. If any differences existed, they were evidently too subtle to be captured by physiological tests of any ordinary kind. West's efforts to demonstrate the role of heredity in stuttering were likewise in vain. True, stuttering was remarkably common in the family backgrounds of stutterers. And a study of twins showed a much higher concordance for stuttering in identical than fraternal pairs. But neither observation constituted indisputable proof; both could be explained on the basis of social environment. And in the 1930s environmental explanations of stuttering were beginning to be appealing.

Theories of stuttering of a broadly psychological nature had emerged much earlier from time to time. In particular, a number of nineteenth-century physicians, some of whom intimately knew the subjective side of stuttering from personal experience, wrote about the problem as a symptom of the speaker's mistaken belief in the difficulty of speech. The coming of the Freudian era gave a powerful impetus to psychological speculations, and by the 1930s the enormous prestige of psychoanalysis had convinced the majority of workers in the helping professions and most of the educated public that stuttering was the expression of deep-seated emotional conflicts. The long series of conflicting and inconclusive personality studies of stutterers that were done between 1930 and 1960 finally led to an almost total rejection of the neurotic theory in the field of speech pathology. But by then, the influence of Freud had created a pervasive new intellectual climate in which biological heredity counted for relatively little in human development and early environmental influences were seen as decisive. In this climate, Wendell Johnson's theory that stuttering is caused chiefly by parents who diagnose their child's normal speech hesitations as stuttering found an unprecedented degree of acceptance on the part of speech pathologists. The diagnosogenic theory proved difficult to verify due to the practical impossibility of observing a child's speech at the moment of original diagnosis by the parent, but it led to much useful research on the phenomena of stuttering. The theory implied that a moment of stuttering was nothing more than an effort of avoidance that a speaker makes in anticipation of stuttering, an idea that was closely allied to the century-old notion that stuttering is the attempt to avoid an imagined difficulty in speech. The research that Johnson and his students did in an attempt to verify this concept by no means settled the question of the nature of the stuttering block, but it resulted in new or more precise knowledge of the conditions under which stuttering occurs and the manner in which it is distributed in the speech sequence. Johnson's view of stuttering as wholly learned behavior gave rise to interpretations of stuttering phenomena in terms of psychological theories of learning.

In the 1950s, when the assumption that stuttering is learned behavior held full sway, a dormant organic interest showed the first signs of reawakening. The discovery of the white noise effect in stutterers and the demonstration of "artificial stutter" in normal speakers through delayed auditory feedback created a brief preoccupation with the possibility that stutterers possess an anomaly of some type in the auditory perception of their own speech. Then in 1966 came Jones's curious report of four stutterers whose Wada tests showed an absence of cerebral dominance for speech before brain surgery, followed by normal dominance as well as remission of stuttering after surgery. The result was a long series of studies of stutterers' cerebral dominance for speech by dichotic listening tests, electroencephalography, and other techniques. Although the findings were not entirely consistent, by the 1980s they had created a distinct suspicion that right-sided or deficient cerebral dominance for speech was unusually prevalent among stutterers. In addition, it had been conclusively shown that stutterers have longer vocal reaction times, on the average, than nonstutterers. What such observations might mean is still not known at this writing.

Along with the revival of constitutional research came renewed interest in the heredity of stuttering. By the 1980s more studies of stuttering in twins had confirmed the high concordance for the disorder in identical pairs. And the research of Kidd and his associates on stutterers' family histories had convinced most workers that the familial transmission of stuttering was indeed biological. But these very same lines of investigation produced the most conclusive evidence that environment also plays a significant part in the development of stuttering, and this inference drew additional support from a report of discordance for stuttering in several pairs of identical twins who had been separated at birth. Exactly what it is about a child's home environment or developmental experience that increases the risk of stuttering is something we cannot yet state dogmatically, but clinical observations and some research findings hint strongly at pressures or failures that have to do specifically with a child's speech competence. As I write this in April of 1992, the best guess I can make about the cause of stuttering is that many, though perhaps not all, stutterers have a hereditary something that has predisposed them in some way to stutter and that the disorder is often, though perhaps not always, precipitated by circumstances that imbue the child with an expectation of failure at language, articulation, or some other aspect of speech.

Like theories of the cause of stuttering, assumptions about its treatment have vacillated between widely divergent views. Relaxation, suggestion, psychotherapy, hypnosis, drugs, operant conditioning, and many other forms of therapy have been tried. But reduced to its simplest essentials, our attempt to aid stutterers has veered back and forth between methods that teach them to talk differently and methods that teach them to stutter differently. The talk-differently methods were used widely in the nineteenth century, when many stutterers were taught to achieve immediate fluency by prolonging syllables, speaking in time to rhythm, using a monotone or unusual inflections, or changing the way they breathed or articulated in some way. One disadvantage of this approach was that it resulted in a bizarre speech pattern. Another serious drawback was that the benefit was often only temporary. The approach consequently came under a cloud of disapprobation in the United States, and by the early decades of the twentieth century it had been largely relegated to commercial "stammering schools" of doubtful reputation. Some advocated psychoanalysis in its place, but after many decades of experience with psychoanalytic and other forms of psychotherapy as a treatment for stuttering, it can be said with some assurance that they have not been outstandingly effective in the great majority of cases.

The 1930s witnessed the beginning of speech pathology as a profession in the United States. Along with some short-lived attempts to treat stutterers by changing their handedness, three students of Travis—Bryngelson, Johnson, and Van Riper—developed the form of stuttering therapy that speech pathologists were to use almost exclusively for the next thirty years. The University of Iowa therapists were motivated by a deep distrust of techniques that resulted in immediate fluency. Together with the management and reduction of fear, they aimed at the amelioration of stuttering by analysis with the stutterer of the behavior of which it consisted and the substitution of a mild, simple form of voluntary disfluency for the old stuttering reactions. Iowa therapy proved to be of benefit to many stutterers, but it had an outstanding drawback: by its very nature it almost never resulted in completely normal fluency. By the 1960s, clinical psychologists had borrowed the conditioning techniques of experimental psychology to develop a treatment for human problems that they called behavior modification or behavior therapy. In this innovation a new generation of speech pathologists glimpsed the possibility of a total cure for stuttering. For a brief period their efforts were confined to the use of conditioning, but set free as they were to experiment with cures for stuttering, they soon found a simpler and quicker way to establish fluency in the talk-differently techniques. In the space of a few years the practitioners of Iowa therapy became a minority; most clinicians were employing rhythmic speech, syllable prolongation, gentle onsets of phonation, or a breath management method called "airflow." For a short time optimism reigned. In time, however, the clinicians who had rediscovered the talk-differently approach rediscovered its problems. By the 1980s, speech pathologists were assiduously working on techniques aimed at ameliorating relapse, enhancing speech "naturalness," and transferring fluency to situations outside the speech clinic. In the end, a major development was the search for ways to integrate features of behavior therapy and Iowa therapy in order to secure some of the benefits of each.

EPILOGUE

Decades ago, Wendell Johnson marvelled at the vast amount of intellectual effort that has been expended in the attempt to account for stuttering. At the date of this book, the thinking and writing are continuing at a greater pace than ever before, and so the effort has clearly not attained its goal. Yet it has been far from futile. We have virtually ruled out the prevalent notion that stuttering is due to an underlying emotional conflict created by parents. And the old theory that it is simply a neurological symptom appears equally untenable. It is almost certain that heredity plays a significant role and we may be on the trail of some subtle features of brain functioning that have a bearing in some as yet unknown way. We can also make some plausible guesses about speech pressures in a child's environment that seem to precipitate the problem or lead to its persistence.

Perhaps it is hardly to be wondered at that stuttering appears to be a complex product of both social environment and heredity. On the one hand, speech is by far the most important function through which we make an impression on the world; how surprising if it were not vulnerable to social pressures. As for heredity, it was Robert West who pointed out that stuttering is ultimately to be viewed as a predictable outcome of biological evolution. Human speech is a function overlaid on ancient systems for eating and respiration. Because it is one of the latest abilities we acquired, he mused, it is one of the most readily lost or impaired.

We have not yet totally succeeded in our endeavor to find the cause and cure for stuttering, but there is far more hope for stutterers than ever before. Where children are concerned, the outlook for recovery is generally excellent. This is not to say that we always help children to achieve it, but we do so often enough that recovery is a realistic expectation where adequate remediation is available. A major qualification is that the help that stuttering children receive is by no means always adequate. This is especially true of much of the remediation that is offered by schools. Too many school systems employ speech personnel with a minimum of training and burden them with heavy case loads. Some of these "speech teachers" seem to achieve outstanding results by dint of sheer devotion. But more often their failures imbue them with a false belief in the difficulty of overcoming stuttering that may communicate itself to the children with unfortunate effect. To be adequately prepared to work with stutterers, a clinician must have as a bare minimum the *Certificate of Clinical Competence* in speech pathology from the American Speech-Language-Hearing Association (ASHA).[1] ASHA requires a masters degree from an approved training program and a year of supervised professional experience. In many states, comparable standards are enforced by governmental licensing of speech pathologists, but these requirements are often circumvented by the use of titles such as "speech improvement teacher" or the like. As a result, many schoolchildren are receiving speech therapy from workers who are neither certified nor licensed. It is evident that the willingness of society to bear the cost of ridding children of stuttering often lags behind our knowledge of how to do it.

In adulthood, totally overcoming stuttering is far more difficult, but adults who stutter can today realistically hope for marked improvement, by modifying either the way they stutter or the way they speak. Although this may seem only a modest achievement, the difference between the problem of a person who is panicked and tormented by stuttering and that of someone who stutters mildly and occasionally and can master such occasions calmly is incalculable. Nevertheless, the question remains whether we will be able to offer adult stutterers in the foreseeable future a realistic expectation of attaining completely normal speech. A compelling argument that this may be an achievable goal is that occasional recoveries from stuttering do take place in adulthood.

There appear to be two conditions under which adults recover. One is treatment, and it is a remarkable fact that virtually any kind of treatment seems to have this capability. The methods that have been reported to have cured people of stuttering in isolated cases include the application of a foam rubber vibrator, speaking with gestures, hypnosis, speaking on inhalation of breath, psychotherapy, and dozens of others. To be sure, in most of these cases the cure was very probably temporary, but in rare instances it seems to have been long lasting. It is difficult to think of any other explanation for these recoveries than the stutterer's faith that the treatment was going to work.

The other condition under which adults completely recover from stuttering is a life experience that radically alters their values and priorities. A narrow escape from death has been known to have that effect. One woman stopped stuttering when she survived an airplane crash. A young man was cured when he almost lost his life in a machine-shop accident. The incident is said to have made his old problems and anxieties

---

1. Address: 10801 Rockville Pike, Rockville, Maryland 20852. Phone: (301) 897-5700.

seem like trifles. Born again religious experiences have also been reported to result in sudden recoveries. A student with whom I was acquainted was convinced by a friend that she could overcome her stuttering by becoming a Christian Scientist. She did, and had no further difficulty with her speech. The same process may occur slowly and unobtrusively, as when a young college student goes on to postgraduate study, becomes established in a profession and responsible for a family, experiences changes in his view of himself and his outlook on life, and gradually seems to forget to stutter.

In all of these examples the common factor seems to be the eradication of a person's self-concept as a stutterer. No wonder that adult recoveries happen so seldom. Under ordinary conditions, it is virtually impossible to forget that one is a stutterer. The power of a belief can hardly be overestimated. But rare as such recoveries are, they show that even in adulthood the difficulty is in principle remediable. Stuttering is not an incurable disease. There is reason to believe that in the future we will be able to offer adult stutterers more hope of totally normal speech. But the fact that we cannot do so as yet means that for the time being we must apply ourselves unstintingly to the treatment of stuttering in children. How well we will fulfill both of these aims depends on how soon we as a society awaken fully to the seriousness of stuttering as a disorder. Fortunately, this recognition seems to be developing at a quickening pace. Stuttering is receiving an increasing share of moderately sensible media attention. Among professional workers, a consensus is in the making that an adequate response to the problem requires the training of specialists in its treatment. Organized efforts in behalf of stutterers are multiplying year by year. The American Speech-Language-Hearing Association has established a special division for clinicians and researchers concerned with stuttering. The International Fluency Association was founded in 1990 with the aim of promoting research and therapy for stuttering worldwide. The Stuttering Foundation of America sponsors and distributes literature for parents, stutterers, and clinicians.[2] The Stuttering Resource Foundation has developed videotaped public service announcements concerning stuttering and a directory of speech clinics and therapists adequately prepared to deal with stuttering.[3] Especially promising is the rise of consumer advocacy on the part of stutterers in a vigorous new self-help movement. In short, there are hopeful signs that we are moving closer to the possibility of a world with fewer people who live with a hobble on the faculty that makes them human.

2. Address: P.O. Box 11749, Memphis, Tennessee 38111-0749. Phone: (800) 992-9392.

3. Address: 123 Oxford Road, New Rochelle, New York 10804. Phones: (914) 632-3925, (800) 232-4773.

Bibliography

Chapter 1

Suggested Reading
Bloodstein, O. (1987). *A Handbook on Stuttering*, 4th ed. (Chicago: National Easter Seal Society), Chapters 1-3.
Van Riper, C. (1982). *The Nature of Stuttering*, 2nd ed. (Englewood Cliffs, N.J.: Prentice-Hall), Chapters 1-3.

Chapter 2

Suggested Reading
Freund, H. (1966). *Psychopathology and the Problems of Stuttering* (Springfield, Ill.: Charles C. Thomas), Chapters 1-3.
Rieber, R. W., and Wollock, J., "The Historical Roots of the Theory and Therapy of Stuttering," *Journal of Communication Disorders*, 10 (1977), 3-24.

Chapter 3

References
Brill, A. A., "Speech Disturbances in Nervous and Mental Diseases," *Quarterly Journal of Speech Education*, 9 (1923), 129-135.
Coriat, I. H., "Stammering. A Psychoanalytic Interpretation," *Nervous and Mental Diseases Monographs*, 47 (1928), 1-68.
Dahlstrom, W. G., and Craven, D. D., "The MMPI and Stuttering Phenomena in Young Adults," *American Psychologist*, 7 (1952), 341.
Fenichel, O. (1945). *The Psychoanalytic Theory of Neurosis* (New York: W. W. Norton).

Suggested Reading
Bloodstein, O. (1987). *A Handbook on Stuttering*, 4th ed. (Chicago: National Easter Seal Society), Chapter 5.
Bloom, L., "Notes for a History of Speech Pathology," *Psychoanalytic Review*, 65 (1978), 433-463.
Glauber, I. P. (1958). "The Psychoanalysis of Stuttering," in Eisenson, J. (ed.), *Stuttering: A Symposium* (New York: Harper & Row).
Goodstein, L. D., "Functional Speech Disorders and Personality: A Survey of the Research," *Journal of Speech and Hearing Research*, 1 (1958), 359-376.
Sheehan, J. G. (1970). *Stuttering: Research and Therapy* (New York: Harper & Row), Chapter 3.

Chapter 4

References
Daniels, E. M., "An Analysis of the Relation Between Handedness and Stuttering with Special Reference to the Orton-Travis Theory of Cerebral Dominance," *Journal of Speech Disorders*, 5 (1940), 309-326.
Johnson, W. and King, A., "An Angle Board and Hand Usage Study of Stutterers and Non-Stutterers," *Journal of Experimental Psychology*, 31 (1942), 293-311.
Travis, L. E. (1931). *Speech Pathology* (New York: D. Appleton-Century).
Travis, L. E., "Dissociation of the Homologous Muscle Function in Stuttering," *Archives of Neurology and Psychiatry*, 31 (1934), 127-133.
Van Riper, C., "The Quantitative Measurement of Laterality," *Journal of Experimental Psychology*, 18 (1935), 372-382.
Williams, D. E., "Masseter Muscle Action Potentials in Stuttered and Nonstuttered Speech," *Journal of Speech and Hearing Disorders*, 20 (1955), 242-261.

Chapter 5

References
Berry, M. F., "Developmental History of Stuttering Children," *Journal of Pediatrics*, 12 (1938), 209-217.
Berry, M. F., "A Study of the Medical History of Stuttering Children," *Speech Monographs*, 5 (1938), 97-114.
Nelson, S. E., "Personal Contact as a Factor in the Transfer of Stuttering," *Human Biology*, 11 (1939), 393-401.
Nelson, S. E., Hunter, N., and Walter, M., "Stuttering in Twin Types," *Journal of Speech Disorders*, 10 (1945), 335-343.
West, R. (1958). "An Agnostic's Speculations About Stuttering," in Eisenson, J. (ed.), *Stuttering: A Symposium* (New York: Harper & Row).
West, R., Nelson, S., and Berry, M. F., "The Heredity of Stuttering," *Quarterly Journal of Speech*, 25 (1939), 23-30.

Chapter 6

References
Dunlap, K. (1932). *Habits: Their Making and Unmaking* (New York: Liveright).
Korzybski, A. (1941). *Science and Sanity: An Introduction to Non-Aristotelian Systems and General Semantics*. 2nd ed. (New York: Int. Non-Aristotelian Library Publishing Co.).
Van Riper, C., "The Preparatory Set in Stuttering," *Journal of Speech Disorders*, 2 (1937), 149-154.

Suggested Reading
Johnson, W. (1961). *Stuttering and What You Can Do About It* (Minneapolis: Univ. Minn. Press), Chapter 11.
Johnson, W. et al (1967). *Speech Handicapped School-Children*, 3rd ed. (New York: Harper & Row).
Van Riper, C. (1958). "Experiments in Stuttering Therapy," in Eisenson, J. (ed.), *Stuttering: A Symposium* (New York: Harper & Row).

Van Riper, C. (1973). *The Treatment of Stuttering* (Englewood Cliffs, N.J.: Prentice-Hall), Chapters 8-13.
Williams, D. E., "A Point of View About 'Stuttering,'" *Journal of Speech and Hearing Disorders*, 22 (1957), 390-397.

Chapter 7

References
Andrews, G. and Harris, M. (1964). *The Syndrome of Stuttering* (London: Wm. Heinemann Medical Books), Chapter 3.
Bender, J. F. (1939). *The Personality Structure of Stuttering* (New York: Pitman Publishing Corp.).
Bluemel, C. S., "Primary and Secondary Stammering," *Quarterly Journal of Speech,* 18 (1932), 187-200.
Bullen, A. K., "A Cross-Cultural Approach to the Problem of Stuttering," *Child Development,* 16 (1945), 1-88.
Froeschels, E., "Beitrage Zur Symptomatologie des Stotterns," *Monatsschrift fuer Ohrenheilkunde,* 55 (1921), 1109-1112.
Gray, M., "The X Family: A Clinical and Laboratory Study of a 'Stuttering' Family," *Journal of Speech Disorders,* 5 (1940), 343-348.
Johnson, W., "The Indians Have No Word for It. I. Stuttering in Children," *Quarterly Journal of Speech,* 30 (1944), 330-337.
Johnson, W. et al, "A Study of the Onset and Development of Stuttering," *Journal of Speech Disorders,* 7 (1942), 251-257.
Lemert, E. M., "Some Indians Who Stutter," *Journal of Speech and Hearing Disorders,* 18 (1953), 168-174.
Morgenstern, J. J., "Socio-Economic Factors in Stuttering," *Journal of Speech and Hearing Disorders,* 21 (1956), 25-33.
Morgenstern, J. J. (1953). *Psychological and Social Factors in Children's Stammering.* Ph.D. Dissert., Univ. Edinburgh.
Zimmermann, G., Liljeblad, S., Frank, A., and Cleeland, C., "The Indians Have Many Terms for It: Stuttering Among the Bannock-Shoshoni," *Journal of Speech and Hearing Research,* 26 (1983), 315-318.

Suggested Reading
Johnson, W. and Associates (1959). *The Onset of Stuttering* (Minneapolis: Univ. Minn. Press).
Johnson, W. (1961). *Stuttering and What You Can Do About It* (Minneapolis: Univ. Minn. Press), Chapters 1-9.

Chapter 8

References
Avari, D. N. and Bloodstein, O., "Adjacency and Prediction in School-Age Stutterers," *Journal of Speech and Hearing Research,* 17 (1974), 33-40.
Bloodstein, O., "A Rating Scale Study of Conditions under which Stuttering is Reduced or Absent," *Journal of Speech and Hearing Disorders,* 15 (1950), 29-36.
Bloodstein, O., "Hypothetical Conditions under which Stuttering is Reduced or Absent," *Journal of Speech and Hearing Disorders,* 15 (1950), 142-153.

Brown, S. F., "The Influence of Grammatical Function on the Incidence of Stuttering," *Journal of Speech Disorders*, 2 (1937), 207-215.

Brown, S. F., "Stuttering with Relation to Word Accent and Word Position," *Journal of Abnormal and Social Psychology*, 33 (1938), 112-120.

Brown, S. F., "The Loci of Stutterings in the Speech Sequence," *Journal of Speech Disorders*, 10 (1945), 181-192.

Brown, S. F. and Moren, A., "The Frequency of Stuttering in Relation to Word Length in Oral Reading," *Journal of Speech Disorders*, 7 (1942), 153-159.

Forte, M. and Schlesinger, I. M., "Stuttering as a Function of Time of Expectation," *Journal of Communication Disorders*, 5 (1972), 347-358.

Goss, A. E., "Stuttering Behavior and Anxiety Theory: I. Stuttering Behavior and Anxiety as a Function of the Duration of Stimulus Words," *Journal of Abnormal and Social Psychology*, 47 (1952), 38-50.

Hendel, D. and Bloodstein, O., "Consistency in Relation to Inter-Subject Congruity in the Loci of Stutterings," *Journal of Communication Disorders*, 6 (1973), 37-43.

Johnson, W. and Brown, S. F., "Stuttering in Relation to Various Speech Sounds," *Quarterly Journal of Speech*, 21 (1935), 481-496.

Johnson, W. and Knott, J. R., "The Moment of Stuttering," *Journal of Genetic Psychology*, 48 (1936), 475-479.

Johnson, W. and Knott, J. R., "Studies in the Psychology of Stuttering: I. The Distribution of Moments of Stuttering in Successive Readings of the Same Material," *Journal of Speech Disorders*, 2 (1937), 17-19.

Johnson, W., Larson, R. P., and Knott, J. R., "Studies in the Psychology of Stuttering: III. Certain Objective Cues Related to the Precipitation of Moments of Stuttering," *Journal of Speech Disorders*, 2 (1937), 23-25.

Johnson, W. and Millsapps, L. S., "Studies in the Psychology of Stuttering: VI. The Role of Cues Representative of Moments of Stuttering During Oral Reading, *Journal of Speech Disorders*, 2 (1937), 101-104.

Knott, J. R., Johnson, W., and Webster, M. J., "Studies in the Psychology of Stuttering: II. A Quantitative Evaluation of Expectation of Stuttering in Relation to the Occurrence of Stuttering," *Journal of Speech Disorders*, 2 (1937), 20-22.

Quarrington, B., "Stuttering as a Function of the Information Value and Sentence Position of Words," *Journal of Abnormal Psychology*, 70 (1965), 221-224.

Rappaport, B, and Bloodstein, O., "The Role of Random Blackout Cues in the Distribution of Moments of Stuttering," *Journal of Speech and Hearing Research*, 14 (1971), 874-879.

Schlesinger, I. M., Forte, M., Fried, B., and Melkman, R., "Stuttering, Information Load, and Response Strength," *Journal of Speech and Hearing* Disorders, 30 (1965), 32-36.

Silverman, F. H. and Williams, D. E., "Prediction of Stuttering by School-Age Stutterers," *Journal of Speech and Hearing Research*, 15 (1972), 189-193.

Stefankiewicz, S. P. and Bloodstein, O., "The Effect of a Four-Week Interval on the Consistency of Stuttering," *Journal of Speech and Hearing Research*, 17 (1974), 141-145.

Tornick, G. B. and Bloodstein, O., "Stuttering and Sentence Length," *Journal of Speech and Hearing Research*, 19 (1976), 651-654.

Van Riper, C., "Study of the Thoracic Breathing of Stutterers during Expectancy and Occurrence of Stuttering Spasm," *Journal of Speech Disorders*, 1 (1936), 61-72.

Chapter 9

References
Hull, C. L. (1943). *Principles of Behavior* (New York: D. Appleton-Century).
Miller, N. E. (1944). "Experimental Studies of Conflict," in Hunt, J. McV. (ed.), *Personality and the Behavior Disorders* (New York: Ronald Press).
Sheehan, J. G., "Theory and Treatment of Stuttering as Approach-Avoidance Conflict," *Journal of Psychology*, 36 (1953), 27-49.

Suggested Reading
Sheehan, J. G. (1975). "Conflict Theory of Stuttering," in Eisenson, J. (ed.), *Stuttering: A Second Symposium*, (New York: Harper & Row).
Wischner, G. J., "Stuttering Behavior and Learning: A Preliminary Theoretical Formulation," *Journal of Speech and Hearing Disorders*, 15 (1950), 324-335.
Wischner, G. J., "An Experimental Approach to Expectancy and Anxiety in Stuttering Behavior," *Journal of Speech and Hearing Disorders*, 17 (1952), 139-154.

Chapter 10

References
Andrews, G. and Dozsa, M., "Haloperidol and the Treatment of Stuttering," *Journal of Fluency Disorders*, 2 (1977), 217-224.
Burns, D., Brady, J. P., and Kuruvilla, K., "The Acute Effect of Haloperidol and Apomorphine on the Severity of Stuttering," *Biological Psychiatry*, 13 (1978), 255-264.
Murray, T. J., Kelly, P., Campbell, L., and Stefanik, K., "Haloperidol in the Treatment of Stuttering," *British Journal of Psychiatry*, 130 (1977), 370-373.

Suggested Reading
Brady, J. P., "The Pharmacology of Stuttering: A Critical Review," *American Journal of Psychiatry*, 148 (1991), 1309-1316.
Burr, H. G. and Mullendore, J. M., "Recent Investigations on Tranquilizers and Stuttering," *Journal of Speech and Hearing Disorders*, 25 (1960), 33-37.
Kent, L. R., "The Use of Tranquilizers in the Treatment of Stuttering," *Journal of Speech and Hearing Disorders*, 28 (1963), 288–294.

Chapter 11

References
Cherry, C. and Sayers, B., "Experiments upon the Total Inhibition of Stammering by External Control and Some Clinical Results," *Journal of Psychosomatic Research*, 1 (1956), 233-246.
Cherry, C., Sayers, B., and Marland, P. M., "Experiments on the Complete Suppression of Stammering," *Nature*, 176 (1955), 874-875.
Fairbanks, G., "Systematic Research in Experimental Phonetics: I. A Theory of the Speech Mechanism as a Servosystem," *Journal of Speech and Hearing Disorders*, 19 (1954), 133-139.

Lee, B. S., "Artificial Stutter," *Journal of Speech and Hearing Disorders*, 16 (1951), 53-55.
Shane, M. L. S. (1955), "Effect on Stuttering of Alteration in Auditory Feedback," in Johnson, W. and Leutenegger, R. R. (eds.), *Stuttering in Children and Adults* (Minneapolis: Univ. Minn. Press).
Sutton, S. and Chase, R. A., "White Noise and Stuttering," *Journal of Speech and Hearing Research*, 4 (1961), 72.

Suggested Reading
Mysak, E. D., "Servo Theory and Stuttering," *Journal of Speech and Hearing Disorders*, 25 (1960), 188-195.

Chapter 12

References
Andrews, G. and Harris, M. (1964). *The Syndrome of Stuttering* (London: Wm. Heinemann Medical Books), Chapter 8.
Brady, J. P., "A Behavioral Approach to the Treatment of Stuttering," *American Journal of Psychiatry*, 125 (1968), 843-848.
Brady, J. P., "Metronome-Conditioned Speech Retraining for Stuttering," *Behavior Therapy*, 2 (1971), 129-150.
Cooper, E. B., Cady, B. B., and Robbins, C. J., "The Effect of the Verbal Stimulus Words *Wrong, Right,* and *Tree* on the Disfluency Rates of Stutterers and Nonstutterers," *Journal of Speech and Hearing Research*, 13 (1970), 239-244.
Curlee, R. F. and Perkins, W. H., "Effectiveness of a DAF Conditioning Program for Adolescent and Adult Stutterers," *Behavior Research and Therapy*, 11 (1973), 395-401.
Flanagan, B., Goldiamond, I., and Azrin, N. "Operant Stuttering: The Control of Stuttering Behavior through Response-Contingent Consequences," *Journal of the Experimental Analysis of Behavior*, 1 (1958), 173-177.
Goldiamond, I. (1965). "Stuttering and Fluency as Manipulatable Response Classes," in Krasner, L. and Ullmann, L. P. (eds.), *Research in Behavior Modification* (New York: Holt, Rinehart & Winston).
Guitar, B., "Reduction of Stuttering Frequency using Analog Electromyographic Feedback," *Journal of Speech and Hearing Research*, 18 (1975), 672-685.
Ingham, R. J. and Andrews, G., "An Analysis of a Token Economy in Stuttering Therapy," *Journal of Applied Behavioral Analysis*, 6 (1973), 219-229.
Ingham, R. J., Southwood, H., and Horsburgh, G., "Some Effects of the Edinburgh Masker on Stuttering during Oral Reading and Spontaneous Speech," *Journal of Fluency Disorders*, 6 (1981), 135-154.
Martin, R. R. (1981). "Introduction and Perspective: Review of Published Studies," in Boberg, E. (ed.), *Maintenance of Fluency: Proceedings of the Banff Conference* (New York: Elsevier North-Holland).
Martin, R. R., Kuhl, P., and Haroldson, S., "An Experimental Treatment with Two Preschool Stuttering Children," *Journal of Speech and Hearing Research*, 15 (1972), 743-752.
Martin, R. R. and Siegel, G. M., "The Effects of Response Contingent Shock on Stuttering," *Journal of Speech and Hearing Research*, 9 (1966), 340-352.
Martin, R. R. and Siegel, G. M., "The Effects of Simultaneously Punishing Stuttering and Rewarding Fluency," *Journal of Speech and Hearing Research*, 9 (1966), 466-475.

Perkins, W. H., "Replacement of Stuttering with Normal Speech. II. Clinical Procedures," *Journal of Speech and Hearing Disorders*, 38 (1973), 295-303.

Perkins, W. H. and Curlee, R. F., "Clinical Impressions of Portable Masking Unit Effects in Stuttering," *Journal of Speech and Hearing Disorders*, 34 (1969), 360-362.

Ryan, B. P. (1974). *Programmed Therapy for Stuttering in Children and Adults* (Springfield, Ill.: Charles C Thomas).

Shames, G. H. and Sherrick, C. E. Jr., "A Discussion of Nonfluency and Stuttering as Operant Behavior," *Journal of Speech and Hearing Disorders*, 28 (1963), 3-18.

Shaw, C. K. and Shrum, W. F., "The Effects of Response-Contingent Reward on the Connected Speech of Children Who Stutter," *Journal of Speech and Hearing Disorders*, 37 (1972), 75-88.

Webster, R. L., "Evolution of a Target-Based Behavioral Therapy for Stuttering," *Journal of Fluency Disorders*, 5 (1980), 303-320.

Wolpe, J. (1958). *Psychotherapy by Reciprocal Inhibition* (Stanford, California: Stanford Univ. Press).

Suggested Reading

Brutten, E. J. and Shoemaker, D. J. (1967). *The Modification of Stuttering* (Englewood Cliffs, N.J.: Prentice-Hall), Chapter 5.

Gregory, H. H. (ed.) (1979). *Controversies About Stuttering Therapy* (Baltimore: University Park Press).

Ingham, R. J. (1984). *Stuttering and Behavior Therapy* (San Diego: College-Hill Press).

Shames, G. H. and Egolf, D. B. (1976). *Operant Conditioning and the Management of Stuttering: A Book for Clinicians* (Englewood Cliffs, N.J.: Prentice-Hall).

Chapter 13

References

Adams, M. R. and Hayden, P., "The Ability of Stutterers and Nonstutterers to Initiate and Terminate Phonation During Production of an Isolated Vowel," *Journal of Speech and Hearing Research*, 19 (1976), 290-296.

Andrews, G., Quinn, P. T., and Sorby, W. A., "Stuttering: An Investigation into Cerebral Dominance for Speech," *Journal of Neurology, Neurosurgery, and Psychiatry*, 35 (1972), 414-418.

Bakker, K. and Brutten, G. J., "A Comparative Investigation of the Laryngeal Premotor, Adjustment, and Reaction Times of Stutterers and Nonstutterers," *Journal of Speech and Hearing Research*, 32 (1989), 239-244.

Boberg, E., Yeudall, L. T., Schopflocher, D., and Bo-Lassen, P., "The Effect of an Intensive Behavioral Program on the Distribution of EEG Alpha Power in Stutterers During the Processing of Verbal and Visuospatial Information," *Journal of Fluency Disorders*, 8 (1983), 245-263.

Cullinan, W. L. and Springer, M. T., "Voice Initiation Times in Stuttering and Nonstuttering Children," *Journal of Speech and Hearing Research*, 23 (1980), 344-360.

Curry, F. K. W. and Gregory, H. H., "The Performance of Stutterers on Dichotic Listening Tasks Thought to Reflect Cerebral Dominance," *Journal of Speech and Hearing Research*, 12 (1969), 73-82.

Doms, M. C. and Lissens, D. (1973). "Stuttering and the Laryngectomee," in Lebrun, Y. and Hoops, R. (eds.), *Neurolinguistic Approaches to Stuttering* (The Hague: Mouton).

Freeman, F. J. and Ushijima, T., "Laryngeal Muscle Activity During Stuttering," *Journal of Speech and Hearing Research*, 21 (1978), 538-562.

Hand, C. R. and Haynes, W. O., "Linguistic Processing and Reaction Time Differences in Stutterers and Nonstutterers," *Journal of Speech and Hearing Research*, 26 (1983), 181-185.

Jones, R. K., "Observations on Stammering after Localized Cerebral Injury," *Journal of Neurology, Neurosurgery and Psychiatry*, 29 (1966), 192-195.

Luessenhop, A. J., Boggs, J. S., LaBorwit, L. J., and Walle, E. L., "Cerebral Dominance in Stutterers Determined by Wada Testing," *Neurology*, 23 (1973), 1190-1192.

Moore, W. H., Jr., "Bilateral Tachistoscopic Word Perception of Stutterers and Normal Subjects," *Brain and Language*, 3 (1976), 434-442.

Moore, W. H., Jr., "Hemispheric Alpha Asymmetries of Stutterers and Nonstutterers for the Recall and Recognition of Words and Connected Reading Passages," *Journal of Fluency Disorders*, 11 (1986), 71-89.

Moore, W. H., Jr., Craven, D. C., and Faber, M. M., "Hemispheric Alpha Asymmetries of Words with Positive, Negative, and Neutral Arousal Values Preceding Tasks of Recall and Recognition: Electrophysiological and Behavioral Results from Stuttering Males and Nonstuttering Males and Females," *Brain and Language*, 17 (1982), 211-224.

Moore, W. H., Jr. and Haynes, W. O., "Alpha Hemispheric Asymmetry and Stuttering: Some Support for a Segmentation Dysfunction Hypothesis," *Journal of Speech and Hearing Research*, 23 (1980), 229-247.

Moore, W. H., Jr. and Lang, M. K., "Alpha Asymmetry over the Left and Right Hemispheres of Stutterers and Control Subjects Preceding Massed Oral Readings: A Preliminary Investigation," *Perceptual and Motor Skills*, 44 (1977), 223-230.

Moore, W. H., Jr. and Lorendo, L. C., "Hemispheric Alpha Asymmetries of Stuttering Males and Nonstuttering Males and Females for Words of High and Low Imagery," *Journal of Fluency Disorders*, 5 (1980), 11-26.

Pinsky, S. D. and McAdam, D. W., "Electroencephalographic and Dichotic Indices of Cerebral Laterality in Stutterers," *Brain and Language*, 11 (1980), 374-397.

Prosek, R. A., Montgomery, A. A., Walden, B. E., and Schwartz, D. M., "Reaction-Time Measures of Stutterers and Nonstutterers," *Journal of Fluency Disorders*, 4 (1979), 269-278.

Quinn, P. T., "Stuttering: Cerebral Dominance and the Dichotic Word Test," *Medical Journal of Australia*, 2 (1972), 639-643.

Reich, A., Till, J., and Goldsmith, H., "Laryngeal and Manual Reaction Times of Stuttering and Nonstuttering Adults," *Journal of Speech and Hearing Research*, 24 (1981), 192-196.

Rosenfield, D. B. and Freeman, F. J., "Stuttering Onset after Laryngectomy," *Journal of Fluency Disorders*, 8 (1983), 265-268.

Sussman, H. M., "Contractive Patterns of Interhemispheric Interference to Verbal and Spatial Concurrent Tasks in Right-Handed, Left-Handed and Stuttering Populations," *Neuropsychologica*, 20 (1982), 675-684.

Tuck, A. E., "An Alaryngeal Stutterer: A Case History," *Journal of Fluency Disorders*, 4 (1979), 239-243.

Victor, C. and Johannsen, H. S., "Untersuchung zur Zerebralen Dominanz fuer Sprache bei Stotterer mittels Tachistoskopie," *Sprache-Stimme-Gehoer*, 8 (1984), 74-77.

Walle, E. L., "Intracarotid Sodium Amytal Testing on Normal, Chronic Adult Stutterers," *Journal of Speech and Hearing Disorders*, 36 (1971), 561.

Watson, B. C. and Alfonso, P. J., "Foreperiod and Stuttering Severity Effects on Acoustic Laryngeal Reaction Time," *Journal of Fluency Disorders*, 8 (1983), 183-205.

Wingate, M. E., "Questionnaire Study of Laryngectomee Stutterers," *Journal of Fluency Disorders*, 6 (1981), 273-281.

Zimmermann, G. N. and Knott, R. R., "Slow Potentials of the Brain Related to Speech Processing in Normal Speakers and Stutterers," *Electroencephalography and Clinical Neurophysiology*, 37 (1974), 599-607.

Suggested Reading

Bloodstein, O. (1987). *A Handbook on Stuttering*, 4th ed. (Chicago: National Easter Seal Society), Chapter 4.

Chapter 14

References

Andrews, G. and Harris, M. (1964). *The Syndrome of Stuttering* (London: Wm. Heinemann Medical Books), Chapter 7.

Eisenson, J., "Observations on the Incidence of Stuttering in a Special Culture," *Asha*, 8 (1966), 391-394.

Farber, S. (1981). *Identical Twins Reared Apart: A Reanalysis* (New York: Basic Books).

Geschwind, N. and Galaburda, A. M., "Cerebral Lateralization: Biological Mechanisms, Associations, and Pathology: I. A Hypothesis and a Program for Research," *Archives of Neurology*, 42 (1985), 429-459.

Godai, U., Tatarelli, R., and Bonanni, G., "Stuttering and Tics in Twins," *Acta Geneticae Medicae et Gemellologiae*, 25 (1976), 369-375.

Goldman, R., "Cultural Influences on the Sex Ratio in the Incidence of Stuttering," *American Anthropologist*, 69 (1967), 78-81.

Graf, O. I. (1955). "Incidence of Stuttering among Twins," in Johnson, W. and Leutenegger, R. R. (eds.), *Stuttering in Children and Adults* (Minneapolis: Univ. Minn. Press).

Howie, P. M., "Concordance for Stuttering in Monozygotic and Dizygotic Twin Pairs," *Journal of Speech and Hearing Research*, 24 (1981), 317-321.

Kidd, K. K., Reich, T., and Kessler, S., *Genetics*, 74 (1973), No. 2, Part 2: s137.

Luchsinger, R., "Die Vererbung von Sprach-und Stimmstoerungen," *Folia Phoniatrica*, 11 (1959), 7-64.

Meyer, B. C., "Psychosomatic Aspects of Stuttering," *Journal of Nervous and Mental Diseases*, 101 (1945), 127-157.

Suggested Reading

Kidd, K. K., "A Genetic Perspective on Stuttering," *Journal of Fluency Disorders*, 2 (1977), 259-269.

Kidd, K. K., Kidd, J. R., and Records, M.A., "The Possible Causes of the Sex Ratio in Stuttering and Its Implications," *Journal of Fluency Disorders*, 3 (1978), 13-23.

Chapter 15

References
Bloodstein, O., "The Development of Stuttering: I. Changes in Nine Basic Features," *Journal of Speech and Hearing Disorders*, 25 (1960), 219-237.
Bloodstein, O., "The Development of Stuttering: III. Theoretical and Clinical Implications," *Journal of Speech and Hearing Disorders*, 26 (1961), 67-82.
Bloodstein, O., "Stuttering and Normal Nonfluency—A Continuity Hypothesis," *British Journal of Disorders of Communication*, 5 (1970), 30-39.
Bloodstein, O. and Gantwerk, B. F., "Grammatical Function in Relation to Stuttering in Young Children," *Journal of Speech and Hearing Research*, 10 (1967), 786-789.
Bloodstein, O. and Grossman, M., "Early Stutterings: Some Aspects of their Form and Distribution," *Journal of Speech and Hearing Research*, 24 (1981), 298-302.
Bluemel, C. S., "Primary and Secondary Stammering," *Quarterly Journal of Speech*, 18 (1932), 187-200.
Hall, P. K., "The Occurrence of Disfluencies in Language-Disordered School-Age Children," *Journal of Speech and Hearing Disorders*, 42 (1977), 364-369.
Hegde, M. N. and Hartman, D. E., "Factors Affecting Judgments of Fluency: I. Interjections," *Journal of Fluency Disorders*. 4 (1979), 1-11.
Hegde, M. N. and Hartman, D. E., "Factors Affecting Judgments of Fluency: II. Word Repetitions," *Journal of Fluency Disorders*, 4 (1979), 13-22.
Johnson, W. and Associates (1959). *The Onset of Stuttering* (Minneapolis: Univ. Minn. Press), Chapter 8.
Merits-Patterson, R. and Reed, C. G., "Disfluencies in the Speech of Language-Delayed Children," *Journal of Speech and Hearing Research*, 24 (1981), 55-58.
Wall, M. J., Starkweather, C. W., and Harris, K. S., "The Influence of Voicing Adjustments on the Location of Stuttering in the Spontaneous Speech of Young Child Stutterers," *Journal of Fluency Disorders*, 6 (1981), 299-310.

Suggested Reading
Bloodstein, O., "The Development of Stuttering: II. Developmental Phases," *Journal of Speech and Hearing Disorders*, 25 (1960), 366-376.
Bloodstein, O., "The Rules of Early Stuttering," *Journal of Speech and Hearing Disorders*, 39 (1974), 379-394.
Bloodstein, O. (1975). "Stuttering as Tension and Fragmentation," in Eisenson, J. (ed.), *Stuttering: A Second Symposium* (New York: Harper & Row).
Bloodstein, O. (1987). *A Handbook on Stuttering*, 4th ed. (Chicago: National Easter Seal Society), Chapter 9.

Chapter 16

Suggested Reading
Egolf, D. B., Shames, G. H., Johnson, P. R., and Kasprisin-Burelli, A., "The Use of Parent-Child Interaction Patterns in Therapy for Young Stutterers," *Journal of Speech and Hearing Disorders*, 37 (1972), 222-232.
Johnson, W. (1961). *Stuttering and What You Can Do About It* (Minneapolis: Univ. Minn. Press), Chapter 10.
Luper, H. L. and Mulder, R. L. (1964). *Stuttering: Therapy for Children* (Englewood Cliffs, N.J.: Prentice-Hall).

Prins, D. and Ingham, R. J. (1983). *Treatment of Stuttering in Early Childhood: Methods and Issues* (San Diego: College-Hill Press).
Van Riper, C. (1973). *The Treatment of Stuttering* (Englewood Cliffs, N.J.: Prentice-Hall), Chapters 14 and 15.
Wall, M. J. and Meyers, F. L. (1984). *Clinical Management of Childhood Stuttering* (Baltimore: University Park Press).
Williams, D. E. (1971). "Stuttering Therapy for Children," in Travis, L. E. (ed.), *Handbook of Speech Pathology and Audiology* (New York: Appleton-Century-Crofts).

Chapter 17

References
Gregory, H. H. (1986). *Stuttering: Differential Evaluation and Therapy* (Austin, Texas: Pro-Ed).
Perkins, W. H. (1984). "Techniques for Establishing Fluency," in Perkins, W. H. (ed.), *Current Therapy of Communication Disorders: Stuttering Disorders* (New York: Thieme-Stratton).
Peters, T. J. and Guitar, B. (1991). *Stuttering: An Integrated Approach to Its Nature and Treatment* (Baltimore: Williams & Wilkins).
Ryan, B. P. and Van Kirk, B. (1971). *Monterey Fluency Program* (Monterey, California: Monterey Learning Systems).
Schwartz, M. (1976). *Stuttering Solved* (New York: Lippencott).
Shames, G. H. and Florance, C. L. (1980). *Stutter-Free Speech: A Goal for Therapy* (Columbus, Ohio: Merrill).
Sheehan, J. G. (1970). *Stuttering: Research and Therapy* (New York: Harper & Row).
Starkweather, C. W. (1984). "A Multiprocess Behavioral Approach to Stuttering Therapy," in Perkins, W. H. (ed.), *Current Therapy of Communication Disorders: Stuttering Disorders* (New York: Thieme-Stratton).
Van Riper, C. (1973). *The Treatment of Stuttering* (Englewood Cliffs, N.J.: Prentice-Hall), Chapters 8-13.
Webster, R. L. (1975). *The Precision Fluency Shaping Program: Speech Reconstruction for Stutterers* (Roanoke, Va: Communication Development Corp.).
Williams, D. E. (1971). "Stuttering Therapy for Children," in Travis, L. E. (ed.), *Handbook of Speech Pathology and Audiology* (New York: Appleton-Century-Crofts).

Index

Disfluencies, normal child-
hood, 47–48, 57–61, 69,
98, 140–141, 146–149
See also Fluency
Distraction, 16–17, 77–78,
100
white noise as, 91, 93–94,
105n, 157, 177
Dopamine, 90
Drive state, 83, 84, 96
Drug therapy, 89–90, 178
Dunlap, Knight, 43
Dysphemia, 39–41

Early stuttering
Bleumel's "primary stut-
tering" as, 58, 139–140,
150–156
normal disfluencies vs.,
57–61, 69, 98, 140–141,
146–149
onset of, 56–70, 139–145
symptoms of, 69
treatment of, 150–156
See also Childhood
Eggshell fluency, 107
Eisenson, Jon, 125–126
Electroencephaly, 114, 115,
177
Electrolarynx, 120
Electromyography, 31, 35
Elektra stage, 20, 21
Emergency situations, 77
Environment
intrauterine, 127, 132–
133n
social. *See* Social environment
Esophageal speech, 120
Expectancy. *See* Anticipation
Experimental extinction,
81–84, 97
Eyedness, 32
Eysenck, Hans J., 96

Fairbanks, Grant, 92n
Faking, 46–47, 54
Family incidence of stutter-
ing, 39, 67–68, 123–125,
127, 177
Farber, Susan, 129–130
Fear of stuttering, 13, 46–55,
101, 140, 157
See also Anxiety
Fenichel, Otto, 19, 20, 85
Finland, 170

Fish Called Wanda, A (film),
169
Flanagan, Bruce, 97
Florance, Cheri L., 163–165
Fluency
conditions for, 76–79, 87
delayed auditory feed-
back and, 104–105, 158,
164
immediate, 17, 43–46. *See
also* Artificial speech
patterns
intimacy with speech
therapist and, 106
relapse and, 95–99, 106–
109
unrealistic demands for,
153
white noise effect and, 91,
92–94, 105n, 157, 177
See also Disfluencies,
normal childhood;
Treatment of stuttering
"Fluent stuttering," 49–51,
161–162
Foot preference, 32
Fortune, Henry, 65
Fragmentations, 138–139,
143–145, 148
France, 12, 15, 17
Frank, Arthur, 64–65
Freud, Sigmund, 13, 19–20,
21, 25, 59–60, 133, 176
Froeschels, Emil, 58

Galaburda, Albert M., 127
Galen, 11
Gantwerk, Barbara F., 141–
145
Gaspard, Jean-Marc, 17
Gathman, Antoinette, 170
Gathman, Bob, 170
General semantics, 52–55
Gentle onset of phonation,
103, 104, 107n, 117,
158–159, 163, 178
Germany, 12–14, 104, 117–
118, 170, 171
Geschwind, Norman, 127
Gilles de la Tourette's dis-
ease, 90
Glenn, Annie, 103
Glenn, John, 103
Goldiamond, Israel, 97, 98,
104–105
Goldman, Bob, 167
Goldman, Ronald, 126

Graf, Odny I., 128
Gray, Marcella, 67–68
Great Britain, 12, 15, 67, 103,
170
Greece, ancient, 11–12
Gregory, Hugo H., 112–113,
162
Grossman, Marcia, 145
Guitar, Barry, 162–163

*Habits—Their Making and
Unmaking* (Dunlap), 43
Habit strength, 83, 96
Habituation to stuttering, 6–
7
Hall, Clark, 83
Haloperidol, 90
Hand, C. Rebekah, 118
Handedness, and stuttering,
29–36, 42, 43, 178
Hard attacks, 137–138
See also Gentle onset of
phonation
Harris, Katherine S., 145
Harris, Mary, 67, 103, 127
Hartford, Michael J., 169
Hartley, Davie, 12
Hartman, David E., 146
Hayakawa, S. I., 52
Hayden, Paul, 119
Haynes, William O., 118
Hearing, 93, 94, 120
delayed auditory feed-
back, 91–94, 104–105,
158, 164, 177
dichotic listening, 112–
114, 117, 177
Hegde, M. N., 146
Heraclitus, 62
Heredity and stuttering, 2,
123–131, 151, 177, 179
adoption studies, 125,
129, 130–131
diagnosogenic theory
and, 67–68
familial incidence of stuttering and, 39, 67–68,
123–125, 127, 177
in medical model, 39–41,
175–176
sex ratio, 2, 124, 125–128
twin studies, 40, 128–130,
176, 177
Hippocrates, 11
Hollins College, 103, 159
Hostility, 20, 21
Howie, Pauline M., 128